A DAILY CALENDAR of SAINTS

A Synaxarion for Today's North American Church

ARCHPRIEST LAWRENCE R. FARLEY

ANCIENT FAITH PUBLISHING
CHESTERTON, INDIANA

A Daily Calendar of Saints: A Synaxarion for Today's Orthodox Church
Copyright © 2018 Lawrence R. Farley
Revised from a book of the same title previously published by the author.

All rights reserved. No part of this publication may be reproduced by any means, electronic, mechanical, photocopying, recording, scanning, or otherwise, without the prior written permission of the Publisher.

Published by:
Ancient Faith Publishing
A Division of Ancient Faith Ministries
P.O. Box 748
Chesterton, IN 46304

Unless otherwise noted, Scripture quotations are taken from the New King James Version, © 1979, 1980, 1982 by Thomas Nelson, Inc. Used by permission.

ISBN: 978-1-944967-41-3

30 29 28 27 26 25 24 23 22 21   17 16 15 14 12 11 10 9 8 7 6 5 4 3 2

CONTENTS

Introduction ~: 5

January ~: 7

February ~: 39

March ~: 63

April ~: 89

May ~: 111

June ~: 133

July ~: 157

August ~: 181

September ~: 203

October ~: 221

November ~: 243

December ~: 265

Readings for the Paschal Cycle ~: 287

~ INTRODUCTION ~

Living with the Saints

Living as a disciple of Jesus means never living alone. That is, while we may sometimes (or often) experience life as a social solitary, we always have the company of the saints. God has saved us by setting us in the Body of His Son, His holy Church, and working out our salvation means that we find eternal life as part of that Body. That is why we are taught to say the "Our Father," not the "My Father"— our salvation is fundamentally and relentlessly corporate. We are surrounded by God's People, who support us and nourish us by their prayers. Some of these people we see every Sunday at church when we go to the divine liturgy. Some of these people we may never see unless we travel abroad, since they live in other earthly countries. And some of them (most of them, actually) we will never see with the eyes of the flesh because they live in heaven.

It is these heavenly saints that form the focus of this book. Every day we say our prayers and invoke the help of our guardian angel, of the Most Holy Theotokos, and of all the saints. Our church calendar gives us the names of these saints, but little else. Who were they? When did they live? What did they say that can help us? How did they die? We are called to cultivate the friendship of the saints, trusting in their love, asking for their prayers, and it is easier to cultivate their friendship if we feel we can know something reliable about them. They are not two-dimensional clones of each other. They were (and are) real people, each one different from the others, each one with his or her own struggles, gifts, and insights. What they all have in common is love for the Lord—and for us.

This book is offered to the earthly people of God still *in via*, on the road home, in the hope that it will help us to cultivate the friendship of the saints who are now *in patria*, in our heavenly homeland. Through their holy prayers, may we also find our way home and there continue to glorify our gracious and loving Lord.

–Archpriest Lawrence R. Farley

JANUARY 1

St. Basil the Great, Archbishop of Caesarea

Basil was born into a wealthy Christian family in Caesarea in Cappadocia in 330 and was educated in the schools of Caesarea, Constantinople, and Athens, where he formed a deep friendship with Gregory (later known as St. Gregory Nazianzus). Shaken by the sudden death of his younger brother, he was converted by his pious sister Macrina. After visiting monastic centers, the young Basil formed a monastic community of his own in Ibora, near his home in Annesi, and lived there with his monks for about five years. He wrote many rules and guidelines for monastics, so all Eastern monasticism owes something to his spirit. Recognizing his gifts, the Church ordained him priest in 365 and Bishop of Caesarea in 370.

As a bishop Basil greatly cared for the poor and suffering, and built an estate which included houses for travelers, a church, a hospital, and a hospice, all with a complete staff. A famine, striking the area, sent many poor and starving into his care. Their pain grieved him, and he labored to feed them with his own hands. He wrote:

> If you are reduced to your last loaf of bread and a beggar appears at your door, then take that loaf and lift your hands to heaven and say, "O Lord, I have but this one loaf; hunger lies in wait for me but I revere Your commandments more than all other things." If you should say this, then the bread you gave in your poverty will be changed for an abundant harvest.

St. Basil greatly strove against the Arian heresy, in which he stood up against the Arian Emperor Valens. When called to account by the state for his orthodoxy, he conducted himself in such a way that the examining prefect (accustomed, as he was, to more pliable hierarchs) expressed astonishment at his boldness. Basil retorted, "Perhaps you have never had to deal with a proper bishop before!"

Basil wrote to his nephews to make full use of pagan literature (a rare attitude in those days) in order to gain a deep understanding of the Christian Faith.

Aware of his own shortcomings and dispirited by disappointments in his life of struggles, Basil wrote, "For my sins, I seem to fail in everything." Nevertheless, he was far from a failure: his labors, including the writing of the works *On the Holy Spirit* and *Against Eunomius*, contributed greatly to the final triumph of Nicene orthodoxy at the Second Ecumenical Council of Constantinople in 381. The liturgy which bears his name is largely his own work. He died peacefully in the Lord in 379.

~: JANUARY 2 :~

Our Holy Father Sylvester, Pope of Rome

Sylvester was born of pious Christian parents in Rome in the third century. He courageously offered to shelter fugitive Christians during the persecutions. He was ordained priest by the Bishop of Rome Miltiades, and when the bishop died in 314, the Roman church chose Sylvester as his successor. As Constantine established peace for the Church just before this time, Sylvester was the first Bishop of Rome to rule his see without persecution.

Sylvester labored as a kind pastor to his church, making sure that the Roman church cared for the many poor who relied upon it for support. He also strove mightily to convert to the Christian Faith the Jews of Rome and the many pagans there. When the emperor convened the Council of Nicaea in the East in 325, Sylvester sent two legates there as his representatives, being too old to travel that far himself. St. Sylvester died in peace on the last day of the year 335 and was buried in the cemetery of Priscilla on the Salarian Way, the first non-martyr to be venerated as a saint in Rome.

Our Holy Father Seraphim of Sarov

Born in Kursk, Russia, in 1759 with the name Prokhor, the future saint was a son of devout Christian parents of the merchant class. At the age of eighteen, he entered a monastery in Sarov, devoting himself to saying the Jesus Prayer and continuing in humble service in the monastery, baking bread and working in the woodwork shop. After four years the young man fell quite ill and was near death. While the brothers prayed for him in church, he had a vision of the Mother of God, who told him he would recover, which he eventually did. He was finally tonsured a monk in 1786 with the name Seraphim and ordained priest in 1793.

Seraphim served liturgy daily and exhorted the people to receive Holy Communion frequently. Soon he asked for a blessing to live a life of solitude in the nearby forest. During his time in the forest he devoted himself to prayer, praying for a thousand days upon a hard rock. He subsisted each week on a loaf of bread and a few vegetables, out of which he fed the animals that came to his cell. Every Saturday and Sunday he returned to the monastery and served liturgy.

Later, St. Seraphim moved into further isolation in the forest, not returning to the monastery for three years but living in total silence. Ill health brought an order from the monastery for him to return. After spending another five years in solitude within the monastery walls, the saint began to receive visitors, guiding many as a true elder and confessor. He also guided the Diveyevo convent of nuns, whose care he inherited after the former abbot of Sarov had reposed.

One of St. Seraphim's many visitors was Nicholas Motovilov. In a visit with the saint, Nicholas saw him shine with the uncreated light of God. St. Seraphim was a man filled with God and the joy of His Kingdom. Year round, he would greet each visitor with the salutation, "Christ is risen, my joy!" He taught that the goal of the Christian life was the acquisition of the Holy Spirit, and that if one acquired the Spirit of peace, thousands would be saved by example. The saint died, kneeling in prayer, at the age of eighty, in 1833.

~ JANUARY 3 ~

The Prophet Malachi

Malachi was a member of the Jewish community that settled in Judea after the return from the Babylonian exile. He prophesied in about 420 BC. He spoke to encourage the small embattled community, leading them closer to God by rebuking their sins and spiritual complacency. Malachi especially strove against the people's practice of divorcing their Jewish wives to marry Gentile women and their non-payment of tithes to the temple. His name appropriately means "My messenger," for he was a true messenger of God. He prophesied of the coming Kingdom, which would be heralded by the return of Elijah (fulfilled in the life of St. John the Forerunner) and which would be brought in by Christ, "the Sun of Righteousness." After St. Malachi, no prophet arose in Israel until his words were fulfilled four hundred years later in the coming of the Forerunner John.

~ JANUARY 4 ~

The Synaxis of the Seventy Apostles

In addition to the Twelve, our Lord chose seventy other apostles, whom He sent out, two by two, to preach, to heal, and to prepare the way in every Israelite town into which He was preparing to go (Luke 10:1). He sent out these apostles as lambs into the midst of wolves, having nothing prepared for their journeys save reliance upon God. Their words were the words of God, so that whoever rejected their message would themselves be rejected on the Last Day (Luke 10:11–12). After their mission, the Seventy returned to their Master with joy, saying, "Lord, even the demons are subject to us in Your Name!" To them, that is, to His Church, the Lord gave authority over all power of the enemy so that nothing may hurt us. The Seventy were told not to rejoice primarily in this bestowal of authority, but to rejoice in their eternal salvation in heaven (Luke 10:17–20).

JANUARY 5

Hieromartyr Theopemptus and the Holy Martyr Theonas

Theopemptus was Bishop of Nicomedia in the time of Emperor Diocletian. When the emperor began his persecution of the Christians, the bishop was one of the first to suffer. Refusing to deny Christ, he was imprisoned, suffering starvation, beatings, and torture. At length a pagan man, Theonas, was brought in to persuade the noble bishop to deny the Faith, but by his steadfastness and the power of Christ, Theopemptus instead converted Theonas, who then also confessed himself a Christian. They were both condemned to death: Bishop Theopemptus was slain with the sword, while Theonas was buried alive. They suffered for the Lord in 298.

JANUARY 6

Holy Theophany

Our Lord Jesus came to St. John the Forerunner when he was baptizing in the wilderness of Judea. St. John was proclaiming the imminence of the Kingdom of God and telling his countrymen that they must repent, even as the unclean Gentiles, to prepare themselves for the coming of the Messiah; otherwise, God would destroy them in the judgment He would bring. As a sign of their dedication to the Kingdom, the penitents would be baptized by John in the Jordan.

Though the Lord Jesus was sinless and had nothing of which to repent, He wanted to fulfill all the righteousness of the Kingdom by consecrating Himself to His Father's mission, and thus He presented Himself to John to be baptized. At our Lord's insistence, John baptized Him (recognizing that He was the more righteous). Afterward, as our Lord stood praying beside the Jordan, John saw a vision of the Holy Spirit descending as a dove upon Him. He heard the voice of the Father designating Jesus as the Messiah, saying, "This is My Beloved Son, in whom I am well pleased."

The Feast of Theophany commemorates this manifestation of God as Trinity (for the Spirit descended on the Son as the Father spoke) and testifies to the Son's identification with us sinners for the sake of our salvation.

❦ JANUARY 7 ❧

St. John the Holy Prophet, Forerunner, and Baptizer

Through St. John, God restored prophecy to Israel, making John to be the herald of the Kingdom of God, so that before Christ, there was no one greater born of woman (Matt. 11:11). John was born to righteous Zachariah and Elizabeth, God having made the barren woman fertile in her old age. While yet in the womb, John leaped for joy as the greeting of the Mother of God reached the ears of his mother, Elizabeth. Named John by his father in obedience to the Archangel Gabriel's word, he came in the spirit and power of Elijah to restore righteousness to Israel through the preaching of repentance.

From his early years John would frequent the Judean desert, fasting and praying. The Word of God came to him in the wilderness in about the year 26, and he began to proclaim that Israel must repent to be worthy of the coming Messiah and must accept baptism as a sign of their repentance. He baptized our Lord (though reluctantly, for he knew Him to be more righteous than himself) and received a vision designating Him to be the Messiah. Thereafter he rejoiced in our Lord's growing popularity, pointing to Him as the Lamb of God and the messianic goal of his own ministry.

Herod arrested John because he rebuked him for his unrighteous life, such as his unlawful marriage to his brother's wife. At the instigation of Herod's wife's daughter, John was beheaded in prison. His disciples buried his body. His relics were eventually taken by the Church to Antioch and thence to Constantinople. St. John was a true messenger (Gr. *angelos*) of God; thus he is often portrayed in his icons as having wings—an earthly angel and a heavenly man.

JANUARY 8

The Venerable St. Dominica the Righteous

Dominica was born to pagan parents in the comfortable middle class in 384 in Carthage. Her parents had great plans for her education, marriage, and social advancement, but God had other plans for the independent young girl. When twenty-one, she prevailed upon her parents to allow her to go and visit the recently completed capital of Constantinople with four of her girlfriends. While there she was greatly impressed by the culture and grandeur of the sprawling metropolis but even more impressed by the glory of the newly ascendant Christian Faith. At length the young girl gained an audience with the city's bishop, Patriarch Nectarius, who was himself so impressed by her fervor that he personally officiated at her baptism.

Desirous of devoting herself completely to Christ through a life of asceticism and monastic service at the capital, she dutifully wrote her parents to inform them of her new faith and to ask their permission for her to live this new life. Her parents were aghast but were at length persuaded by her. Dominica began her ascetic life at age twenty-five, along with her four girlfriends. She lived a life of peace and service to God, and throughout the next seventy-five years her godly reputation spread throughout the empire. Those who came to visit her spoke of her healing ministry and her miracles. She entered into rest at the age of one hundred in 484.

JANUARY 9

The Holy Martyr Polyeuctos

Polyeuctos served as an officer along with his close friend Nearchus in the Twelfth Legion, stationed in Melitene in Armenia in the middle of the third century. Nearchus was a Christian, but Polyeuctos was still a pagan. When the persecution broke out against the Church, the army officers were required to prove their loyalty to the state by offering the customary sacrifices to the pagan gods. Nearchus told his friend that he would have to refuse to do so and therefore expected to pay the inevitable penalty of martyrdom. Thus, he said, the two dear friends would be separated forever.

Nearchus's witness to Christ must have been working on the soul of his friend Polyeuctos, and the pagan Polyeuctos shared how he had a dream of Christ appearing to him, exchanging his military uniform for a shining robe and giving him a winged horse on which he could ride up to heaven. Convinced now of the Faith, he was eager to join his Christian friend in martyrdom and was determined himself to defy the imperial order to sacrifice to the pagan gods.

When the fateful day came, the two friends approached the place where the emperor's edict was posted, ordering the sacrifices to be made. To the great astonishment of the gathered crowd, Polyeuctos pulled down the edict and tore it to pieces. He rushed into the midst of the pagan procession and smashed the idols carried by the pagan priests. He was instantly arrested and condemned for the crime of being a Christian.

At his trial, his family gathered to try to induce him to deny Christ, offer the sacrifices, and save himself. His wife Pauline especially was in tears and cried out, "What madness has got into you?"

He refused to be moved by these entreaties and replied, "There is nothing for it, Pauline, but to join me in worshipping the true God and hurry to exchange this passing life for heavenly and eternal life." Since he refused to recant, the judges condemned him to death. He was executed by beheading, thus experiencing Christian baptism in his own blood. His friend Nearchus later joined him the Kingdom, suffering martyrdom and winning the robe of victory.

St. Philip, Metropolitan of Moscow

The future St. Philip was born to aristocratic Russian parents in 1507 and baptized with the name Theodore. In accord with family wishes, he began a military career, serving in the Crimea. But though he advanced in the world, his soul could find no rest, for he had a heart to seek God as well and felt himself torn between these two desires. Then, while in church, he heard a priest cite the Savior's words, "No one can serve two masters." He decided at length to resign his commission at the age of thirty, leave the world, and seek God in the remote monastery on Solovky Island in the White Sea. In humility, the new monk took an assignment as gardener and woodcutter. He fulfilled his novitiate, and the abbot tonsured him with the name Philip.

At the abbot's death, Philip succeeded to the office, donating his share of his family estate to the monastery. Under his astute administration, the monastery grew and was soon known all over Russia for its wealth and piety. As the pride of Russia, Philip became well known to the government and in 1566 was appointed Metropolitan of Moscow by Tsar Ivan ("the Terrible").

For a while all went well, and the tsar allowed himself to be counseled by Philip. But when the tsar began a reign of terror, in paranoia jailing all he feared would be a threat to him, Philip challenged him. While the tsar was in church, in his royal pew, Patriarch Philip pointed an accusing finger at him and called for an end to the reign of terror. "Silence lays sin upon my soul," he said. "Here we are offering up the bloodless sacrifice to the Lord while behind the altar flows the innocent blood of Christian men!"

The tsar stormed out of the church and ordered his patriarch to preach no more sermons on the subject, but Philip refused to comply, continuing his public denunciation of the tsar. For this he was stripped of all rank and, as a mere monk, banished to a monastery, to be later assassinated there by being smothered with a pillow in 1569. After twenty-one years, Philip's body was disinterred and his relics found to be incorrupt. They remain in the Cathedral of the Assumption in Moscow.

~: JANUARY 10 :~

St. Gregory, Bishop of Nyssa

St. Gregory lived as a man of peace and simplicity of spirit, a joyful lover of God who hated the strife of high politics and worldly administration. He was born about 335, being five or six years younger than his older brother Basil (January 1). He also loved his beautiful and devout sister Macrina (later St. Macrina). His father died when he was young, and he lived on his share of his father's estate.

His mother, an enthusiastic Christian and devotee of relics, obtained the relics of the Forty Martyrs of Sebaste and prepared to house them in a chapel built for them on her estate in Annesi. Young Gregory, not yet fervent, was bored by the all-night vigil of psalm-singing and at length, annoyed and angry at it all, left the garden chapel and fell asleep elsewhere. There he dreamed of the Forty Martyrs and was converted. He returned to the vigil and prayed for God's pardon.

Though Basil and his friend Gregory of Nazianzus had taken vows of chastity, our present Gregory chose to be married to a girl named Theosebia, though they lived together as man and wife for only a short while. Gregory lived in Caesarea, then joined Basil for a while at his monastic community. Basil soon appointed him to the nearby see of Nyssa so that he might help him in his struggle against Arianism.

Gregory hated the strife and responsibility he knew the episcopate would bring—he later said the day of his consecration (in 372) was the most miserable of his life. As Gregory had no tact and no head for money, two years later his Arian foes were able to trump up false embezzlement charges against him, and he was dismissed from his see and arrested. He escaped, however, and went into hiding until the Arian emperor responsible for his imprisonment died. He helped Basil to further monasticism by writing his treatise *On Virginity*.

In 377 Gregory was restored to his see, and after Basil's sad death two years later, he began a brilliant career as a teacher and theologian. Soon, his sister Macrina died. He was present with her on her deathbed, where they spoke of the soul and the hope of resurrection. (He later condensed her teaching into a book, *On the Soul and Resurrection*.) He also wrote against Arianism and composed the brilliant *Great Catechism*, as well as a commentary on the Song of Songs (at the suggestion of the deaconess Olympia) and a mystical *Life of Moses*. He was acclaimed by the emperor's court, and the work in the Creed on the Holy Spirit is probably his own composition. He died in peace in about 395.

Gregory loved to pray; he wrote, "Prayer is the delight of the joyful, the consolation of the weary, the crown of the bride, the feast on the birthday, the shroud that covers us in our graves." So great was he that the fathers of the Seventh Ecumenical Council called him "the Father of fathers."

~: JANUARY 11 :~

St. Theodosius the Great

Theodosius was born of pious parents at Mogarisses in Cappadocia in 423 and later became a cantor in his village church. In about 456 he was reading of the call of God to Abraham to "get out of your country . . . to a land that I will show you" (Gen. 12:1), and he felt as if God was speaking to him. He said goodbye to his family and departed for a life of monastic holiness in Palestine, taking a side trip on the way to visit the famous St. Simeon the Stylite to ask for his blessing.

Theodosius spent some time in a monastic community on the road to Bethlehem before setting out on his own. He lived in a cave, and soon others joined him. In seeking the place God willed, it is said he went into the wilderness swinging an unlit censer, and at the place where it spontaneously lit and smoked, he founded his community. This was in 479—a year after St. Sabbas founded his hermit community nearby.

Theodosius's community (called a cenobium) soon developed and grew, containing hostels for travelers and hospitals for the sick, a residence for mentally ill monks, and an old-age home. By the time of his death, the community included over four hundred monks, who came from all over. There were also several churches—one for Armenians, one for Georgians, and the largest one using Greek, which was then the international language. Each group met on its own for the liturgy up until the end of the Gospel, then came together for the Eucharist in the Greek language.

Abbot Theodosius was a model of piety. Once when two brothers were quarreling, he fell down at their feet and would not rise until they had reconciled. As abbot, he strove to keep remembrance of death before the minds of his monks, and he had a common grave dug for them in clear view that it might serve as a daily reminder.

He was also a man of faith and miracles. One Lent, with Pascha soon approaching, the monks had no food, not even bread for the liturgy. Some murmured, but he told them God would provide—which He did, as mules soon arrived bearing the monastery's provisions. The Bishop of Jerusalem, under whom Theodosius served, appointed him leader (or "archimandrite") of all cenobitic communities (even as Sabbas was appointed leader of all hermit communities). Theodosius often met with Sabbas as the two friends consulted together.

In 513, the emperor supported the Monophysite heresy (which denied the full humanity of Christ), banished the Bishop of Jerusalem, and appointed his own man in his place. Theodosius (with Sabbas also) refused to recognize the new heretical replacement, despite imperial pressure. The emperor once sent Theodosius a "gift for the poor"—in reality a bribe—to win him over. Theodosius kept the money and spent it on the poor, but refused to agree with the emperor's false profession of faith. Instead, he wrote him refuting his heresy and proclaiming himself ready to die for the truth.

As the controversy heated up, Theodosius traveled throughout Palestine, urging monks to hold fast to Orthodoxy and the Fourth Ecumenical Council of Chalcedon, which condemned the Monophysite heresy. At Jerusalem, he and Sabbas supported the Orthodox patriarch, proclaiming in church, "If anyone receives not the four councils as the four Gospels, let him be anathema!" Theodosius was eventually banished but was later recalled when the emperor died. Theodosius lived in continued austerity and peace, dying at last in the year 529.

JANUARY 12

Holy Martyr Tatiana of Rome

In about the early third century, Tatiana was born of wealthy and eminent parents in Rome. She became a Christian and served as a deaconess in the Church. When persecution broke out against the Church there, she was among those arrested. Refusing to worship the gods (but praying instead to Christ, to the rage of her interrogators), she was sentenced to be tortured and killed.

Her torture was particularly drawn out—she was flogged, disfigured, and torn with iron hooks. Seeing the courage and steadfastness of the woman, some of her guards were themselves converted. When she was at last brought to the public arena to meet the lion, the public was especially anxious to see the daughter of a distinguished citizen suffer. But the lion, when released, did her no harm. She was at length executed by beheading in about the year 225.

St. Sava, Archbishop of Serbia

Sava was born in 1169, one of three royal sons of Stephan Nemanja, King of Serbia. As a youth, he had a great desire to serve God as a monk on Mount Athos. In 1191, when some Athonite monks came to visit his father, he secretly slipped away with them to live on Mount Athos. At length his father found out where he was and pleaded with him to return to his royal destiny in the world. He wrote back to his father, telling of the joys he had found there—a letter, it is said, some four hundred pages long! His father came down to the Holy Mountain himself to see his son and was so moved by what he found there that he too embraced the monastic way, resigning his throne to his two remaining sons. Together Sava and his father founded an Athonite monastery for their Serbian countrymen—Chilandari—which still exists as one of the ruling houses on the Holy Mountain.

The tumultuous times would not leave Sava in the peace he desired: strife and anarchy in his homeland sent him back there in 1208 at the request of the Patriarch of Constantinople. He established himself at Studenitsa, built monasteries, schools, and churches throughout the land, and strove to bring political peace. To consolidate the work, he asked for and gained the autocephaly of his church from Constantinople and was himself consecrated its first archbishop in 1219. He strove to serve his church, founding a hospice for Serbs in Jerusalem and arranging for Serbian monks to be received in Mount Sinai and other monasteries.

Depending not on the princes of men but on God, Sava would

often withdraw to an inaccessible hermitage in Studenitsa for prayer and divine guidance. He died in Trnovo, Bulgaria, in 1236, on his way back from a journey to the east. He is rightly hailed as the true founder of the Serbian church and nation.

~: JANUARY 13 :~

The Holy Martyrs Hermylus and Stratonicus

Hermylus was a deacon in the church in Singidunum (modern Belgrade) in the early fourth century. When the persecution ravaged the church there, the deacon was arrested and asked to renounce the Christian Faith. This he refused to do, answering his interrogators with such spirit that they slashed his cheeks before throwing him into the dungeon. When he was next interrogated, he was even more defiant. Six men beat him with rods, but he did not seem to feel the pain, being rapt in prayer and asking Christ that He would allow him to partake of His Passion.

The jailer, Stratonicus, observed all this and was won over to the Faith by the constancy and faith of Hermylus, though he did not dare to confess it. The next day, his captors led Hermylus from his cell, stretched him upon the ground, and beat him relentlessly with sharp rods while his entrails were gashed with eagle's claws. Stratonicus could bear it no longer. He was overcome by his crisis of faith and conscience and began to weep uncontrollably. When asked the reason, he finally confessed himself a Christian. For this he too was arrested and imprisoned.

At length the two martyrs, Hermylus and his new convert friend Stratonicus, were tied up in a net and thrown into the Danube River to be drowned. Filled with joy, they began singing, "Glory to God in the highest, and on earth, peace, goodwill to men!" They perished in the river, and their souls were received by the Most High God in the Kingdom. When their bodies were found washed up on the shore after a few days, the local Christians buried them with honor. The martyrs suffered and were glorified with Christ in the early fourth century.

St. James, Bishop of Nisibis

James was born in Nisibis in about the late third century. Tired of the world's pomp and vanity, he sought out a life of solitary holiness and asceticism, living in the high mountains in a cave in the winter and in the woods in the summer. His holiness and austerities were soon discovered, and his fame grew, especially his reputation for prophetic insight and miracles. James visited churches in pagan Persia and strengthened the brethren there. He suffered for the Faith in the persecution of the pagan Emperor Maximinus. For his reputation for holiness, the Christians of Nisibis elected him as their bishop. James continued in his great personal austerity. As Bishop of Nisibis, he built a stately church there whose majesty greatly impressed visitors.

When the city was under siege by the nearby pagan Persian Empire, it was more than once safeguarded by the prayers of the church and its saintly bishop within. After an initial siege in 338, a second siege was attempted in 350. Bishop James encouraged his flock to hold out against the invaders, praying all the time in church for their deliverance.

A deacon, Ephraim (later St. Ephraim the Syrian), visiting from nearby Edessa, brought the bishop up to the walls to see the enemy and urged him to pray for their overthrow. St. James went then to the top of a high tower and prayed, "O Lord, You are able by the weakest means to humble the pride of Your enemies—defeat these multitudes by an army, not of men but of gnats!"

Soon a swarm of gnats and flies afflicted the foe, throwing them into confusion. Famine and pestilence soon followed, so that after a three-month siege, the Persian king abandoned his attempt and returned home. St. James reposed peacefully in his Lord soon after, in about the year 350.

❧ JANUARY 14 ☙

The Holy Martyrs of Mount Sinai and Raithu

Before the Emperor Justinian built the fortress-like monastery at its present site on Mount Sinai, many monks lived there in the desert,

JANUARY

scattered in the wilderness. A Saracen chief was encamped in the area at that time, near the place where the monks gathered for Sunday liturgy. When the chief suddenly died, the Saracens blamed the monks and massacred Doulas, the head of the community, along with thirty-eight of the monks. The slaughter was particularly terrible: some of the monks' heads were chopped off almost completely, hanging only by some skin. Other monks lay cut in half; others had been disemboweled or dismembered. The monks were found soon and buried with tears.

Only two monks survived the carnage. One died of his wounds that evening. The other (by the name of Sabas) lingered somewhat longer, in great distress. He could not stand to survive alone, when so many of his beloved brothers had fallen. He prayed, "Woe is me, wretched and unworthy sinner that I am, alone excluded from the eternal blessedness acquired by these martyrs today!" The Lord evidently heard his prayer, for he expired soon after from his trauma and distress, a martyr like his brethren.

There was another monastic community near Raithu on the shores of the Red Sea, led by their abbot, Paul. This community contained several monastics of exceptional holiness: Moses of Pharan, who had lived in the desert for seventy-three years, keeping vigil all through the night, and having a gift for exorcism; and Joseph of Aila, who, it was said, was covered by a divine fire from head to foot while he prayed.

The villagers of nearby Pharan had mobilized against the Blemmyes from Ethiopia, and in retaliation, three hundred of the Blemmyes came ashore to destroy and pillage the town of Raithu. Forty-three of the monks fled before them to take shelter in the fortified church in the city. The Blemmyes killed one hundred forty-seven villagers and besieged the church. Eventually they burst into the church, massacring its inhabitants. One monk was dragged into the courtyard and shot with arrows; another had his head split with a sword. A fifteen-year-old novice seized a sword and struck one of the invaders on the shoulder, whereupon they hacked him to pieces. One monk alone escaped the slaughter to bring news of the disaster to the wider Christian world. These massacres occurred in about the fourth century.

St. Nina, Enlightener of Georgia

In the late third century, a girl, Nina, was captured and taken to Georgia as a slave. She was a girl of goodness and great faith in the healing power of Christ. The pagan Georgians had a custom of taking a child, when sick, from door to door, hoping to find a cure at some house. A child of a wealthy woman fell dangerously sick, and in desperation the mother resorted to the old custom. She thus came at last to the house where Nina was.

Nina's owners, aware of her faith in her God, let her pray. She prayed in faith, and the sick child was instantly healed. News spread to the queen of Georgia, who was herself ill with a painful and incurable disease, and it was arranged for the queen to visit young Nina. She did, and Nina prayed long and hard for the queen. She touched her with a cross of reeds she had made (seen often in her icon). The queen too was instantly healed, and she converted in her heart to Nina's God, Jesus Christ.

King Mirian, however, was not converted despite his wife's entreaties until, lost in the woods while hunting, he found his way to safety after calling upon Christ for help. The king too was then converted, and he helped Nina and her church in the work of converting the Georgian people. He built a church in the capital city with miraculous help from God. The king sent to Emperor Constantine to ask for bishops to be sent to evangelize the people.

Nina herself continued to bear witness, traveling throughout Georgia, telling everyone about Christ. She died in peace in 338, not in her old home from which she was taken, but in her new home in Georgia, which she had brought to Christ.

~: JANUARY 15 :~

Our Holy Father Paul of Thebes

Paul was born to a wealthy family in Lower Thebes in Egypt in 229. When persecution under the Emperor Decius broke out in 250, his brother-in-law, wanting to seize Paul's property, planned to betray him to the persecuting authorities. Paul then arose and fled to the desert to await the end of the persecution. He found a cave near a palm tree and a spring, and there he lived, clothing himself in the palm leaves, eating the tree's fruit, and drinking water from the spring.

Paul at length found that he so loved this solitude and peaceful communion with God that, even after the storms of persecution ended, he remained in his hermitage. There he lived his long life, being cared for by God as Elijah was cared for in the wilderness. Anthony the Great came to visit him once, being told by God that in Paul there was one greater even than himself. After the visit, Anthony returned to his friends saying, "Woe is me, my children, for I am a sinful, false monk, a monk in name only! I have seen Elijah; I have seen John the Baptizer in the desert: Paul, in Paradise!"

Paul lived one hundred thirteen years and died in peace in 342. He was buried, at his own request, by St. Anthony in the robe which Anthony was given by St. Athanasius of Alexandria. A lion, as if in mourning for a friend, helped Anthony dig the grave. Paul is hailed as the first and father of hermits.

~ JANUARY 16 ~

The Chains of the Holy Apostle St. Peter

The Church has always venerated its martyrs, especially revering the chains they wore. Thus it was that the Church kept the chains St. Peter wore after he was imprisoned by Herod in Jerusalem (Acts 12:7). Later the Patriarch of Jerusalem, St. Juvenal, made a gift of these relics to the Empress Eudoxia. Together with the chains with which he was shackled by Nero in Rome before his death, they were placed in the Church of St. Peter in Rome. Some were also sent and placed in the New Rome, in the Church of the Holy Apostles in Constantinople.

⁕ JANUARY 17 ⁕

Our Holy Father St. Anthony the Great

Anthony was born of wealthy parents in middle Egypt, in a village near Herakleopolis, in 251 and was raised a Christian. Anthony's parents died when he was about twenty, and he was left with the care of his sister. At liturgy one day he heard the Savior's words, "If you would be perfect, sell all you have and give it to the poor." Struck to the heart by these words, he sold all his property, arranged for the care of his sister, and gave all the rest to the poor. The young man then moved to live in a tiny hut on the edge of his parents' estate, devoting himself to poverty, fasting, and prayer according to the custom of those days.

There Anthony began a struggle with the demonic enemy. He left his hut for a cave used as a tomb and was so set upon by the spiritual enemy that he was found unconscious and carried to a nearby church. Anthony insisted on returning to the cave to finish the struggle. When at length he won and Christ's light chased the horrors away, he asked, "Where were you, Lord? Why didn't you come earlier to relieve me of my agony?"

The Lord replied, "Anthony, I was there, but I was waiting to see you in action. Now, because you have triumphed, I will always help you and make your efforts known everywhere."

Anthony soon left for the great solitude of the desert—a novelty in those days. He lived in an abandoned fort for the next twenty years, being brought his supply of bread only twice a year. Afterwards, friends broke down the door and Anthony came forth—"neither dried up nor fat through idleness but as God-borne and standing in his natural condition." Word spread everywhere, and crowds came to see him. The desert soon became populated with those emulating the man of God and looking to him as their father.

As St. Anthony's fame grew, he found it harder to find solitude, so in 313, he moved further into the desert—to the foot of a mountain near the Red Sea, his "Inner Mountain." He returned to Alexandria only twice: once in 311 to strengthen the Christians arrested in the persecution, and once in 338 to strive publicly against Arianism, supporting St. Athanasius, who invited him. In the desert, he continued to pray and care for the monks. So it was that he came, at the age of ninety, to meet St. Paul of Thebes, another hermit who lived in complete solitude.

Anthony was visited by many from the world as well. When challenged by some pagan philosophers as to how he could claim wisdom though he was not educated, he answered, "Which is older—the mind or the book? And which is the source of the other? So, to the man whose mind is sound, there is no need for books to attain wisdom." He was known as one who had frequent visions and revelations, who drove out demons and healed the sick by his prayer, and who lived in cheerfulness and joy. Anthony died in peace after a full eighty-five years in the desert.

~: JANUARY 18 :~

Ss. Athanasius and Cyril, Archbishops of Alexandria

These men shone as two great lights of the great city of Alexandria. They strove mightily to uphold the Orthodox doctrine of Christ, withstanding the heresies of their day so that the truth might be preserved for the ages to come. In the fourth century, Athanasius battled against the Arian heresy at great personal cost, being exiled many times from his see. In the fifth century, Cyril battled the Nestorian heresy in the midst of great turmoil. Though these two were vilified by many in their generation, the Church has ever after glorified them as great defenders of the Faith, standards of Orthodoxy, and true Fathers of the Church. Though separated by years in this life (for they ruled Alexandria in different centuries), yet they are united in the same love for Christ and share the same reward as faithful stewards of the truth.

~: JANUARY 19 :~

Our Holy Father Macarius the Great

Macarius was born in Upper Egypt in about the year 300. As a child he stole some figs and ate one of them—a sin for which he ever after berated himself. As a young man, Macarius devoted himself to asceticism and prayer. When a young girl in his village falsely accused him of being the father of her unborn child, Macarius did not deny it, but accepted the unjust slander and beating from her family and undertook to support the girl. During a hard labor, the girl at length cried out the truth—that the true father was not Macarius but someone else. Macarius refused to accept the adulation of the village for his patient endurance of injustice and fled to Scetis in the vast desert to escape it. He was then about thirty years old, and he remained there for the rest of his life.

Macarius lived a life of great austerity—it is said that he never ate, drank, or slept as much as nature required. Yet his austerity was coupled with mildness, patience, and humility. A demon once confessed, "There is only one thing in which I cannot exceed you—not in fasting, for I never eat; nor in vigils, for I never sleep—but you conquer me by your humility."

In his humility, Macarius was immune to vanity. When a young man came to him for a spiritual word, he directed him to go to a cemetery to insult the dead, and then to flatter them. The young man did so, and Macarius asked him what response he got from them. "None at all," said the young man.

"Then," replied Macarius, "go and learn to be moved neither by insults nor by flatteries."

But though reluctant to discuss his virtues with those who were in awe of him, Macarius would gladly talk with those who treated him without awe. If any of the monks asked, "Abba, when you were a camel-man and used to steal, didn't the wardens beat you?"—to these he would gladly talk about anything.

He would travel forty miles across the desert each week to attend liturgy with the nearby priest Pambo. After ten years, however, he finally allowed himself to be ordained priest to care for the needs of his little community. In 374, the Arians triumphed in Alexandria, and Macarius with other Orthodox was exiled to a small island in the Egyptian delta. Eventually, though, he was allowed to return to his beloved Scetis. He died there in peace in 390.

St. Mark of Ephesus

St. Mark was born to a distinguished family in 1392 and rose in the Church until he became Archbishop of Ephesus. He was with the Orthodox delegation that met with the Roman Catholics at the Council of Ferrara and Florence in 1438. Rome had said it would not give the much-needed military help to defend Constantinople against the invading Turks unless the Orthodox East submitted to the papal faith. So great was the political pressure that the Russian Orthodox delegates unilaterally made their submission to the Pope. Mark, however, refused to betray the Faith and stormed out of the council to rally forces against the false union. Though banished by the beleaguered Eastern emperor for his refusal to submit, he was recalled after two years. He died in peace in Constantinople in 1444.

~: JANUARY 20 :~

Our Holy Father Euthymius the Great

Euthymius was born in Melitene in Armenia in 376. He was tonsured a reader in the Church early in life and raised by the local bishop. Ordained priest at the age of twenty, Euthymius was given care of all the monks of the diocese. But he craved solitude, and so, in the year 405, at the age of thirty, he left for Jerusalem to seek a life of monasticism.

Every year, as was the local custom in Armenia, he would leave his cell to spend all of Great Lent in the desert to fast and pray, returning to the community on Palm Sunday. So he settled in the Palestinian desert with a companion, Theoctistus. One day in the desert, a pagan Arab sheik, led by divine revelation, sought out Euthymius on behalf of his sick paralyzed son. Euthymius healed the boy, and the sheik and his entire tribe converted and were baptized. Fleeing increasing attention from the world, Euthymius soon settled at a distance from Theoctistus and the other monks, though he did return to them on Saturdays and Sundays for the Divine Liturgy.

The monastic settlement grew, and a church was built. As more and more monks desired to join them, Euthymius offered a synthesis of the two forms of monasticism: some monks would live the communal life (under Theoctistus), and some the eremetic, solitary life (under himself). This way soon became characteristic of Palestinian monasticism: the communal life under Theoctistus became the training ground for monks who, when ready, would proceed to the solitary life with Euthymius.

Euthymius was known for his wonders and his wisdom. Regarding those who wished to move from place to place, he said, "A tree that is frequently transplanted does not bear fruit." Siding with those who remained true to the Orthodox Council of Chalcedon of 451, Euthymius was persecuted for his staunch defense of the council. He rallied many to the support of Chalcedon. When the government began to persecute defenders of Chalcedon, he was forced to flee to the desert of Rouba for two years. He never relented in his godly austerity, completing his course and dying in peace in 473. At the moment of his death, a lightning bolt was seen to turn to a pillar of light as his soul rose to heaven.

~: JANUARY 21 :~

St. Maximus the Confessor

Maximus was born at Constantinople in about 580 as a member of the aristocracy. He was appointed chief secretary to the emperor but resigned his career in the world to seek God in monastic solitude at Chrysopolis. Maximus was elected abbot of the community, but when the community had to flee before the Persian invasion in 626, he went to Alexandria and eventually to Rome.

When the heresy of Monothelitism arose (which asserted that Christ had only one will, the divine will, and so was not fully human), he opposed it with all his might, supporting the Bishop of Rome. When the emperor espoused this heresy and commanded all to submit, Maximus refused, and like the Bishop of Rome, he was arrested and taken prisoner to Constantinople. There he suffered years of torture and harassment. Though the church at Constantinople espoused this heresy and Rome joined with them, he still refused to enter into communion with them, saying, "Even if the whole world enters into communion with them, I alone will not!"

For his refusal to submit, his tongue was cut out and his right hand cut off. He was then sent into exile to a lonely fortress at Skhemaris at the far end of the Black Sea. There he died for the truth, having suffered as a confessor for the Faith. The saint was a brilliant and original theologian. He also wrote mystical and ascetical works, such as his *Four Centuries of Charity*. He died in the Lord in 662.

~: JANUARY 22 :~

Holy Apostle Timothy

Timothy was born in Lystra in Asia Minor, son of a Gentile father and a Jewish mother. As a young man he was converted by St. Paul, accompanied him on his missionary journeys, and was the recipient of two of Paul's New Testament epistles. St. Paul wrote to him not to allow any to look down on him for his youth (1 Tim. 4:12), for he had a difficult task to do in Ephesus, and many there would be tempted to disdain him for his youth.

After St. Paul's martyrdom, St. Timothy continued to serve as Bishop of Ephesus, where he was bidden to stay (1 Tim. 1:3), later sharing the work there with St. John the Theologian. In about the year 93, he was martyred by stoning at the hands of a pagan mob when he went out into the street to remonstrate with them for their idolatry and excess at a pagan festival. His relics were taken to the Church of the Holy Apostles in Constantinople in the year 356.

JANUARY 23

Hieromartyr Clement, Bishop of Ancyra

Clement was born in Ancyra in 258 to a pagan father and a Christian mother. He was orphaned at age twelve and brought up by the local church. So great were his zeal and piety that he was chosen by the church to be their bishop when he was only twenty. When persecution broke out soon after, Clement was arrested. He suffered imprisonment and periodic torture as he was transferred from city to city. He was put to public scorn and torture in hope of demoralizing the Christian Church at large.

During one period of torture, when they were hitting his face and breaking his teeth, Clement cried out to his torturers, "You honor me, for the mouth of my Lord Jesus Christ was struck like this and His cheeks were slapped too, and I, unworthy as I am, am now made worthy of this!"

Throughout his imprisonment he was horribly tormented—he was stretched on the rack, seared with hot iron, flung upon a bed of nails, and his flesh was flayed until his bones showed through. At last he was beheaded in Ancyra and was received to heavenly glory in the year 312.

JANUARY 24

Our Venerable Mother Xenia of Rome

St. Xenia was born in the fifth century with the name Eusebia, a daughter of a noble Christian Roman family. Though she wanted to dedicate herself to holy chastity, her family arranged for her to marry. On her wedding night, Eusebia fled with two of her maidservants, taking a ship bound for Alexandria and calling herself Xenia (meaning "a stranger").

When she reached the island of Kos, she disembarked. Remembering the story of how God had sent St. Paul to help Thekla, she prayed that God would help her too. And God indeed sent her help:

a monastic (also named Paul) met her and took her to the city of Mylassa, where his monastery was. He offered her and her two maidservants cells nearby. They accepted his offer and lived there in holy asceticism for many years. Soon others came to be with Xenia, seeking her prayers, and her fame grew.

In the year 450, Xenia died in peace while praying, a true bride of her heavenly Bridegroom, and her soul ascended to heaven. Her two maidservants who had followed her so loyally into the life of monasticism at length died also and were buried, according to their request, at her feet.

Our Holy Mother Xenia of St. Petersburg

Xenia of St. Petersburg was born early in the eighteenth century. She married Andrei, a singer in the royal choir. Suddenly, her husband died and left Xenia a widow at the age of twenty-six. She then took up her husband's persona, using his name and wearing his military uniform. The widow began to sell her husband's house in order to distribute the money to others. Her friends, distressed at her renunciation of wealth, had her medically examined to declare her insane and thus not competent to give away her wealth. But when the doctors examined her, they found Xenia to be quite sound of mind and thus legally entitled to dispose of her property as she wished. So she sold all she had and went to live in the cold streets of St. Petersburg as a fool-for-Christ.

Though mocked by the locals as an insane woman, she went about doing good in secret. For example, when a new stone church was being built, night after night, after all the workers had gone, she would carry bricks up to the roof to be used by them the next day. She accepted only the smallest of alms, often giving them away to her fellow poor.

God granted her the gift of prophetic foresight. Eventually, Xenia's true worth began to become known to the local people, and they would bring themselves and their children to be blessed by her. After forty-five years of prayer and life in the streets, she fell asleep in Christ in the year 1803 and was buried in Smolensk Cemetery.

᛫ JANUARY 25 ᛫

St. Gregory of Nazianzus, the Theologian

Gregory was born in Arianzus in 329, son of the bishop of nearby Nazianzus. He received a fine education, culminating at Athens, where he went to school with his lifelong friend Basil (later St. Basil the Great). Gregory, being a sensitive and quiet man, longed for the prayerful solitude of monasticism and so joined his friend Basil at his monastic community at Ibora in the year 358. He joyfully devoted himself to monastic rigor: he slept on the ground, ate only bread and salt, and drank only water, spending half of each night in prayer and meditation.

Gregory's father, however, called him back home and compelled him to accept ordination as a priest in 361 to serve him as his assistant. Gregory thought himself unworthy for such work and soon fled back to his monastic retreat with his friend Basil. After ten weeks, though, he returned home to Nazianzus to work with his father.

In 370, Basil became Bishop of Caesarea and soon needed his Orthodox friends around him as allies against Arianism. Thus he persuaded Gregory to accept ordination as bishop of the town of Sasima, a small town nearby—"a detestable little place," Gregory wrote of it, "without water or grass or any mark of civilization." He tried to work there but soon thought it futile and returned again to Nazianzus. After the death of Basil, he ended up at Constantinople and, for his famed poetic eloquence, was given charge of the Orthodox community there (all of the other churches of the capital being Arian).

Here Gregory gave many lectures proclaiming the Orthodox Faith, and crowds flocked to hear him. When the Arians were expelled from the churches there, Gregory was elected the archbishop of the city. He contributed greatly to the Second Ecumenical Council held there in 381. But he still had no taste for all the politics and intrigue that attended so powerful an office, and so he withdrew back to Nazianzus a few months later, spending his remaining days in prayer and in writing. Because of the profundity and power of his teaching, he has been given the title "the Theologian." Gregory died in peace in 388.

JANUARY 26

Our Holy Father Xenophon, Our Mother Maria, and their sons, John and Arcadius

In the fifth century, a wealthy senator named Xenophon had a wife, Maria, who bore him two sons, John and Arcadius. It was decided to have them finish their education in Beirut, but on the way there, the boys' ship was lost in a storm. John and Arcadius both survived separately, clinging to timber from the wreck. They reached shore miles from each other, each thinking the other lost.

John, coming ashore north of Tyre and barely alive, was nursed to health by the monks of a desert monastery. In his devotion to God, he decided to stay at the monastery as one of its monks. Two years later, Acadius also, in his devotion to God, decided to become a monk, and so the brothers lived and served God in separate monasteries, unknown to each other.

Later, a monk visiting Constantinople suggested to Xenophon and Maria (who thought themselves bereaved of their two sons) that one of the monks at St. Sava's in Jerusalem was their son Arcadius. Immediately they set out for the Holy Land to see if this was so. By Divine Providence, John also decided to visit Jerusalem as a pilgrim to the holy places. Thus, by God's grace, they all came together and met in a joyful reunion at our Lord's Tomb in the Church of the Resurrection in Jerusalem. The surprise and joy of their unexpected reunion led them to a fresh dedication to God. Xenophon resigned from the senate and joined his sons as a monk at St. Sava's Monastery. Maria also became a nun at a women's monastery not far from there. They died in the fifth century in peace.

JANUARY 27

Translation of the Relics of St. John Chrysostom

St. John's feast day is November 13. This day commemorates his relics being brought with honor from Armenia to the capital city of Constantinople.

St. John died in exile far away in the village of Comana in Armenia, having been banished there by the spiteful Empress Eudoxia for his fearless stand for righteousness and his denunciation of the empress's sins. On unjust and trumped-up charges, he was deposed and banished to Cucusus in Armenia in 407.

In order to further isolate John from his supporters and to pursue him even to death, he was banished further out to Pityus in Iberia in the dead of winter. In his old age and ill health, St. John died from exhaustion along the way. Thirty years later, the Patriarch Proclus roused the people and the Emperor Theodosius to vindicate John's memory and return his venerable relics with glory to the capital. His relics—which had healed the sick even before their translation—were carried with honor back to the patriarchal throne in the Church of the Holy Apostles in Constantinople, while the emperor begged forgiveness over them in the name of his mother, Eudoxia.

To show how complete was his vindication and how he now dwelt among them as formerly, the story is told of how, when his relics were brought to the patriarchal throne (as John himself used to ascend the throne at the start of each liturgy and bless the people), his voice was heard from the relics, blessing the people and saying, "Peace be with you!"—even as he blessed the people from there in former days. The translation of his relics took place in 438.

~: JANUARY 28 :~

Our Holy Father St. Ephraim the Syrian

Ephraim was born at Nisibis around 306, of Christian parents. Early on he had an interest in monastic endeavor. Ephraim was made a catechetical teacher by his bishop, St. James of Nisibis, with whom perhaps he attended the First Ecumenical Council of Nicaea in 325. Eventually he was also ordained deacon. While in Nisibis, Ephraim wrote seventy-seven hymns designed for popular use and to teach the people to resist false doctrines. He became very famous for these—people said, "Ephraim teaches as if a fountain were flowing from his mouth." The people called him "the lyre of the Holy Spirit."

When the emperor signed a peace treaty in 363 giving Nisibis to the Persians, the Christians of the city were forced to move elsewhere. Ephraim settled in Edessa, taking a job as a bathkeeper. Soon he met a monk who persuaded him to join some hermits living in the nearby hills. There, he continued to study and to write, producing many Old and New Testament commentaries. Ephraim's fame grew, and disciples gathered around him. He continued to write hymns to glorify God and to oppose heretical doctrines.

Ephraim heard of the fame of St. Basil in faraway Caesarea. He went there to visit him, arriving at Theophany in 371. Though they could only speak through an interpreter (Ephraim spoke no Greek), Basil still recognized his worth: when Ephraim referred to himself as a sinner, Basil replied, "A sinner! I would that your sins were mine!"

Ephraim was a great ascetical master: the Lenten prayer, "O Lord and Master of my life," is testimony to his ascetic humility and his peaceable spirit. Once, when he had fasted several days, a brother brought him some pottage to eat but accidentally dropped it so that the food was strewn all over the floor and the dish itself was broken. Seeing the brother upset, Ephraim said cheerfully, "Never mind—if the supper won't come to me, I will go to the supper!" and began to eat it from the floor as best he could.

Toward the end of his life, a severe famine struck Edessa. Though seventy years of age, Ephraim undertook famine relief work, caring for the sick, arranging for the burial of the dead, and distributing food to the starving. A month after the crisis, Ephraim died in peace in 373.

~: JANUARY 29 :~

Translation of the Relics of St. Ignatius the God-Bearer

St. Ignatius's principal feast is December 20—today is the feast of the translation of his relics.

Ignatius, Bishop of Antioch, was arrested in his old age and taken to Rome, where he was thrown to the beasts and martyred in the year 107. His companions collected his bones and returned to Antioch, where they buried them, laying them in a chest as a great treasure.

When Antioch was conquered in 637, the relics were translated to Rome and enshrined in the Church of St. Clement.

~: JANUARY 30 :~

The Three Holy Hierarchs

This feast was instituted in the eleventh century. At that time there was a quarrel among the people about which of these three hierarchs was the greatest—St. Basil the Great, St. Gregory the Theologian, or St. John Chrysostom. The quarrel was resolved by a dream divinely sent to Bishop John of Euchaita. In his dream, each of the three hierarchs appeared to John, and then all three of them appeared together, saying to him, "We are one in God, as you see, and there is no dispute among us. Neither is there a first or a second." They advised him to celebrate a common feast for them. This day is testimony to the great heavenly unity of all the saints in Christ.

~: JANUARY 31 :~

Holy Unmercenaries Cyrus and John

Cyrus lived in Alexandria and worked as a physician. As a Christian, he not only treated the bodies of the suffering with his skill but also prayed for them, and by this healed many with the sign of the Cross. When the Emperor Diocletian began his persecution of the Church, Cyrus fled to Arabia, where his ministry of healing continued. There he met John, a former Roman officer from a noble family in Edessa, who had heard of his ministry. They became close friends, and John decided to leave the army and join Cyrus so they could live the ascetic life together.

When they heard of a Christian woman named Athanasia who, with her daughters, was suffering for the Faith in Canopus, they went there to encourage her, fearing that the women might otherwise apostatize. Cyrus and John tried to slip into the prison and minister to the women unseen by the authorities, but they were apprehended as Christians. They were tortured in full sight of the women, in the hope that Athanasia and her daughters might themselves lose heart and recant. Such were the faith and constancy of Cyrus and John that the women did not weaken. All of them were led together to the place of execution, where they were beheaded.

This occurred in 311. In the next century, the holy relics of Cyrus and John were translated to Menuthis so that the miraculous power of the saints might overcome the cult of Isis there. Their relics worked many miracles. The saints abide in the Church, a testimony to the healing love of Christ.

FEBRUARY 1

Holy Martyr Tryphon

Born in the village of Lampsacus in Phrygia in the third century to humble Christian parents, Tryphon worked as a humble peasant, tending his flock of geese. During the persecution under Emperor Decius, he was arrested with other Christians and sent in chains to Nicaea, to the governor Aquilinus. When the governor asked his name and his fortune, Tryphon replied, "There is no fortune or luck among Christians, but all things occur as Divine Providence directs. But if you want to know our condition, we are of honorable birth."

The governor said, "Sacrifice to the gods, for I see you have come to full age and have full powers of intelligence."

He replied again, "We have perfect intelligence in our Lord Jesus Christ, and we want to possess a perfect intelligence for Him and to finish our agony."

With his companions, Tryphon was stripped and tortured, being set in a pillory and beaten for three hours with wooden swords. All this he endured without a sound. As he steadfastly refused to deny his Lord, he was tortured more and then dragged through the city in the cold of winter. Then nails were driven into his feet, and he was dragged into the public forum. Soldiers beat him, dislocating his limbs, and burnt his body with torches. Finally Tryphon and his companions were beheaded and inherited the heavenly Kingdom. This happened in the year 250.

~: FEBRUARY 2 :~

The Meeting of the Lord in the Temple

In obedience to the Law, the Theotokos brought Christ into the temple to present Him to God as her firstborn son and to offer a sacrifice for her ceremonial purification. Thus did Christ, born under the Law, fulfill all the Law for our salvation, beginning a life of obedience and love to the Father.

While in the temple, they were met by aged Simeon, who had been promised by God that he would not die until he had seen the Messiah. Seeing Jesus in His mother's arms, he gave thanks to God, saying, "Lord, now You are letting Your servant depart in peace, for my eyes have seen Your salvation." They were also met by the aged prophetess Anna, who had lived since her early widowhood in chastity—she also recognized Him as the Messiah and spoke of this hope to all she met. Thus was Jesus recognized by Israel as their own Christ, in the persons of these two venerable representatives. This solemn feast dates from 544. Candles are blessed in church on this day and are held by the faithful throughout the liturgy.

~: FEBRUARY 3 :~

St. Simeon the Elder and Anna the Prophetess

Simeon, an old man, was led by the Spirit in the temple to meet the Theotokos and recognize the Child in her arms as the long-awaited Messiah. He had been promised by God that he would not die until he had seen the Christ, and upon seeing Him, in joy he sang, "Lord, now You are letting Your servant depart in peace." He also prophesied that this Divine Child would be a controversial figure in Israel and a judgment on them. He thus revealed in prophecy the nature of Jesus' messiahship—that He would not be a figure of triumphal popularity but One spoken against and crucified. He predicted that a sword of sorrow would pierce the heart of the Theotokos also, which happened when she saw her Son upon the Cross.

Anna was a daughter of Phanuel, of the tribe of Asher. She was widowed at an early age after only seven years of marriage. After this she lived in holy chastity until the age of eighty-four, spending all her time in the temple worshipping with fasting and prayer. As a true prophetess, she also recognized the infant Jesus as the true Messiah and spoke of Him to all who came to the temple, saying that the Redeemer of Jerusalem and Israel had been born.

Simeon and Anna abide in the Church as embodiments of the hope and desire of Israel for its Messiah.

St. Nicholas, Enlightener of Japan

Nicholas was born in 1836 in Russia and named John Kasatkin. He desired to serve as a missionary, and when the Russian Consulate in Japan asked for a priest, he volunteered to go. In 1860, at twenty-four years of age, he was tonsured a monk with the name Nicholas and ordained priest. He left Russia for his new work in Japan.

Waiting to enter the country, he met Bishop Innocent Veniaminov (later St. Innocent), who counseled him to conduct himself with dignity in order to inspire respect among the Japanese. He said, "Go buy yourself some velvet for a good cassock!"

Work in Japan was difficult for foreigners, but Nicholas worked hard to learn Japanese and present the gospel to them in a way they could understand. Conversions were slow. The work grew, however, even when persecution of foreigners began in 1872. A seminary was opened and books were published. Services were held in Japanese, and native Japanese were ordained as priests. In 1880, Nicholas was ordained bishop for his flock.

When war broke out between Japan and Russia, he stayed in Japan and even blessed his people to pray for Japanese victory—though he could not bring himself to do so. After the war, he was made archbishop. He died in peace in 1912 at age seventy-six. His cathedral in Tokyo is known as Nicholai-Do—"the house of Nicholas."

❦ FEBRUARY 4 ❧

Our Holy Father Isidore

Isidore was born in 370 to a well-to-do family in Alexandria, having connections with Patriarch Theophilus and his nephew, Cyril (later St. Cyril of Alexandria). Following an excellent education, Isidore became zealous for Christ, being particularly inspired by the work of St. John Chrysostom. After teaching rhetoric in Pelusium, east of the Nile delta, Isidore felt drawn to a life of monastic solitude and retired to the desert of Nitria to live as an ascetic.

After a year of fruitful struggle there, he returned to Pelusium to be ordained priest and take up a life of teaching in the Church. His great learning and fame for holiness drew multitudes to him, and he converted many to Christ. A new bishop was elected in Pelusium, and Isidore again withdrew from the city, retiring to a monastery near Aphnaion, where he was to remain.

When St. John Chrysostom was exiled by the empress in 407 and his name removed in disgrace from the lists of Orthodox patriarchs, Isidore, long an admirer and supporter of John, was grieved. He wrote in protest to Cyril, the new Patriarch of Alexandria, urging him to restore John's name to the list. He was successful, and peace was restored between Alexandria and the cause of John.

St. Isidore was also a man of great learning—he wrote three thousand commentaries on the Scriptures. Commenting on the five foolish virgins of our Lord's parable (Matt. 25), he said the foolish virgins were rejected "because they had no other virtues, such as compassion. Virginity itself is not sufficient. It is of no use if the virgin is filled with pride and self-seeking." St. Isidore died in peace in 470.

❦ FEBRUARY 5 ❧

Holy Martyr Agatha

Agatha was born to a rich and noble family in Catania in Sicily. At the time of her arrest during the persecution under Decius in the mid-third century, she was only fifteen years of age.

When she appeared before Quintinian the governor, since she was very beautiful and had great wealth, he wanted her for his own. Agatha, however, remained resolute. For a month he tried to break her resolution, but to no avail.

When she appeared before the governor again, he asked her, "Since you are of noble birth, why are you acting like a slave?"

The spirited girl replied, "Because I am the slave of Christ, and slaves of Christ are really the freest of all creatures, because they have acquired mastery of self." For her recalcitrance, she was imprisoned and tortured for the Faith.

She suffered cheerfully. When she was stretched on the rack and beaten, scraped with iron claws, and her wounds were scorched with flame, she said, "Corn does not reach the granary until it is threshed, and my soul cannot attain eternal blessedness until it is separated by sufferings from my body." Her breasts were cut off, and she was thrown bleeding into prison.

In prison she had a vision of St. Peter urging her to constancy and restoring her. She was tortured again until she died. The brave young girl suffered for her King in 251.

❦ FEBRUARY 6 ❧

St. Bucolus of Smyrna

St. Bucolus was entrusted with the care of the church in Smyrna by St. John the Apostle in the first century. Bucolus preached and converted many pagans to the Faith. He tended the church as a true steward of God's radiant grace, caring for God's lampstand there with true devotion and zeal (see Rev. 1:20). When the time for his death approached, he entrusted the community to St. Polycarp, who later ended his course as a martyr. In the following centuries St. Bucolus's tomb became a site of pilgrimage, where many came in faith to find healing from this early saint of the Church.

FEBRUARY

St. Photius, Patriarch of Constantinople

Born in 810 to one of the prominent families in Constantinople, Photius was raised by pious parents, both of whom were martyred during the iconoclast controversy. Photius was devoted to learning and spent whole nights in study. He had a brilliant career in the imperial court.

When the patriarchal throne fell vacant, Photius was elected bishop on account of his great learning. He was hurriedly ordained through all the ranks from monk to reader to bishop in the space of one week and was consecrated bishop of the imperial city in 858. He was reluctant to assume such a position in such perilous political times, saying that he only submitted to it in deference to others and was "enthroned as a prisoner." Nonetheless, he worked tirelessly, restoring churches and monasteries that had been damaged by the iconoclasts, and working to further mission work among the Slavic peoples by sending the missionaries Cyril and Methodius.

His work as patriarch was troubled by politics (he was exiled more than once), but he maintained his integrity in those difficult times. When Nicholas, Pope of Rome, claiming an authority he did not have, excommunicated Photius and sought to depose him, Photius wrote to excommunicate and depose Nicholas in return. Photius stood firm against the growing pretensions of the Roman bishop and against the espousal of the filioque addition to the Creed.

He wrote many books, including his classic Mystagogy of the Holy Spirit, in which he refutes the filioque, championing the patristic interpretation of the procession of the Holy Spirit from Father alone. Despite all the wild accusations of his enemies, Photius retained a peaceful and forgiving spirit. A man of great patience and learning, he died in about 891.

❧ FEBRUARY 7 ☙

St. Parthenius, Bishop of Lampsacus
Parthenius was the pious son of a deacon in Melitopolis. He loved to fish and devoted his life to this work, often donating a sizable portion

of his catch to feed the poor. Though illiterate, he had a retentive memory and knew the Scriptures well. He also had a gift of healing. When the local bishop discovered this, he had him ordained priest, despite his illiteracy. He was chosen Bishop of Lampsacus when the see fell vacant. The Emperor Constantine, greatly impressed by his accomplishments, chose Parthenius for the work of replacing pagan temples with Christian churches.

A story is told of his holiness: When he was casting out a demon, the demon spoke and refused to come out, protesting that Parthenius would cast him into swine. "No," Parthenius replied, "but I will offer you a man—enter me if you can!" But the demon cried out and fled, unable to enter so holy a servant of God. When Parthenius died in peace, he was buried with state honors usually given only to patriarchs and emperors. He reposed in the fourth century.

~: FEBRUARY 8 :~

Holy Great Martyr Theodore Stratelates ("the General")
Theodore was a general under Licentius and a governor whose capital was Heraklea in Pontus. For his faith in Christ, he scorned military and worldly glory and advancement and suffered as a martyr. His sufferings were particularly severe: he was flogged seven hundred times on his back, fifty times on his stomach, and then struck on the back of the neck with a lead-tipped scourge. After this, he was flayed and his wounds were scorched and scraped with potsherds. During all these torments, all the general said was, "Glory to You, my God!"

After this, he was thrown into prison without food. At length he was crucified outside the city. Soldiers pierced his entrails with an iron spike, and young people shot at him with arrows, putting out his eyes. He was finally dispatched by beheading.

St. Theodore, a true military leader in the army of Christ, suffered in the year 319. His relics were later taken to Constantinople and buried with honor at the church in Blachernae.

FEBRUARY 9

Holy Martyr Nicephorus

Nicephorus was a layman who lived in Antioch in the third century with his friend, the priest Sapricius. The two friends, who often debated with each other, one day quarreled and remained at odds with each other. Nicephorus tried to make peace with his friend, but Sapricius would have none of it. When persecution broke out in 258, Sapricius was arrested and, though tortured for Christ, remained firm in his faith. He was therefore sentenced to be beheaded and led out to execution. As Sapricius was on his way there, Nicephorus met him and, falling at his feet, begged pardon from his friend in a last attempt to be reconciled. "Martyr of Jesus Christ," he pleaded, "forgive me my offense!" But Sapricius hardened his heart in pride and did not reply. Despite the continued and urgent entreaties of his former friend, Sapricius would not forgive him but still more hardened his heart.

Thus it was that God in judgment forsook him—when he reached the spot of execution and was ordered to kneel down for beheading, his courage, invincible before, even under torture, failed him. He grew pale and troubled and asked why he was being executed. When they answered that it was for refusing to sacrifice to the gods, he cried out, "Stop, my friends! Do not kill me—I will do what you want—I will sacrifice!"

Nicephorus was dismayed and aghast and said, "What are you doing, brother? Do not renounce Jesus Christ our good Master! Do not lose the crown you've already won by torture and suffering!" When Nicephorus realized that it was to no avail, he cried out, "I am a Christian and believe in Jesus Christ, whom this one renounced! Look—I'm ready to die in his place!" Thus was Nicephorus martyred in his stead and gained the crown which Sapricius despised. This happened in the year 260.

~: FEBRUARY 10 :~

Hieromartyr Charalampus

Charalampus was a priest in the town of Magnesia in Asia Minor, serving there for many years. When persecution raged against the church there, Charalampus, by then over a hundred years old, also was arrested and condemned by Lucianus, the local governor. His torture was terrible and prolonged—for months he suffered, the enraged governor himself joining in the terrible work. But the martyr remained steadfast: while they were flaying him with iron scrapers, he said, "Thank you, brothers, for scraping off the old body and renewing my soul for new, eternal life!"

So great was his torture that he actually died from it before the executioner could behead him. He suffered and was glorified in about 202. His relics are now kept in the monastery of St. Stephen in Meteora, Greece.

~: FEBRUARY 11 :~

Hieromartyr Blaise, Bishop of Sebaste

A man of prayer, Blaise spent much time in the hills of Mount Argea, communing with God and praying in a cave. He was a physician, and his gentleness caused him to be elected Bishop of Sebaste in eastern Anatolia. When persecution arose against the Church in the reign of Emperor Diocletian, Blaise stayed safe in the hills for some time but was at last arrested and taken before Agricolus. Confessing himself a Christian, he was imprisoned and cruelly tortured. He was martyred along with seven women and two young children in 316.

~: FEBRUARY 12 :~

St. Meletius, Archbishop of Antioch

Meletius the bishop, a humble and peaceable man, was translated from his episcopal see of Sebaste to the see of Antioch by the local council of Antioch in 361. In a time of ambiguity and controversy about Arianism, he spoke clearly for Nicene Orthodoxy in the council. For this, his own deacon (of Arian belief) clamped his hand over his bishop's mouth to silence him. At this, Meletius preached with his hands until he could free himself, holding aloft three fingers and then one finger, indicating the three-in-one nature of the Trinity. For his strong stand, the council deposed him. He was banished, and the council elected an Arian bishop in his place.

When a new emperor came to the throne, Meletius was recalled. The Arians still supported their Arian replacement bishop. When another Arian emperor ruled later, Meletius was again exiled until political fortunes changed. So great was his reputation that at the Second Ecumenical Council in 381, Meletius was asked to preside. He died during the council, a martyr to the rigors of his exiles. He was loved and missed by his brother bishops. "Where now," said St. Gregory of Nyssa at his funeral, "is that sweet and calm look, that radiant smile, that kind hand and voice?" His relics were carried with honor to Antioch in 381.

❦ FEBRUARY 13 ❧

The Venerable Martinian

Martinian was born in Caesarea in Palestine in the fourth century. When he was eighteen, he retired to the nearby mountains of Cappadocia to live as a hermit. He lived there in peace and austerity for twenty-five years. One day an immoral woman named Zoe was moved to tempt him to sin. She contrived to be present at his door one night in a storm, pretending to be lost and in need of shelter. He admitted her, and she attempted to seduce him. Filled with holy and desperate resolution, he thrust his legs into the fire and cried out, "Martinian! How does this fire feel now? The fire which the devil will kindle in hell to burn the sinner will be worse than that!"

The woman was horrorstruck and, suddenly ashamed of herself, burst into tears. She repented of her immoral life and eventually entered a monastic community, where she lived as a nun. Martinian, when his legs healed, moved to another place where he was not known, an island cave not far from shore. He lived there in peace for six years.

One day a boat was wrecked on the shore, and one of the passengers, a girl, found her way to his cave and sought shelter. He did not want to refuse her shelter but did not want to cohabit with her for the two months until his regular ship would come bringing food. Thus he abandoned his cave and swam to shore, letting the girl stay there until the ship came to rescue her. He wandered about town for two years, preaching the gospel to all he met. He reached Athens and died there in peace in 422.

❦ FEBRUARY 14 ❧

Our Holy Father Auxentius

Auxentius was the son of a Persian Christian who fled the pagan persecution under King Sapor of Persia, settling in Syria. He visited Constantinople and there began a distinguished career in the imperial guard. While there, he was drawn to monasticism through contacts with local ascetics at the capital, and in about 446 he retired to a mountain near Chalcedon in Bithynia to live as a hermit. There he advanced in holiness and was granted by God gifts of healing.

When the Fourth Ecumenical Council met in Chalcedon in 451, Auxentius was invited to come, and though reluctant to leave his solitary life, he was prevailed upon to accompany those sent for him. The Monophysite heresy (which denied the fullness of Christ's humanity) was unknown to him, and such theological subtleties were beyond him. But he impressed all the council by his venerable holiness. He gave his assent to the Chalcedonian definition of the Faith.

After the council Auxentius established himself in a mountain hermitage nearer to Chalcedon, praying and receiving visitors who came to seek his spiritual counsel. He composed hymns and taught them to those who visited him. Many women renounced the world and placed themselves under his direction, so that a monastery was built for them not far from his own hermitage. He died suddenly of an illness in 470.

F   *Holy Martyr Valentine*
E   Valentine was a presbyter of the church in Rome in the third century.
B   He was arrested and commanded to renounce Christ in the perse-
R   cution that raged there. When he refused, he was beaten with clubs
U   and afterward beheaded outside the Flaminian Gate. A later legend
A   tells of how he wrote to a friend while in prison, encouraging her to
R   remain true to Christ, and signing the letter, "From your Valentine."
Y   It is from this that the modern custom of greeting another in love on
     this day is said to have arisen.

FEBRUARY 15

Holy Apostle Onesimus

Onesimus was a native of Phrygia and a slave to Philemon in Colosse. He ran away from his master and found his way to Rome, where he was converted by St. Paul, who was then a prisoner in Rome. St. Paul sent him back to be reconciled to his master bearing a letter, the New Testament Epistle to Philemon. In this epistle, St. Paul exhorted Philemon to pardon Onesimus and even grant him his liberty. This Philemon did, and Onesimus returned to serve St. Paul in Rome. Onesimus later served as a bishop in Ephesus after St. Timothy. In the persecution under Trajan he was arrested and taken to Rome, where he was imprisoned and martyred. He suffered for his Lord in the year 109.

FEBRUARY 16

Holy Martyrs Pamphilus, Valens, Paul, and the Five Egyptians

Pamphilus was born in Berytus (modern Beirut) of a wealthy family and received an excellent education. He also studied in the great catechetical school of Alexandria (being an admirer of Origen, who once taught there). Pamphilus was a great scholar and collected a vast library. He moved to Caesarea in Palestine and opened a school there, continuing his scholarly work of editing, correcting, and transcribing copies of the Scriptures. He was ordained priest and served with great humility and charity.

In 307, the pagan governor of Palestine persecuted the Church, and Pamphilus was arrested, tortured, and imprisoned for two years. His fellow prisoners were Valens (an aged deacon of Jerusalem) and Paul (a devout layman of Jamnia in Palestine). Like Pamphilus, they endured their tortures with constancy, keeping their Faith.

The governor's successor, Firmilian, continued the persecution. When five travelers from Egypt arrived in Caesarea and confessed themselves to be Christians, they were arrested. When asked their names, they gave the names of the Old Testament saints Elijah, Jeremiah, Isaiah, Samuel, and Daniel; when asked their city, they answered, "Jerusalem!" Finding them uncooperative, the governor had them flogged and sentenced to death.

They were executed by beheading, along with Pamphilus and his companions. Their bodies were left exposed with dishonor to be eaten by the wild beasts, but the beasts did not touch them. Pamphilus's spiritual son, the eighteen-year-old Porphyrius, called out from the crowd and demanded the bodies for burial. He was arrested on the spot and suffered martyrdom as well by being burnt alive.

These martyrs suffered with honor for their Lord in 309.

⁓ FEBRUARY 17 ⁓

St. Theodore the Recruit ("the Tyro")

He was a native of Amasea in Pontus and as a youth enlisted in the Roman army, even though he was a Christian. As a member of the Marmarite regiment he was stationed at Euchaita. When the persecution under Emperors Maximian and Maximin broke out against the Church, the young recruit was seized and asked by the governor how he dared to practice a religion that was illegal. He retorted, "I do not recognize your gods. Jesus Christ, the only Son of God, is my God. Beat, tear, or burn me, and if my words offend you, cut out my tongue—every part of my body is ready when God calls for it as a sacrifice!" Thinking him a mere youth who could be persuaded later, the governor dismissed him.

In his zeal for God and to compel the authorities to take his faith

FEBRUARY

seriously, Theodore set fire to a pagan temple of Cybele, which burned to the ground. This time he was arrested and taken seriously. Proving steadfast in his Christian confession, he was whipped, racked, and tortured. All the while, he kept repeating, "I will bless the Lord at all times; His praise shall always be in my mouth!" He was finally executed by being burnt alive, suffering for the Savior in 306.

The story is told of how, when Julian the Apostate tried to demoralize the Christians by having all the meat in the markets of Constantinople sprinkled with the blood of animals sacrificed to idols, St. Theodore appeared in a dream to the bishop of the city, telling him to command the people to eat only boiled wheat and so avoid the contagion of eating food offered to idols. Thus, thanks to St. Theodore, the Christians of the city were saved from the sin of idolatry. This event is commemorated on the first Saturday of Great Lent, when St. Theodore is celebrated and boiled wheat is eaten as part of the Church's prayer for the departed. Theodore abides in the Church as an image of steadfastness and courage.

↢ FEBRUARY 18 ↣

St. Leo the Great, Pope of Rome

Leo, archdeacon of Rome, was elected bishop in 449 when the previous Pope died. He vigorously opposed the local heresies of Pelagius (who denied the need for God's inner grace) and of the Manichaeans.

When the Fourth Ecumenical Council was convoked by the emperor at Chalcedon in 451 to address the Monophysite heresy (which denied the full humanity of Christ), Leo sent a letter, his "Tome," professing the faith held by Rome—that Christ was one person in two natures, divine and human. When the letter was read at the council, it was acclaimed to be the truth and consistent with the faith of St. Cyril of Alexandria, whom all acknowledged to be a standard of Orthodox truth. The council fathers cried out, "St. Peter has spoken through Leo! Cyril and Leo have taught alike!" Thus the agreement of Rome, necessary to the consensus of East and West, was secured and the truth of Chalcedon proclaimed.

Leo also stood firm in his courageous defense of his own city against the onslaught of barbarian invasion. When Attila, the leader of the Huns, advanced on Rome to destroy it in 455, Leo went out to meet him, unarmed and fearless, leading not an army but a procession of clergy. He urged Attila to use restraint on the conquered city, and it was due to Leo's serene and authoritative courage that the pillage was not worse than it was. Leo survived the sack of Rome by five years, dying in peace in 461.

❦ FEBRUARY 19 ❧

Holy Apostles Archippus, Philemon, and Apphia

Archippus lived with Philemon and his wife, Apphia, at Colosse. Philemon was a man of wealth and had a slave named Onesimus who, after deserting and fleeing to Rome, where he became a Christian under St. Paul, returned to his master, Philemon, and was reconciled to him. Philemon seems to have served as bishop at Colosse, along with Archippus. They were martyred there during a pagan festival of Diana by being scourged, buried alive up to their waists, and finally stoned to death.

The presence of this family in the Church's martyrology reveals the sanctity possible within families—a married life and children are no barriers to reaching the heights of holiness. God calls each of us to His glory, whatever our condition in life, and strengthens us with His grace.

❦ FEBRUARY 20 ❧

St. Leo, Bishop of Catania in Sicily

Leo lived in the eighth century. He was of noble birth and was consecrated as bishop of his native city of Ravenna. So great was his zeal that his fame grew, and he was elected Bishop of Catania in Sicily. He was a true pastor and strove to purge from his Christian flock the remnants of pagan superstition remaining in them. He also tended to the poor, the orphans, and the afflicted. He was notable in striving to convert and then (when this proved impossible) to subdue a local rebel, a magician named Heliodorus. (The rebel was later arrested and executed.) St. Leo was known for his wonderworking prayers and was invited to Constantinople. After his death, myrrh flowed from his relics, bringing healing to those who approached in faith.

Hieromartyr Sadok

Sadok was a bishop in Persia. In about the year 344, the pagan Persian king Sapor arrested many Christians and brought them to trial. They were ordered to desist from the Christian Faith and join the Persians in their worship of fire. Sadok replied, "We are ready with all our hearts to die for our God and will not worship fire!" Thus they were tortured and executed, dying for their Lord.

FEBRUARY 21

St. Eustathius, Archbishop of Antioch

Eustathius was born in Sidon in Pamphylia and was first Bishop of Berea (modern Aleppo). He was then elected Bishop of Antioch in about 325 and attended the First Ecumenical Council of Nicaea in that year. After the council he powerfully resisted the Arians and was persecuted by them: at a council in Antioch, they induced a woman with an infant child to falsely accuse Eustathius of being the child's father. For this he was deposed by the Arian majority at the council and banished to Thrace. There he died and was buried in about 345.

The woman who accused the saint, when later stricken by a serious illness, repented of her complicity in the lying attack of the Arians that resulted in the banishment of Bishop Eustathius. She openly confessed the truth of his innocence. St. John Chrysostom praised the saint from his former town of Antioch as a martyr, hoping the schism provoked by his banishment would end—which it did in 414. Eustathius's relics were translated with honor to Antioch in 482.

FEBRUARY 22

Discovery of the Relics of the Holy Martyrs in Eugenius

In the time of Patriarch Thomas of Constantinople, around 607, the relics of some unknown martyrs were discovered buried in the district of Eugenius in Constantinople. When they were exposed for veneration by the faithful, many miracles occurred.

After many years, a book copyist named Nicolas reported by revelation that the relics of St. Paul's coworkers Andronicus and Junia were among those discovered (see Rom. 16:7).

The presence of these wonderworking relics is a witness of God's love for His Church, for just as the relics of unknown martyrs have power to work wonders after lying undiscovered for many years, so God's grace is never absent from His people. He is able to care for His Church through any instrument He chooses.

Holy Martyr Maurice and the Seventy Companions

During the persecution of the Church under Maximian, Maurice and seventy soldiers with him (including his son Photinus) were arrested for refusing to sacrifice to the gods. They were stripped of their military belts (i.e., degraded from military rank) and imprisoned. When their belts were removed, Maurice said, "Our God will clothe us with clothes and belts that will not corrupt and with eternal glory!" When Maurice's son was slain before his eyes, he said, "You have fulfilled our desire and sent Photinus, Christ's soldier, on before us!" They were at length executed by being tied to trees and smeared with honey, so they would starve and be eaten alive by mosquitoes and hornets. The last man took ten days to die. They suffered honorably for Christ in about 305.

FEBRUARY 23

Hieromartyr Polycarp, Bishop of Smyrna

Polycarp was born a pagan in about AD 70 and was converted to the Faith as a young man, being a disciple of St. John the Theologian. He

FEBRUARY

was appointed by St. John to be Bishop of Smyrna. He was a man of great gravity and holiness, zealous in his defense of Orthodoxy. The heretic Marcion (who denied the Old Testament) met him and was incensed that Polycarp did not greet him. "Don't you know me, Polycarp?" Marcion said.

"I know you," replied Polycarp, "you are the firstborn of Satan!"

Still, he was a man of peace and mildness. One time he visited Rome to confer with the bishop there about the fact that he and the Pope used different calendar dates for Pascha. He refused to quarrel, and they agreed not to break communion over issues of calendar but each to observe their own customs.

In about 155, persecution broke out against the Church. When at last Polycarp was arrested, the soldiers sent for him and were surprised to find him cheerful and hospitable. Polycarp ordered them to be given a meal and asked their leave to pray—which he did, interceding for the members of his flock by name for two hours. He was taken to Smyrna's officials, who tried to persuade him to save his life by denying Christ. "What's the harm in simply saying, 'Caesar is Lord,' and burning a little incense to him?" they asked.

He did not reply, but as they continued to badger him, at last he simply said, "I shall never do what you want of me." Then they insulted him and hauled him to the arena to be put to death.

The arena was filled with shouting, yet Polycarp heard a voice from heaven saying, "Be strong, Polycarp, and play the man!"

The proconsul there still tried to get Polycarp to save his life by apostatizing. "Swear by Caesar," he said, "and I will release you. Curse Christ."

Polycarp replied, "For eighty-six years I have served Him, and He never did me harm but only good. How can I revile my King and my Savior?" For his steadfast confession as a Christian, Polycarp was condemned and burnt alive. He refused to be nailed to the stake but said, "Let me be. He who gives me grace to endure this fire will enable me to stand still without that preparation." He prayed and blessed God in the midst of the fire. Polycarp suffered and died in 155. The Christians lovingly gathered his relics and laid them to rest with honor.

❧ FEBRUARY 24 ☙

Discovery of the Head of St. John the Baptizer

St. John the Forerunner of our Lord was beheaded by King Herod at the instigation of his wife, Herodias. Joanna, wife of Chuza, Herod's steward (Luke 8:3), recovered John's head and buried it with honor. The relic was passed through private hands until it came to rest, by Divine Providence, in the care of Bishop Ouranios of Cappadocia. In the ninth century it was translated to Constantinople. The finding and veneration of this precious relic is testimony to the importance to Christians of St. John, looked upon as the father of ascetics and foremost of the witnesses to Christ.

❧ FEBRUARY 25 ☙

St. Tarasius, Patriarch of Constantinople

Tarasius was a distinguished layman at the imperial court in the eighth century, at the time the iconoclast controversy was shaking the Church. Icons had been banned by imperial order. When the iconoclast emperor died, the Patriarch of Constantinople resigned and the see fell vacant. The Empress Irene wanted to appoint pious Tarasius to the office, but he would not accept it unless she agreed to convene a council of the Church to restore godly order in the matter of the icons. Upon her agreement, he was ordained Archbishop of Constantinople on Christmas Day in 784.

The promised council was called, and it met in 787. This gathering, the Seventh Ecumenical Council, solemnly restored the icons to the churches. Tarasius continued as patriarch, living a life of godly austerity in the midst of the luxury of the capital. He often took food from his table to give to the poor with his own hands, visiting every house and hospital in the city.

Later, when the new emperor (son of the Empress Irene) became infatuated with his wife's handmaiden Theodota, he tried to persuade Tarasius to agree to his divorcing his lawful wife, Mary. Tarasius refused, saying, "I would rather suffer death and all kinds of torture than consent to this." When the emperor himself declared the marriage null and married Theodota anyway, Tarasius excommunicated both the emperor and the priest who performed the marriage.

Tarasius held firm despite imperial plots against him. He died in peace in 806 after an illness. Those with him at the end heard him refuting the demons who falsely accused him of sins and reproaches as he said, "I am not guilty of this sin, nor of that one." When he died, his face shone with heavenly radiance.

~: FEBRUARY 26 :~

St. Porphyrius, Bishop of Gaza

Porphyrius was born in Thessalonica in 353 of wealthy parents. When he was twenty-five, he left the world to live in the monastic desert of Scetis for five years. Then he traveled to the Holy Land to live in a hermitage-cave near the Jordan River. Such were his austerities that after five years there he fell quite ill and so returned to Jerusalem. He sought Christ's healing, daily visiting all the holy places, even though he was in pain and weakness. When at Golgotha, he fainted from exhaustion and had a dream of Christ healing him and charging him to take care of His Cross.

Porphyrius awoke free from pain and in perfect health. He gave away all his wealth and continued in the ascetic way. When he was forty years old, the Bishop of Jerusalem ordained him priest and, in fulfillment of his vision, set him to care for the Holy Cross in the church there. This he did for three years.

In 396 he was elected bishop of nearby Gaza without his knowledge. Gaza had a small, poor Christian population of only 280, set amid a crowd of hostile pagans. Porphyrius had a vision in which Christ told him, "Give up the treasure of the Cross, for I will marry you to a wife—poor and despised but of great piety and virtue. Be careful to adorn her well, for, worthless as she may appear, she is My sister"—the church of Gaza. Thus, much against his will (for he thought himself unworthy of the episcopate), he was ordained Bishop of Gaza in 396. He struggled greatly to convert the pagans there.

A drought in Gaza was blamed on the Christians. Porphyrius, leading his small flock in prayer and fasting, brought rain to the land, which caused several hundreds of pagans to convert to the Faith. Yet persecution against them increased, and Porphyrius appealed to the emperor for protection and help. Help came, and the order was given to demolish the pagan temples and idols of Gaza. This was done, and Porphyrius took the marble from the pagan temples and made it into steps for the church that the work of paganism might be trampled. A beautiful church was built with funds and material from Constantinople, being finished in 408. Thus did Porphyrius "adorn well" the poor church of Gaza as Christ commanded. He died in peace in 421.

❦ FEBRUARY 27 ❧

Repose of St. Raphael of Brooklyn

The future North American saint was born in Damascus, Syria, in 1860 as Rafla Hawaweeny. He was tonsured into monasticism in 1879 with the name Raphael and continued his studies, attending the patriarchal school in Damascus and the theological schools on Halki Island, Turkey (where he was ordained deacon), and in Kiev, Russia (where he was ordained priest). He was called to the New World by the Syrian Orthodox Benevolent Committee in New York and immigrated in 1895 to serve in the Russian Orthodox Mission there.

As well as being rector of St. Nicholas Church in Brooklyn, Raphael traveled throughout the North American continent as a priest for nine years before being consecrated Bishop of Brooklyn in 1904 by the Russian Orthodox hierarchy (then the only canonical Orthodox episcopate in North America). As bishop, he continued to travel throughout the continent, offering pastoral care, encouragement, and aid to struggling Orthodox communities, seeking the lost, tending the faithful, and founding thirty new parishes. Before his untimely death in 1915 at the age of fifty-five, he became known as the "Shepherd of the Lost Sheep in America."

St. Raphael's canonization in 2000 by both the Orthodox Church in America (the original Russian Mission in which he served) and the

Antiochian Orthodox Church (heir to his Arabic work) reflects the past administrative unity of the Orthodox in North America as well as the desire for its future restoration.

Our Holy Father Procopius of Decapolis

Procopius was born in the Decapolis of Palestine in about the eight century and in his youth led a life of monastic rigor. When Emperor Leo banned icons, many in the Church rose against the decree, continuing to venerate icons. Procopius also vigorously defended the holy use of icons, leaving the safety of his monastic retreat to crusade for the truth. He rallied to the cause many monks who went about preaching Christ and denouncing the iconoclast heresy. The emperor in retaliation persecuted the monks, and Procopius himself was imprisoned for a year. When he continued to preach even in prison, he was exiled. After Emperor Leo died, Procopius returned and continued his struggle in Constantinople itself. He went abroad, urging all the clergy to be resolute for the truth. Finally he returned to his monastery. He died in peace in the ninth century.

FEBRUARY 28

The Venerable Basil the Confessor

St. Basil lived in the eighth century and became a monk in his youth, under the direction of St. Procopius (feast day February 27). Like his mentor Procopius, Basil refused the imperial decree banning icons during the iconoclastic struggle against the Church. For this he was arrested and tortured, suffering especially wounds to his face. Despite these trials, his constancy was unshakable. After the death of the emperor, he was released with other confessors and continued his life of ascetic holiness. He died in peace.

Hieromartyr Proterius

Proterius was a priest in Alexandria at the time of the Monophysite heresy (which denied the fullness of Christ's human nature). When the Patriarch of Alexandria, Dioscurus, was deposed for his heresy,

Proterius was elected patriarch in his place. The Monophysites did not accept the Orthodox Proterius and continued to agitate and create a tumult. When they elected their own man, the Monophysite Timothy, as patriarch, Proterius fled for safety to one of the city's churches. The heretical mob broke in on him, dragged him into the streets, and hacked him to pieces along with six of the Orthodox faithful. This occurred in 457.

~: FEBRUARY 29 :~

(commemorated on February 28 in a non-leap year)

Our Holy Father John Cassian the Roman

John was born in about 365 and was probably of Scythian origin, though he seems to have lived in Constantinople. He early sought monastic holiness with his friend Germanus. They visited Bethlehem and the monasteries of Egypt, meeting many holy monks there.

After returning to Bethlehem, John settled in the Egyptian desert of Scetis for some time, learning the Egyptian ways of holiness. In about 400 he went to Constantinople with his friend Germanus, where they were both ordained deacons by St. John Chrysostom and served the community there. When Chrysostom was unjustly condemned, John Cassian was sent to enlist the support of Rome and the West in Chrysostom's defense. At the request of the Roman Archdeacon Leo (later Pope St. Leo the Great), he wrote against the Nestorian heresy in his book *On the Incarnation of the Lord*.

John went to Marseilles to bring the monasticism of the East to those Western lands. He built two monasteries there, one for men and one for women. To further this work, he also wrote *Institutes* (a book for beginner monks) and then *Conferences* (a study in monastic perfection, containing conversations of those monks he met in Egypt). He did not want his monasteries to be like so many others—mere breeding grounds for bishops and advancement in the Church. He said, "It was the advice of the Fathers—always relevant—that a monk should at all costs flee the company of bishops and women, for neither women nor bishops let a monk remain in peace in his cell."

John was a man of discretion, prayer, and wise moderation. He advised the constant repetition of a prayer, such as, "Come to my help, O God!" He entered into heavenly rest in 435. His relics are preserved in Marseilles.

MARCH 1

Our Holy Mother, the Martyr Eudoxia

Eudoxia was a Samaritan who lived in Heliopolis. Being a beautiful woman and making a living as a prostitute, she acquired much wealth. One day an ascetic named Germanus came to stay at the house of a Christian woman who lived next door to her. In the middle of the night, he began to chant the psalms and to read aloud from a book describing the Last Day and the final Judgment. The walls were thin, and Eudoxia could hear him plainly. At first she was annoyed by the noise, but as she listened she became interested and then disturbed. God drove the words into her heart, and after Germanus had finished, she lay awake all night thinking back on her shameful life. At dawn, she sent for him and they talked long about Christ, repentance, and salvation.

She soon requested baptism from the local bishop, Theodotus, and after she had thus surrendered her life to Christ, she gave all her valuables to the Church to be distributed to the poor. She then went to live in an ascetic community of thirty women. Such was her piety that a year or so after her admission, when the superior of the community died, Eudoxia was elected her successor. She lived a total of fifty-six years in holiness there. When a persecution of the Christians arose under the governor, she suffered with the others and was beheaded. This occurred in the second century.

MARCH 2

Hieromartyr Theodotus, Bishop of Cyrenia in Cyprus

Theodotus ruled the see of Cyrenia as bishop. When persecution of the Church arose under Emperor Licinius, he was arrested and put to torture as they hammered nails into his body. During the torture he was urged to save himself by denying Christ, and he replied, "If you knew the goodness of my God, who by these tortures will make me worthy of eternal life, you too would wish to suffer for Him like this!"

While he remained in prison, before his time for execution came, the order went out from the newly converted Emperor Constantine to cease the persecution of the Christians. Thus Theodotus was released and lived another two years. He died in peace in the year 302.

MARCH 3

Holy Martyrs Eutropius, Cleonicus, and Basiliscus

In the reign of Maximian and Maximin, a persecution raged against the Church. In Amasea many were arrested, including St. Theodore the Recruit. Theodore's relative Basiliscus was among those arrested and imprisoned, along with two of Basiliscus's close friends, Eutropius and Cleonicus, who were brothers. They were the closest of friends and said they would stand firm together for Christ. The three declared themselves as inseparable in faith and love as the Holy Trinity were inseparable one from another.

When Eutropius and Cleonicus were martyred, Basiliscus feared he would not have the courage to go it alone, and he prayed, "O Lord Jesus Christ, remember me, even to the end, that I may not be separated from these holy men who have been taken from me and who now are crowned!" The time came for Basiliscus to appear before the governor. He too refused to offer sacrifice to the gods and, after suffering terribly, was also martyred by beheading and so joined his friends in the heavenly Kingdom. This happened in 308.

MARCH 4

Our Holy Father Gerasimus of the Jordan

Gerasimus lived in the fifth century and learned monasticism in the Egyptian Thebaid. Like many in Egypt, he at first tended toward Monophysitism, but he was persuaded to forsake this error and embrace the truth of the Fourth Ecumenical Council at Chalcedon by St. Euthymius, who lived near him in Palestine. He became close friends with Euthymius and would spend the whole of Great Lent with him, fasting in the desert wilderness.

As many disciples wanted to join Gerasimus, he built a monastery for all of them near the Jordan River and lived there in great asceticism. The monks there never lit fire in their cells but endured the cold, and Gerasimus himself would not eat throughout Great Lent, taking only the food of the Holy Communion.

One day Gerasimus was walking beside the Jordan River and saw there a lion. The lion did not attack or flee but merely limped about, roaring in pain and holding out its paw. Gerasimus took the paw in his lap and removed a splinter from it. Then he bathed the swollen paw to ease the pain. The lion gratefully followed him home to his cell and afterwards was his inseparable companion. Gerasimus named him Jordan and sent him out to guard the monastery donkey as it carried water.

After many years of serving God faithfully, Gerasimus died and was buried by the monks. The lion was not with the old man when his master died, and it roamed all over the monastery searching for him. The monks tried to show the agitated and disconsolate beast that his master had died. They brought the lion to Gerasimus's grave and wept there. The lion at last understood. He stretched out on the grave, put his head on the sand, and moaned, refusing to move from the place. He died there a few days later. Gerasimus reposed in his Lord in 475.

MARCH 5

Holy Martyr Conon of Isauria

Conon lived as an ascetic, giving himself to prayer and fasting. Though constrained to marry by his parents, he convinced his wife Anne that they should live together as brother and sister. Relying on angelic assistance (especially from the Archangel Michael), Conon worked miracles through prayer to Christ that brought others in turn to the Faith. During a persecution, he was arrested and tortured. He did not die but lived on for several years after his release. He lived and died in the second century.

MARCH 6

The Forty-Two Holy Martyrs of Ammoria

These were soldiers of the Byzantine Emperor Theophilus. The emperor fought the Muslim Saracens and was defeated, losing the town of Ammoria to them. Many Christians of the town were martyred or sold into slavery. These soldiers were imprisoned and remained there for seven years, nourishing their spirits on the words of the Psalter and praying the divine offices at the prescribed hours. They were urged to deny Christ our God and embrace Islam, but they all refused.

On the night before their execution, they spent the whole night singing to God. The next morning, their captors tried once again to make them renounce their Faith and embrace Islam by attending prayers with the Caliph. They replied that they would certainly pray for their enemies, as Christ commanded, and would pray that the Muslims might embrace the true Faith. They finished by pronouncing an anathema on Mohammed and on all who confessed him a true prophet. Hearing this, the Muslim soldiers bound them and dragged them down to the banks of the river. They were beheaded and their bodies cast into the Euphrates. They suffered for their Lord as true soldiers of the Cross in 845.

↝ MARCH 7 ↜

The Seven Hieromartyrs of Cherson

The Bishop of Jerusalem sent a succession of men to Cherson in the Crimea to bring the pagans there to faith in Christ. They were sent as missionary bishops—Basil, Ephraim, Eugene, Elpidius, Agathodorus, Aetherius, and Capito. The first five encountered great opposition and were martyred. Aetherius, living at the time of Emperor Constantine, enjoyed greater success, building a church in Cherson and dying in peace. The last-sent, Capito, converted many of the town to the Faith when he worked a wonder for them: they challenged him, if his God were the true God, to stand unscorched amid a fiery furnace. With fervent prayer Capito did so, and many were converted. But those who refused to convert rose up and drowned him in the Dnieper River. St. Capito was praised for his faith at the First Ecumenical Council in 325.

↝ MARCH 8 ↜

St. Theophylactus, Bishop of Nicomedia

Theophylactus was born in about 765 and left his own country to go to Constantinople. There he became the friend of St. Tarasius, who lived in Constantinople. When Tarasius became patriarch there, Theophylactus, under Tarasius's influence, embraced the monastic way, going to a monastery Tarasius had founded. There Theophylactus progressed in the ways of ascetic holiness.

Recognizing his spiritual gifts, Tarasius had Theophylactus consecrated bishop for the great city of Nicomedia in Bithynia. Theophylactus served the church there with great devotion, caring for its poor and needy, organizing hospitals, and distributing alms to the unemployed of the city. Each week Bishop Theophylactus went himself to the hospitals after keeping vigil all night, visiting and caring for the sick there and tending their wounds.

When the iconoclast controversy broke out and icons were banned, Theophylactus refused to comply with the emperor's decree to destroy the icons. Rather, in an interview with the emperor, he boldly withstood him to his face, declaring God would destroy him for his impiety. For this Theophylactus was deposed, beaten, and banished. He spent thirty years in exile. While in exile, he maintained a great correspondence, guiding others with his wisdom. Despite his exile, he continued to care for the poor and afflicted. He finally died, after many struggles, in 845.

MARCH 9

The Forty Holy Martyrs of Sebaste

When Emperor Licinius persecuted the Church in the early fourth century, Agricola, governor of Cappadocia and Lesser Armenia, enforced the decree, and many Christians became martyrs for Christ. The so-called Thundering Legion of the Roman army, quartered there in the city of Sebaste, contained forty Christians—men drawn from all over the world but united in their faith in Christ. When imprisoned for their faith, they decided among themselves to remain steadfast and to ask God to send the forty together to receive their crowns. They prayed that Christ, who consecrated the number forty to Himself by fasting forty days, would enable all forty men to receive the heavenly prize.

After a week, they were condemned to death by exposure—they were made to stand naked in the bitter cold of the nearby lake in the dead of the winter's night until they died. To further tempt them to apostatize, a fire and a warm bath were prepared in a hut near the lake and within sight. They were told they could leave the icy lake for the warmth of the bath hut any time they chose—on condition that they would deny Christ. All stood in the freezing lake. Some fell, dying sooner than others of the cold; some walked about, trying to preserve body warmth; some stood still as if lost in prayer.

One of the soldiers guarding the martyrs fell asleep and dreamed that an angel, beautiful and radiant with light, repeatedly came down to the lake, bearing crowns for those who had died. He brought thirty nine crowns in all. Then the soldier awoke and saw one of the forty apostatizing, dragging his frozen body to the warmth of the bath hut. The others remaining in the lake shouted after him to remain steadfast: "Forty wrestlers have entered the arena—let forty victors receive the prize!" The apostate reached the bath hut but died anyway, forfeiting both his life and his crown.

The guard, moved by the faith of the sufferers, converted to Christ and cried out, "One has fallen from his crown—I may attain to it!" Thus confessing himself to be a Christian and being also condemned, he joined the others in the lake and with them won the crown of martyrdom. The forty suffered in the year 320.

~: MARCH 10 :~

Holy Martyr Quadratus and Companions

During a persecution of the Church, many Christians fled to the mountains and forests to escape, including the mother of Quadratus. She was pregnant at the time and gave birth to him while yet hiding in the forest. She raised him in the safety of the desert during his infancy. When older, he returned to town and lived there. He established himself in Corinth, where he studied medicine. When another persecution of the Church arose, he was arrested with his friends, taken before Governor Jason in Corinth, and condemned to death. The friends suffered for the truth in 250.

~: MARCH 11 :~

St. Sophronius, Bishop of Jerusalem

Sophronius was born to a pious couple in Damascus in about 550. He worked as a teacher of rhetoric for a while but was restless for the heavenly wisdom. He went on a pilgrimage to Palestine to venerate the holy places there. Here he met a true friend, John Moschus, who was somewhat older and was working on his ascetical collection *The Spiritual Meadow*. Sophronius joined his friend and mentor in a search for spiritual philosophy. The two went to Alexandria in 578 to learn from the teachers there and to visit the monks of Egypt as well.

MARCH

At length they returned to Palestine, and Sophronius made his monastic profession there. They went then to the monastery in Mount Sinai, and after ten years resumed their spiritual wanderings through Egypt and Palestine. John died in 619 during their stay in Rome.

Around 633, Sophronius was again in Jerusalem as the church there mourned the death of their bishop. The Christians of the city unanimously chose him for their bishop, and he was consecrated bishop of the Holy City in 634. Sophronius was steadfast in opposing the Monothelite heresy (which denied the full humanity of Christ's will), keeping the Faith in a difficult time.

Soon after, the Arabs invaded and took the Holy City in 638. Sophronius died in peace in his see in about 640. He wrote many works, including *The Life of St. Mary of Egypt* and the prayer for the Great Blessing of Water used at Theophany. He was a great lover of spiritual wisdom.

~: MARCH 12 :~

Our Holy Father Theophanes the Confessor

Theophanes was born to a wealthy family in Constantinople in 759. He was betrothed at the age of twelve to a rich young lady. At the age of twenty, when the time of their marriage drew near, he persuaded his bride that they should live together as brother and sister. She agreed, and they lived together in continence, despite family pressure from the girl's father.

Theophanes spent all his available free time visiting the ascetics in the area and seeking their wisdom. After his father-in-law's death, he gave away his wealth and freed his slaves, and he and his wife became monastics. She lived in a monastery on the Princes' Islands, and he became a monk on Mount Sigriane near Cyzicus. They never saw each other again, though they kept in touch by writing.

Theophanes became a great spiritual authority, and many sought him out, impressed by his gentleness and zeal. In 787 he attended the Seventh Ecumenical Council, meeting in Nicaea to defend the veneration of icons. He appeared before the council poorly dressed but rich in holy insight. After he returned to his monastery, he was seized by an attack of kidney stones, which left him bedridden.

When Emperor Leo began to persecute the Church, waging war on those who venerated icons, Theophanes was taken to Constantinople and urged to recant and to renounce the Church's stand regarding icons. This he steadfastly refused to do. For this he was imprisoned for two years and then exiled to the island of Samothrace. Old and ill, St. Theophanes succumbed to the hardships of the journey after only three weeks. He died on March 12 in about 817, a confessor for the truth and a lover of God.

St. Gregory the Great, the Dialogist, Pope of Rome

Gregory was born in Rome in about 540, the son of wealthy parents, and for a time had a career as a civil magistrate there. He gave away all his wealth and established a monastery in Rome and six monasteries in Sicily, becoming a monk himself at the age of thirty-five. So great were his ascetic labors that he often fainted from his fasting and ruined his health, remaining weak and sickly for the rest of his life. For a while he was obliged to cease from fasting altogether—even on Paschal eve, which caused him great distress.

Gregory was called to serve as papal representative to Constantinople from about 578 to 585. On returning to Rome, he saw some slaves from faraway Anglia at the slave market. He was moved by the sight of those poor pagans and asked their country of origin. On hearing they were Angles, he replied, "Not Angles, but Angels"—that is, "not slaves, but souls." He determined that he would one day send missionaries to Anglia in Britain to convert those souls to Christ (which he later did, sending St. Augustine of Canterbury and forty monks).

In 590 Gregory was elected Pope of Rome, and he served in that office for fourteen years. It was a time of war and great upheaval from the invading barbarian tribes, and he labored much to help victims of war and famine and to ransom prisoners. He also objected to the Patriarch of Constantinople calling himself "Ecumenical Patriarch" (which in Greek only meant "Patriarch of the ecumenical or imperial city" of Constantinople), because in Latin the title was translated as "universal

Patriarch." He thought the patriarch was claiming an authority over all, and he objected to such perceived pride. He wrote, "Whoever calls himself 'Universal Patriarch' is in his elation the forerunner of Antichrist, because he proudly puts himself above all others."

This remark was based on a misunderstanding. Gregory was a truly humble man. He was a true pastor as well and wrote many pastoral works—including *Pastoral Care* (a handbook for bishops), *Moralia* (a commentary on the Book of Job), and his famous *Dialogues* (a book on local Italian saints), which gave him his title, "the Dialogist." He died in peace in 604. The title he used to describe himself was later used by all his successors—"servant of the servants of God."

St. Symeon the New Theologian

Symeon was born with the name George in 949 at Galatea in Paphlagonia in Asia Minor, the son of wealthy and influential parents. A career in refined Byzantine society was marked out for him, and he was brought to Constantinople at age eleven. But he had no interest in that, and at about age twenty dropped out of higher studies, living a dissolute life.

George was attracted, though, to a holy man, Symeon the Pious, who lived at the Studium monastery there. George attached himself to Symeon in devotion as a spiritual son, working during the day and praying long into the night. After another lapse into worldly living, he returned to following his spiritual father and joined his monastery as a monk at age twenty-seven, taking the name Symeon.

Such close relations of spiritual father to son were discouraged at the monastery then, and Symeon was expelled from the Studium. He then joined the monastery of St. Mamas in a nearby suburb, still remaining under Symeon the Pious's direction. After three years there he was elected abbot. The monastery of St. Mamas was exceedingly lax and run-down, and Symeon attempted, by preaching, encouragement, and counsel, to reform it and rekindle his brothers' zeal for holiness.

There he began to receive visions of Christ in His brilliant uncreated light. He remained abbot there for twenty-five years, enduring and struggling with the opposition of some of his monks who did not appreciate his reforming zeal. He constantly stressed that mere externals were not enough—one must have true inner contrition for sin with tears. "To wash a soiled garment without water is impossible," he said, "and to purify a stained soul without tears is even more inconceivable." He proclaimed that a tangible experience of God was necessary: "I teach all to seek grace and the conscious coming of the Holy Spirit," he wrote. "Without this neither forgiveness of sins nor freedom from passions is ever bestowed on any mortal."

In 1005 Symeon resigned as abbot of St. Mamas, worn out by the opposition of some of his monks and desiring the quiet of unbroken prayer and contemplation. He humbly submitted to his replacement abbot, even though he was famous and popular as a theologian. His popularity drew the jealousy of some who were high in the Church, including Metropolitan Stephen. After a lengthy struggle between them, Stephen succeeded in having Symeon exiled on false charges in 1009. He was banished to a small village in the dead of winter, deprived of everything, including food. The first thing Symeon did there was to thank God with joy for all he had suffered.

He was eventually recalled from exile. However, he voluntarily stayed in the little village-monastery, using it as a place of retreat and quiet prayer. He died in peace in 1022.

MARCH 13

Transfer of the Relics of St. Nicephorus

When St. Methodius became Bishop of Constantinople in 842, he immediately besought the emperor and empress to return the relics of St. Nicephorus to the imperial city. St. Nicephorus (whose feast day is June 2) had earlier been driven into exile for his fearless stand for the truth during the iconoclastic controversy, dying far from his see in 828. Receiving imperial permission, Methodius went with the envoys to the monastery of St. Theodore, where Nicephorus lay buried. His holy relics were returned with honor to the capital, being carried first to his Church of the Holy Wisdom for an all-night vigil. St.

Nicephorus was finally laid to rest in the Church of the Holy Apostles, amid the saints and emperors who reposed before him.

~: MARCH 14 :~

Our Holy Father Benedict
Benedict was born in 480 of rich parents in Nursia in Italy. He studied in Rome but was upset by the sinful worldly ways he found there and fled to the peace of the monastic way when still a young man. He lived as a hermit in Subiaco, sharing that rough state with a companion, the monk Romanus. He was unrelenting in his asceticism—once when a passion of lust came upon him, he rolled himself among thorns and nettles to drive out the lustful thoughts. He was soon discovered by others seeking holiness and was persuaded to become abbot of a community of monks. He founded near him twelve small monastic communities of twelve monks each.

After thirty-five years there, Benedict left these now-thriving communities to sojourn elsewhere. He ended his sojourn in Monte Cassino, where he stayed for the remaining fourteen years of his life. He established a monastery there, and men came from all over. His fame grew, and he was even visited by the Gothic King Totila.

Benedict's sister Scholastica lived in a women's monastery nearby. Three days before her death, the two siblings spoke together all night long of God's love. Benedict survived Scholastica by only forty days, dying from a sudden fever. He reposed in about 550 while standing in prayer, supported by two of the brothers. He was buried, at his request, with his sister. He was a man of charity, holy moderation, and peace. He wrote a rule for monks, based on previous monastic rules, which he called "a little rule for beginners."

St. Benedict's influence was especially felt in the Western Church of the Middle Ages, where much of monasticism looked to his inspiration.

~: MARCH 15 :~

Holy Martyr Agapius and Companions

When Urban was governor of Caesarea in Palestine under Diocletian, Agapius and others were condemned to death on the charge of being Christians. Though he faced the beasts in the arena, Agapius did not die, but was imprisoned for a further two years and again brought to Caesarea.

When some Christians in the crowd saw the constancy and joyful zeal with which the martyrs were suffering, they confessed their Faith, running into the amphitheater and crying out that they too were Christians. These were Timolaus from Pontus, Dionysius from Phoenicia, a subdeacon of the church in Diospolis named Romulus, two Egyptians named Alexander and Paisius, and Alexander, from Gaza.

The governor was astonished at such a spectacle and promptly had them arrested. As all remained obdurate in their confession of faith, they were martyred along with Agapius. They all suffered for God and were beheaded in 303.

~: MARCH 16 :~

Holy Martyr Sabinas the Egyptian

Sabinas was born to an illustrious family in Hermopolis on the Nile. His zeal for the Christian Faith became known to the authorities during the great persecution of the Church under Diocletian in the early fourth century, and they were seeking to arrest him. With six other believers, he hid in a hut some way outside the town, fasting and praying.

Their presence was betrayed, however, by a beggar to whom they had given alms, and Sabinas was brought in chains before the governor. They flogged him until his blood ran, but the saint said nothing. Someone present suggested that he was mad, and he spoke up, "It is nothing of the kind; I am of sound mind, and that is why I refuse to renounce Christ in order to sacrifice to demons."

He was taken in a boat across the river back into town and cruelly tortured. When he refused to recant his faith, he was taken out in a boat to the middle of the river and thrown overboard with a heavy stone tied to his feet. He drowned, and his body was found three days later by local Christians. They buried him with honor, together with the stone which had been the instrument of his going to God.

~: MARCH 17 :~

St. Patrick, Enlightener of Ireland

Patrick was born on the west coast of Roman Britain in about 385, the son of the deacon Calpurnius and the grandson of a priest. When he was sixteen he was abducted by pagan raiders and carried off to Slemish in Ireland, where he served in misery as a slave and swineherd. His faith in Christ deepened in those years, and he would often spend all night in prayer. One day he found an opportunity to escape from his masters back home to Britain. He wandered for a time and ended up in a monastery in Lérins in Gaul.

Patrick returned to Britain, yet still found himself restless, wanting to serve God as a missionary. He repeatedly had a dream in which Irish voices called to him, "We pray you, holy youth, come to us and walk among us as before!" He went to Auxerre on the continent to prepare himself for his apostolic labors, then returned again, with the blessing of the Pope of Rome, to Ireland.

Patrick taught the people about the Holy Trinity, using the three-leaf clover as an illustration of God being three and also one. He worked long and hard among the Irish, striving to win over the high kings to Christ and to vanquish the rival pagan druids. One evening, when no fires were to be lit until the great pagan sacred fire had been lit at the royal castle at Tara, Patrick lit a fire first anyway—the great Paschal fire for the celebration of Pascha. It was a challenge to paganism. The king sent soldiers to arrest Patrick, but God protected him and he escaped their hands.

At length Patrick won the friendship of the king, and the gospel spread more and more throughout the land. He established his see at Armagh and traveled abroad, preaching to all. Patrick was a wise and sensitive missionary. He refused to use coercion but won all by simple preaching and humble service. He invited lepers to live near him and washed their sores with his own hands. A breakthrough in his work came when he destroyed the great idol Cenn Cruaich. After he tumbled the idol to the ground with his own staff, the hold of paganism on the people's hearts was broken.

Patrick died in peace in 461. His surviving writings include his *Confession* and a *Letter to Coroticus*, a pagan soldier, denouncing his raid on a Christian congregation. For all his great success, Patrick remained a humble man of steadfast faith. He wrote, "I Patrick, a sinner, am the most ignorant and of least account among the faithful, despised by many. I owe it to God's grace that so many people should through me be born again to Him."

St. Alexis, Man of God

Alexis was born in Rome around the turn of the fifth century. He was given a good education, and his parents had high hopes that he would follow their own course. Accordingly, it was arranged that he be married to a wealthy girl of similar Roman nobility. Alexis, however, did not want to marry but to pursue monastic asceticism. On his wedding night, therefore, he bade his bride farewell, returned his ring to her, and fled, taking the first ship he could find. He sailed to Laodicea, where he joined a merchant caravan bound for Edessa.

There he found a church dedicated to the Mother of God and made this his new home. He stayed in the narthex of the church (thus avoiding detection and being identified, for his parents were looking everywhere for him), and spent the next seventeen years there, fed by the charitable alms of the people who came. His family never ceased to look for him, and some sent by them even came to the church in their searching and gave Alexis alms, though they did not recognize his changed and ragged appearance.

Eventually the monks of the monastery realized that the beggar in their narthex was a true ascetic, and they went to bring the holy man of God into the church with them. Wanting to avoid both honor and detection, Alexis set off again, taking a ship bound for

Tarsus. Contrary winds, however, pushed the ship to the Roman port.

Alexis, discerning the hand of Providence, went back to his home, asking alms from the servants there like any other beggar. Alexis's father, not realizing the beggar at the gate was his own son, commanded the servants to house and feed him as long as he wanted. Thus Alexis lived a further seventeen years in his own home, unknown by family, suffering abuse and insults from the servants.

As his death approached, he asked for pen and paper and wrote out the story of his life and wandering so that it might be discovered after his repose. Thus his secret was at last uncovered, to the stupefaction of all. The saint's life remains a testimony to the value of choosing the holiness of the Kingdom over all things, even over the claims of family.

MARCH 18

St. Cyril, Bishop of Jerusalem

Cyril was born in Jerusalem in 315 and, for his piety, was elected Archbishop of Jerusalem in about 350. The Arian controversy was then racking the Church. Acacius, Metropolitan of Caesarea and an Arian, opposed Cyril because he was Orthodox. He also opposed him because Cyril, taking his stand on the decrees of Nicaea that gave Jerusalem a position of honor, declared his independence of Caesarea.

Acacius called a council of his own party to depose Cyril. He was officially condemned for selling church property—in fact, during a famine, he had sold a gold bishop's vestment Constantine had given him and used the money to feed the poor. Cyril was banished by the Arians in 358—the first of three separate exiles which would last a total of sixteen years in all. He finally returned, old and frail, to Jerusalem from his last exile in 378 and found his see in deplorable and corrupt condition. He labored to restore godly order.

In 381 Cyril attended the Second Ecumenical Council at Constantinople, which condemned afresh the Arian heresy, especially as regards the Divinity of the Holy Spirit. He died in peace in 386. He is best remembered for the baptismal sermons he gave, his *Mystagogic Catecheses*.

St. Nicholas of Zhicha

Saint Nicholas of Zhicha was born in western Serbia on January 4, 1881. Though a sickly child, he used to walk three miles to Chelije Monastery with his mother to attend services. He had an excellent mind and went to school in Belgrade, graduating in 1905. He also earned doctoral degrees in Berne in 1908 and from Oxford in 1909. When as a priest-monk he applied to the Theological Academy in St. Petersburg so that he could teach in Belgrade, the provost asked him why he had come. He replied, "I wanted to be a shepherd. As a child, I tended my father's sheep. Now that I am a man, I wish to tend the rational flock of my heavenly Father."

Nicholas indeed became a true shepherd. After traveling to England and America, he returned to Serbia in 1919, where he was consecrated as Bishop of Zhicha and later transferred to Ochrid. There he assisted those who were suffering from the ravages of war by establishing orphanages and helping all in distress. When Germany invaded his homeland in 1941, Bishop Nicholas, a fearless critic of the Nazis, was arrested and confined to a monastery. In 1944, he was sent to the concentration camp at Dachau, where he was tortured before the camp was liberated in 1945. He then went again to England and America, believing he could serve his beloved Serbian church better in freedom from abroad.

He taught for three years at St. Sava's Seminary in Illinois before settling at St. Tikhon's Monastery in Pennsylvania in 1951, eventually as its dean. St. Nicholas died in peace in 1956 and was found in his room kneeling in an attitude of prayer. He was buried at St. Sava's Monastery in Illinois. His relics were later transferred to a monastery in Serbia, fulfilling his desire to be buried in his homeland. He is best known for his devotional classic, *Prologue from Ochrid*. For his zeal in preaching, he is known as "the Serbian Chrysostom."

MARCH 19

Holy Martyrs Chrysanthus and Daria

Chrysanthus was born to a wealthy Alexandrian who settled in Rome in the late third century. He began to study philosophy but found, through his contact with the Christian gospel, that the true wisdom was in Christ alone. He therefore found a priest, a certain Carpophorus, who was hiding from the persecution then raging against the Church, and requested baptism. Chrysanthus returned home a Christian seven days later, zealously preaching the Faith to all his friends, to the great distress of his parents.

His parents tried to dissuade the young man, holding out to him the prospect of riches and a career. When this failed, they shut him up in the house, hoping that this would break his spirit and cause him (as they thought) to come to his senses. It is said that when this seemed not to work, they brought in a number of beautiful girls, hoping perhaps that attraction to one of them would draw him back to the secular life he once led.

One of these girls was a young lady named Daria, and in their conversations, far from her converting him, he managed to convert her. Seeing the difficulty of his situation, they decided to tell the parents they would marry, though they were determined to live in chastity as brother and sister. In their life together, however, it was apparent that they were Christians, for they devoted their time to sharing their faith with other young people in Rome.

They were at length arrested and tortured to make them deny their faith. When this proved fruitless, Chrysanthus was imprisoned in the notorious Mamertine prison to break his spirit, and Daria was taken to a brothel. The young people still held to their faith and so were finally executed by being buried alive in a sandpit on the Salarian Way. They suffered for their Lord and together inherited the crown of life. Their story abides in the Church as an inspiration for youth to hold to their integrity and faith in Christ in a hostile world.

MARCH 20

Our Holy Father John and Companions

The monastery of St. Sava had several times been plundered by Arabs but was always restored and reoccupied. The monks who lived there in the eighth century heard of another imminent Arab attack but decided not to flee. "We fled from the world to this wilderness for love of Christ," they said. "It would be shameful to flee from this wilderness for fear of men!" So they stayed where they were, unarmed, to meet their armed foe. The plundering Arabs came and martyred them all. Some were shot with arrows, others suffocated by smoke. They suffered and inherited eternal glory in 796.

MARCH 21

St. James the Confessor, Bishop of Catania

James lived in the eighth century. He lived in ascetic holiness from his youth and entered the Studium monastery in Constantinople, where he became the spiritual son of St. Theodore. For his virtuous life, he was consecrated Bishop (it is said) of Catania. He suffered during the iconoclastic controversy, finally giving his soul to God.

MARCH 22

Hieromartyr Basil, Priest of Ancrya

Basil was a priest in Ancyra in the fourth century and fought hard against Arianism. When Julian the Apostate became emperor, some occasional persecution of Christians was tolerated. Thus Basil was arrested by local pagans. "What do you mean," said the interrogator, "going about agitating the people and speaking against the religion established by the emperor?"

"God break your jaws, you servant of Satan," retorted the zealous priest, "It is not I who ruin your religion, but He who in heaven confounds your plans and scatters your lies!" For his steadfastness he was hung up by his wrists and ankles and his flesh was torn with hooks. Seven thongs were cut from his skin each day, and he was tortured with red-hot irons. He suffered and entered the heavenly courts in 363.

~: MARCH 23 :~

Hieromartyr Nikon

Born in the third century, Nikon was converted to Christ while a soldier in the Roman army. He was at length baptized by Theodosius, the Bishop of Cyzicus in Asia Minor. After his baptism he zealously served the church there, finally becoming bishop. He went to Sicily and cared for a monastic community of 199 men. The community became an active center for propagating the Faith and so attracted the attention of the government. When a persecution under the Emperor Decius arose in 250, Nikon was arrested and tortured with his community. Nikon himself was cruelly tortured, being thrown from a high cliff, beaten, and flayed. He was finally executed by beheading and entered, with his 199 brethren, into the Kingdom.

~: MARCH 24 :~

St. Artemon, Bishop of Seleucia

Artemon was born and educated in Seleucia and was converted by the Apostle Paul, serving as bishop there. He strove not only to lead the church there but also to provide for the orphans and the poor. He took care to secure the education of the clergy and assembled his flock every day to celebrate the Divine Liturgy with them. He died in peace after a long and holy life.

~: MARCH 25 :~

The Annunciation

When the time came for God to call the humble Mary of Nazareth to the work for which she was born, the Archangel Gabriel was sent to her house in Nazareth. She was then, at the normal age of about thirteen, betrothed to Joseph. Gabriel found her prayerfully pursuing her normal women's work, such as spinning with a spindle (as she is portrayed in some icons of the Feast), and he announced to her God's choice of her. He said, "Rejoice, O full of grace! The Lord is with you!"

Mary was troubled by this greeting, and Gabriel said, "Fear not, Mary, for you have found grace with God. Behold, you are now to conceive and bear a Son, and you will call His name Jesus." Mary knew not how she was about to conceive, since she was still a virgin, and asked how this was to be. Gabriel said, "The Holy Spirit will come upon you, and the power of the Most High will overshadow you."

Mary, while knowing all the misunderstanding and suffering a virgin birth would cause her because of her unbelieving neighbors, humbly submitted to God's will, saying, "Behold the handmaid of the Lord! Let it be to me according to your word." Thus did the holy Virgin of Nazareth open the Kingdom and become the foundation of our faith, becoming by her assent our most pure and immaculate Lady, the Mother of God.

MARCH 26

The Holy Archangel Gabriel

Gabriel's name means "mighty one of God," and he is one of the seven archangels. His greatest deed for our salvation was his announcement to the Virgin Mary of Nazareth that she was chosen to be the Mother of Jesus. After announcing to Zechariah that his wife Elizabeth was to conceive and give birth to John the Forerunner, in the sixth month of Elizabeth's pregnancy Gabriel was sent to Mary in Galilee. He greeted her, saying, "Rejoice, O full of grace! The Lord is with you!" He announced to her the good news that she was the one chosen for the work of bringing the long-awaited Messiah into the world through her virginal womb by the power of the Holy Spirit.

The Virgin humbly accepted his divine word, saying, "Behold the handmaid of the Lord! Let it be to me according to your word." Upon this, he departed from her. Gabriel seems to be the archangel specially charged with revealing the will and plan of God to mankind. With

St. Michael the Archangel, his icon adorns the deacon's door of the church's icon-screen.

~: MARCH 27 :~

Our Holy Mother Matrona

Matrona was an orphan who became the slave of a rich Jewish woman named Pautilla in Thessalonica. She lived quietly as a Christian, secretly praying to Christ our God. When her mistress went to the synagogue every day, Matrona would accompany her to the door of the synagogue, then hurry to the church to offer prayers there. She would return before her mistress left the synagogue so that her secret visits to the church would go unnoticed.

When the Jewish Passover came, her mistress went to the synagogue, and Matrona, after accompanying her to the synagogue's door, went to her church as usual. This time, however, she was late in returning, and one of the other servants reported her to her mistress. Pautilla was furious, declaring that if Matrona had deceived her in this matter, she was doubtless deceiving her in other things as well, pilfering and stealing behind her back. Matrona denied any such wrongdoing, but Pautilla was adamant. She had Matrona strapped to a bench and beaten with rods.

Matrona was defiant, and when asked why she had snuck off to the church, she replied, "Because God lives in the Christian Church, but He has departed from the synagogue of the Jews." This further enraged her mistress, and after locking the servant girl up for three days to break her spirit, she beat Matrona so severely that she died. The Christian community took her body and buried it with honor.

~: MARCH 28 :~

Our Holy Father Hilarion the New

Hilarion was a friendly and humble monk with a generous heart. One day he met a poor beggar and, having nothing else to give him, gave him the garment he was wearing. Hilarion departed naked, so great was his devotion to his Master Christ and his desire to serve Him through serving the poor. He was abbot of the monastery of Pelekete on Mount Olympus in Bithynia. During the iconoclast controversy, he was exiled to a place near Ephesus with forty of his monks. He died in prison for the truth in 754. Many mighty miracles were accomplished at his tomb. He was a true confessor for the Faith, enduring steadfastly during dark and difficult years.

MARCH 29

St. Mark the Confessor, Bishop of Arethusa

Mark was Bishop of Arethusa and was responsible for the destruction of the local pagan temple. The Emperor Julian ordered in his law that Mark should either repay the cost of the destroyed temple (which he was not able to do) or rebuild the temple (which he was not willing to do, it being a house of idols). Mark then fled, but seeing that this put others in the Church in danger, he returned and gave himself up. The pagan mob fell upon the venerable old man, stripping, scourging, and stabbing him, and finally dragging him through the streets. Almost dead, he was smeared with honey and then hung up and left exposed to be eaten by bees and wasps. Not wanting him to die a hero to the Christians, however, the emperor released him. Mark suffered as a confessor for the Faith in 362.

MARCH 30

Our Holy Father John of the Ladder

John was born about 579 and came to the monastery at Mount Sinai when he was sixteen, learning from his spiritual father Martyrius, who tonsured him a monk at about age twenty. Martyrius died soon after, and John retired to Tholas, five miles from the monastery, to live as a hermit. He lived in prudent moderation, eating everything allowed but in small amounts. He slept very little and received the grace of continual prayer and the gift of tears. He became famous as a spiritual guide and received many visitors—so many that some criticized him as a chatterbox. After this he kept silence for a year, finally speaking only when entreated by those who had once criticized him.

John visited a large monastery in Egypt but continued to live at his hermitage. After forty years there he was elected abbot of Mount Sinai. John was a great spiritual director, and he placed much emphasis on mourning for one's sins, attaining inner stillness, and being constantly in prayer, invoking the Name of Jesus. It was for his monks that he wrote his famous book of monastic direction, *The Ladder of Divine Ascent*, which is read by monks during Great Lent. In it, he said, "When we die, we will not be criticized for having failed to work miracles. We will not be accused of having failed to be theologians or contemplatives. But we will certainly have to offer some explanation to God for not having mourned unceasingly." Before his death he resigned as abbot and returned to the quiet of a hermitage. He died in peace in about 649.

~: MARCH 31 :~

St. Innocent, Metropolitan of Moscow, Apostle to America
St. Innocent was born with the name John in the district of Irkutsk in Russia in 1797. His father died when he was six, and he was cared for by his uncle Dimitri, a deacon. In 1806 he went to the seminary school for clerical families in Irkutsk. He married and in 1821 was ordained priest for the local church. The bishop wanted to find a volunteer to go to faraway Russian Alaska to work as a missionary. John volunteered—much to the horror of his wife, who burst into tears when he broke the news to her.

After a year's traveling, the family arrived in Alaska in 1824. Fr. John worked hard at his apostolic endeavors, building a church with his own hands and going all over to preach to the natives, traveling by canoe and later by dogsled. He learned their language and wrote the first grammar for them, translating the sacred church books into their own tongue. He lived on Unalaska Island for ten years, then was transferred to Sitka for another five years. He continued his work there, opening a seminary. The work grew as Fr. John traveled many hundreds of miles, and many were converted to Christ.

He decided to return to Russia to get extra help for his mission. While there, his wife died in 1839, leaving him with his six growing children. After much prayer, he settled them in schools, received monastic tonsure with the name Innocent, and was ordained bishop for his new missionary territory in 1840. He returned to his New World flock and spent the next ten years journeying throughout his far-flung diocese, preaching the gospel and strengthening his people in their new Faith. He gave directions for mission work, encouraging the use of English for North America and the use of North American-born clergy.

In 1850 he was raised to the dignity of archbishop, given more territory to care for, and his see was moved to Yakutsk in Siberia. After much apostolic labor, he was elected Metropolitan of Moscow in 1867. When he received the news of his election, he was greatly shocked, feeling quite inadequate. He said, "Who am I to take the word and power of my predecessors? A pupil of a remote country who passed more than half a lifetime on the frontiers, one who is only a common worker in Christ's vineyard . . ." Yet, at age seventy, worn out with sickness from years of hard travel and nearly blind, he worked hard as metropolitan, building care homes for widows and orphans, working to help needy clergy, and establishing an Orthodox Missionary Society.

He passed away on Holy Saturday in 1879. Dying, he said, "Tell them that no eulogies are to be said at my funeral. Rather, let them preach an instructive sermon." When he died, he had laid the foundation for Orthodoxy in the New World as a true Apostle to America.

St. Hypatius, Bishop of Gangra

Hypatius was Bishop of Gangra in Paphlagonia (in the north of Asia Minor). He was a hardworking pastor, building churches, training clergy, teaching the faithful, writing, and establishing hospices. When he traveled, he always went by donkey, in humility, imitating the

MARCH

Savior. He lived in stillness of spirit, often withdrawing to the solitude of a cave to pray. His prayers were very powerful, and he had the reputation of being a wonderworker.

In the reign of the Emperor Constans (352–360), Hypatius was summoned for a visit to Constantinople. On the way home, he was set upon in the Luziana Gorge (possibly by bandits) and killed. The criminals hid his body in a pile of straw and then fled. Eventually he was discovered, and his body was returned with honor to his home church in Gangra.

~ APRIL 1 ~

St. Mary of Egypt

Mary was born in the fifth century and lived as a prostitute in Alexandria from the age of twelve. She was quite sick spiritually and often had sex with partners for no charge, engaging in all kinds of unnatural sexual practices. One day when she was about twenty-nine years old, out of boredom, she followed a crowd heading for the Holy Land for the Feast of the Elevation of the Holy Cross. She had no money and so paid for her passage by sleeping with the crew, consumed as she was with a desire to seduce as many as she could.

With the crowd of pilgrims, Mary tried to enter the Church of the Resurrection but found herself physically unable to do so. At last she understood—God Himself was rejecting her from His presence. All the shame of her past came flooding upon her, and she broke down and wept. Seeing an icon of the Theotokos, she prayed that if she might by Our Lady's intercession be allowed to enter, she would dedicate the rest of her life to holiness. Then she effortlessly entered the church and venerated the Holy Cross there. Mary then set out for the Palestinian desert, where she lived in seclusion and repentant prayer for the next forty-seven years.

At first she was tormented by vivid memories of her old life. But she persevered in the struggle for holiness, depending on the intercessions of the Mother of God, and after seventeen years found sanctity and peace.

At the end of the forty-seven years, a priest-monk named Zosimas chanced to find Mary during his journey in the desert during Great Lent. He found her naked in the desert and, giving her his cloak to cover her, learned her story. She prayed with him, and Zosimas was awestruck to see that when she prayed fervently, she was raised and floated over a foot off the ground. She had received the gift of prophetic insight and knew all about him.

Upon her request, he brought her Holy Communion on Holy Thursday of the next year. She came to him, walking on the water of the Jordan River. She received the Holy Mysteries and asked him to come to her again the next year. Taking leave of him, she said, "Pray, for God's sake, pray for me and remember a miserable wretch."

When Zosimas returned to her the next year, he found her dead, with the words she had traced in the sand before she died: "Abba Zosimas, bury on this spot the body of humble Mary. Return the dust to the dust and pray to the Lord for me." The earth was too hard to allow him to bury her with no tools, but a lion came and dug in the earth a place for her grave. Mary, formerly a wretched and sick prostitute, had become through repentance and grace a bride of the Kingdom. She entered into glory about 530.

APRIL 2

Our Holy Father Titus the Wonderworker

Titus was consecrated to God from his earliest childhood, serving as a monk in a monastery in the region of Constantinople. He served God in great humility and obedience, showing great gentleness and affectionate care to his monks as their abbot. He was steadfast to the truth despite the pressure put on the monks by the iconoclasts of his time. For his faith, he received the gift of prophetic insight, and his prayers worked miracles for those who came to him for help. He died in peace in the ninth century.

APRIL 3

St. Nicetas the Confessor

Nicetas was born in Caesarea in Bithynia. His mother died when he was only eight days old, and he was put into the service of the Church by his father, who then became a monk. Nicetas lived with his grandmother until he finished his education, which was supervised by the bishop of the city. He was a zealous child, and the bishop tonsured him a reader at the age of twelve.

He entered the monastery at Midikion as a monk and after about seven years was also ordained priest. At length he was elected abbot. When the iconoclast heresy sprang up again in the reign of Emperor Leo the Armenian in 813, Nicetas was imprisoned and tortured for his defense of the holy icons. After a while, Nicetas, exhausted by his imprisonment, relented and was reconciled to the heretical emperor. Then, consumed with remorse, he publicly recanted and resumed his original steadfastness. He was immediately arrested again and was imprisoned for six years in a lightless and dank dungeon on the island of St. Glykeria on Cape Akritas.

After the death of Leo, Nicetas was released. He did not consider himself worthy to return to rule his monastery because of his lapse, and so he returned to a quiet place near Constantinople, where he passed his remaining days in peace. He was a confessor for the truth in dangerous times. At his funeral in 824, his body was returned to his monastery at Medikion.

~: APRIL 4 :~

Our Holy Father Joseph the Hymnographer

Joseph was born of pious parents in Sicily in 816. He early devoted himself to the study of the Scriptures. When he was fifteen years old, Sicily was occupied by the Muslims, and Joseph fled to Thessalonica, where he became a monk. He led an austere life, sleeping on the ground and spending most nights making prostrations and praying to God. He worked at his monastic obedience of copying manuscripts.

He accompanied his friend St. Gregory of Decapolis (feast day November 20) back to Constantinople. In 813 Emperor Leo assumed the throne, and the iconoclasts persecuted the Orthodox. Joseph, with others, was banished and fled to Rome, but his ship was captured by pirates along the way, and he was taken captive to Crete. There he languished in prison for six years. After his release, he returned once more to Constantinople and eventually served as head of the sacristy for the great church there. He wrote countless hymns and canons for the Church.

After a life full of imprisonments, adventures, and exiles, Joseph died quietly in the Lord in 886 at the age of seventy. St. Photius called him "Father of Fathers, equal to the angels, and a man of God."

~: APRIL 5 :~

Holy Martyrs Agathopodes and Theodulus

Agathopodes was an elderly deacon and Theodulus a young reader in the church in Thessalonica in the third century. During the persecution of the Church under Emperor Diocletian, they were arrested by Governor Faustinus and imprisoned. While in prison they had a vision of being on board a ship that was caught in a storm. In their vision, they were plunged into the sea but escaped to a rock and ascended a hill. The divine vision was fulfilled in their martyrdom: they were killed by being thrown into the sea with great stones tied around their necks. But though they drowned, yet they found their way to the heavenly rock of Christ and ascended the celestial hill of the Kingdom. Their bodies were buried with honor by the Church. They suffered for the Lord in 303.

Holy Martyrs Claudius and Companions

Claudius and six of his companions were arrested in Corinth during the persecution under the emperor Decius in the middle of the third century. They were horribly tortured: one, named Victorinus, had his right eye gouged out and his fingers and toes cut off; another, named Nicephorus, was beaten, strung up by his hair, and had his fingers broken one by one. One martyr suffered lacerations from a spear; one was hanged upside down and his limbs broken by clubs; yet another had his hands cut off. Claudius himself was hanged on a gibbet and had his cheeks, hands, and feet cut off. All seven, enduring all these torments for the love of Christ, entered the glory of the Kingdom and inherited eternal bliss around 251.

~ APRIL 6 ~

St. Eutychius, Patriarch of Constantinople

Eutychius was born to pious parents in Phrygia about 512 and became a monk in Amasea. He was elected abbot at the age of thirty and in that capacity attended a church council, being sent as the delegate of his bishop, who was unable to attend the council. The Emperor Justinian often consulted him for his piety and learning. When the see fell vacant, Eutychius was appointed Patriarch of Constantinople. As patriarch, he presided over the Fifth Ecumenical Council at Constantinople in 533.

He served there over twelve years until he provoked the wrath of the emperor when he refused to embrace a Monophysite view which held that Christ's body was incorruptible even before His Resurrection. For this refusal, Eutychius was arrested while in the middle of serving the Divine Liturgy and was locked up in a monastery in Chalcedon. Eventually he was allowed to spend his exile back in his monastery at Amasea. After the emperor died twelve years later, he was recalled to the patriarchal throne at Constantinople. He died in peace four years later, in 582.

~ APRIL 7 ~

Repose of St. Tikhon, Enlightener of North America

St. Tikhon was born Basil Belavin in 1865 to a priest's family in Toropets, near Pskov in Russia. A pious boy, he was tonsured a monk and ordained priest, serving as a teacher at various seminaries. At age thirty-two he was ordained Bishop of Lublin in Poland. He served only a short time before being appointed bishop for the North American mission.

Bishop Tikhon arrived in New York in 1898, the "bishop of the Aleutians and Alaska." At that time, all Orthodox in North America looked to the Russian bishop for leadership, as the Russian church was the only one with a hierarch present on the continent. His diocese therefore was multi-ethnic, encompassing not only Russians but

APRIL

also Greeks, Serbs, Arabs, Romanians, Bulgarians, Ukrainians, and native Alaskans. Tikhon traveled throughout the U.S. and Canada for nine years, strengthening the new churches. He established a seminary in Minneapolis and a monastery in South Canaan, Pennsylvania. He commissioned a translation of the church services into the common language of English.

In 1905, Tikhon's see was moved from San Francisco to New York. He had a clear vision for the future of North American Orthodoxy. He wanted it to be an indigenous North American church and suggested to his fellow bishops in Russia that the diocese be autonomous, if not autocephalous. He was tireless in his promotion of Orthodoxy as the Faith for all Christians. He said, "Orthodox people must care for the spread of the Orthodox Faith among the heterodox. The light of Orthodoxy is not lit for a small circle of people. It is our obligation to share our spiritual treasures, our truth, and our joy with those who do not have these gifts."

In 1907 he was recalled to Russia to take important posts there. His work culminated with his election as Metropolitan of Moscow in 1917. As metropolitan he presided over the church council of 1917, which restored the patriarchate (abolished by a tsar two hundred years earlier). When the Communist Revolution broke out, the Church suffered great persecution. Tikhon stood firm against the atheists, excommunicating the Bolsheviks and recalling them to Christ. "Recover your senses, madmen," he wrote. "You are committing the deeds of Satan, which are condemning you to the flames of hell in the next world."

In 1922 the Communists placed him under house arrest for a time. They constantly harassed him in his work, and his health deteriorated. He was given a dose of morphine to "ease the pain"—which proved fatal. He fell asleep in God, a confessor and sufferer for Christ, in 1925.

APRIL 8

Apostles Herodion, Agabus, Rufus, Asyncritus, Phlegon, and Hermas

These apostolic men were all known to St. Paul, and some are mentioned in his Epistle to the Romans (Rom. 16:11, 13, 14).

Herodion was a fellow Jew, a "kinsman" of St. Paul. He served in Thessaly and in Neo-Parthia. He was martyred by being crushed in the face with stones and then run through with a sword.

Agabus was a wandering apostolic prophet (Acts 11:28). He met St. Paul in Caesarea and prophesied that he would be arrested in Jerusalem and bound in chains (Acts 21:11).

Rufus was (possibly) the son of Simon of Cyrene, and he served as Bishop of Thebes in Greece.

Asyncritus served in Hyrcania, where he was martyred.

Phlegon served, it is said, in Dalmatia.

APRIL 9

Holy Martyr Eupsychius of Caesarea

Eupsychius was a native of Caesarea in Cappadocia in the fourth century. The Christians of Caesarea had closed the pagan temples and destroyed the temple dedicated to "Fortune." Under Emperor Julian the Apostate, the Christians responsible for the temple's destruction were arrested for this and condemned to death or exiled. Eupsychius (who had just married a wife) was also arrested, tortured, and executed. When some of the Christians of the city were ordered by the emperor to rebuild the pagan temple, they instead built a church dedicated to the holy martyr Eupsychius. St. Basil the Great celebrated the saint's feast there, inviting all the neighboring bishops in Pontus to serve with him. Eupsychius suffered with honor in 362.

APRIL 10

Holy Martyrs Terence, Africanus, Maximus, Pompeius, and Companions

When the Emperor Decius raged against the church in Carthage in the mid-third century, he demanded that all the people there sacrifice to the gods. Terence, Africanus, Maximus, Pompeius, and thirty-six other Christians refused to submit. When the governor reproached the Christians for worshipping as divine a criminal the Jews had crucified, Terence retorted, "This crucified man is the Son of God, who united divinity to His human nature and was crucified for our salvation!"

Despite further threatening, all the Christians remained steadfast. They were imprisoned overnight. The next day, three of their number—Zeno, Alexander, and Theodore—since they still refused to sacrifice to the gods, were flogged with whips and rods and burnt by a lit pyre, where they sang the Song of the Three Holy Youths in the Babylonian furnace (Dan. 3). They were then hung on stakes to tear their flesh to their entrails. At length they were beheaded. Terence and the others were returned to prison and tortured. Since they refused to submit to the imperial decree and deny their Faith, they too were beheaded. All suffered with honor for their true King in the year 250.

APRIL 11

Hieromartyr Antipas, Bishop of Pergamum

Antipas lived in the first century in Pergamum, a city steeped in idolatry. It was also the official cult center of Asia Minor for the worship of the emperor. There was a temple there to Augustus Caesar (built 29 BC). Thus Pergamum was referred to by Christ as the city "where Satan's throne is" (Rev. 2:13). Antipas was a zealous and faithful witness to Christ there, refusing to participate in idolatrous practices, for which he was martyred. Some say he died by being roasted to death, suffocating in a bronze bull. Christ commended him and his faithful steadfastness, referring to him as "My witness, My faithful one" (Rev. 2:13, RSV). He suffered for his Lord in about 92.

APRIL 12

St. Basil the Confessor

In the eighth century, Basil was Bishop of Parium in Asia Minor. When the Emperor Leo the Isaurian ordered that icons be destroyed, he refused to comply with the impious decree. He was arrested and tortured, then sent into exile, where he moved from place to place, encouraging the brethren. He died in peace in the early eighth century, a confessor of the Faith.

APRIL 13

Hieromartyr Artemon

Artemon served as a priest in Laodicea in the reign of Emperor Diocletian. He was very aged at the time of the persecution. He refused to sacrifice to the gods or to honor Asclepius, the god of healing. The god's symbol was the serpent (embodying wisdom) and he was called "savior" by his devotees. Artemon refused to participate in such things, serving Christ as the only true Savior. When urged to sacrifice and save his life, he replied, "I spent sixteen years reading the Holy Books to the people of God, twenty-eight years as a deacon, and twenty-five years as a priest, teaching a devout life. How could I now sacrifice to idols?" For his obstinacy, he was tortured and roasted on a gridiron. Finally he was executed with a sword. He suffered for his faith in 303 and inherited the Savior's Kingdom.

Holy Martyr Crescens

Crescens was an old and distinguished citizen of Myra in Lycia. He was arrested and dragged before the governor with his hands tied behind his back. When asked why he subverted the emperor's orders and insulted the gods, he boldly answered back, "I am a Christian and desire only one thing: to remain faithful to my God to the end. As for your gods, I call them idols, the work of men's hands, incapable of helping those who trust in them!"

Crescens was flogged and tied to a stake, and his flesh was torn with iron nails. Even covered with blood, his face shone with joy, and he kept repeating, "Lord Jesus Christ, come to my aid!" When his torturers burned his side with torches, he prayed that God would grant them grace to know Him.

After being imprisoned overnight, Crescens was again brought forth and tortured. As they cast him into a red-hot furnace, he prayed that the God who had kept the Three Holy Youths safe in the furnace would enable him also to finish his course and not betray his faith. After he gave up his soul in peace to God, his body was thrown out as carrion. The Christians came to take up his holy relics and bury them in safety. Crescens suffered for his God in the mid-third century.

~: APRIL 14 :~

St. Martin, Confessor, Pope of Rome

Martin was elected Pope of Rome in 649, a time when the Monothelite heresy (which denied the full humanity of Christ's will) was shaking the Church. The Emperor Constans II attempted to bring peace to the Church by forcing all to agree to his statement of faith (called the "Typos") which was, however, basically of heretical Monothelite leanings.

At Rome, Martin held a council of 105 bishops, which condemned not only Monothelitism but also the Typos of the emperor. The emperor was furious. He ordered Martin to be arrested on trumped-up charges and brought to Constantinople. Martin reached the capital (after being imprisoned on the island of Naxos along the way) and was imprisoned there for three months, being so ill by then that he had to be taken to prison on a stretcher. He wrote, "For forty-seven days have I not been given water to wash in. I am frozen through and wasting away from dysentery. The food I get makes me vomit. But God sees all things, and I trust in Him."

He was condemned by the emperor for rebellion and lifted up on a platform. One said to him, "You have struggled against the emperor, and what hope remains for you? You abandoned God, and now God has abandoned you!" Then his episcopal vestments were plucked off.

He was imprisoned for another three months and then banished in 655 to Cherson in the Crimea. Ill and short of food, he died a few months later, abandoned by his clergy and neglected by his friends. Thus this pious and steadfast man suffered as a confessor for the truth and gloriously inherited the eternal Kingdom.

APRIL 15

Holy Apostles Aristarchus, Pudens, and Trophimus

Aristarchus was apparently a native of Thessalonica. He was with St. Paul during the riot at the theater in Ephesus (Acts 19:29). He went with Paul when he was sent under arrest from Jerusalem to Rome (Acts 27:2) and voluntarily shared his imprisonment in Rome. Thus Paul hails him as his "fellow prisoner" (Col. 4:10) and his "fellow worker" (Philem. 24, RSV). He seems to have served the church in Apamea in Syria.

Pudens was a distinguished Roman. St. Paul mentions him, sending him greetings during his first imprisonment (2 Tim. 4:21).

Trophimus was from Asia Minor and accompanied St. Paul on his apostolic journey (Acts 20:4), though he was left sick at Miletus (2 Tim. 4:20). It is said that all three suffered as martyrs in Rome under Nero.

APRIL 16

Holy Martyrs Agape, Chionia, and Irene

These were three beautiful virgin sisters from a rich and influential family in Thessalonica. In a persecution of the Church under Diocletian they were arrested along with others and tried on charges of refusing to eat food sacrificed to idols. The governor, Dulcetius, asked them where they got their strange ideas from. Chionia said, "From our Lord Jesus Christ"—thereby confessing themselves to be Christians. The governor could not make them apostatize, and so Agape and Chionia were burnt alive.

It was learned that Irene had kept copies of the Christian

APRIL

Scriptures, which was against the law. The governor ordered Irene stripped and given over to a brothel so that she might be humiliated and her spirit broken. But Irene was defiant. "Even so I will not forsake my God!" she said. "Those defilements which the mind does not consent to do not pollute—just as the saints of God had sacrifices forced down their throats but they were not polluted or defiled by them." Irene was sentenced to death, and the Scriptures she had were publicly burnt. The three sisters, pure brides of the Kingdom, suffered for the Lord in about 304.

❧ APRIL 17 ☙

Hieromartyr Simeon, Bishop in Persia

Simeon was the son of a fuller, or launderer, and a disciple of Papias, Bishop of Ctesiphon. He was ordained bishop in 316 and sent a priest as his representative to the First Ecumenical Council in 325. He was one day accused of being a friend of the Roman emperor and of secretly being in correspondence with him. The Persian King Sapor was infuriated and ordered Christian clergy slain as rebels. Simeon, the catholicos and head of the local church in that region, was arrested and loaded with chains. Refusing to deny Christ and embrace the Persian religion (worshipping the sun), he was beheaded with one hundred others of the faithful on Great and Holy Friday at the ninth hour (three PM). They all suffered for Christ in about 341.

❧ APRIL 18 ☙

Holy New Martyr John of Epirus

John was born in Ioannina. When his parents died, he went to live in Constantinople and worked as a craftsman. The Turks had occupied Constantinople not long before, and men who worked nearby had apostatized and become Muslims. They argued together about the Faith, John rebuking them for their apostasy. The men then falsely accused John of embracing Islam and then apostatizing to the Christian Faith, which was a capital offense. John was imprisoned and tortured. The next day, Pascha, he was brought out for more torture, and he emerged with joy, crying, "Christ is risen!" Seeing his joy and his desire to die for Christ, they raged and condemned him to death. He was beheaded and entered the Kingdom of God. This happened in 1526.

Our Venerable Father John the Isaurian
John was born in Isauria and from his youth loved the Lord Jesus. He became a disciple of Saint Gregory of Decapolis, serving his spiritual father in humility and learning the ways of ascetic holiness. John took part in Gregory's valiant defense of the holy icons during the persecution under Emperor Leo. He died in peace in 820.

APRIL 19

Blessed Matrona of Moscow
Matrona was born in 1881 to a poor family in the village of Sebino-Epifaniskaya, in the Tula region. She was blind from birth, having no pupils in her eyes. From the age of about six, God gave the child extraordinary gifts of prophecy and healing. When she was taken to see the then-famous Fr. John of Kronstadt, the saint cried out, "Matrona, come here!" adding that she would be his heir and a pillar of Russia. Illness struck the young girl again at the age of seventeen, so that she was ever after unable to walk. She remained steadfast and patient throughout her life, quietly praying, receiving all the visitors who came to her, and foretelling the terrible fortunes which would befall her country at the hands of the Bolsheviks.

God continued to bless His child with miraculous gifts. One day, when visitors were commiserating with her about her lack of sight, she shared the following miracle: "A day came on which God opened my eyes, and I saw the light of the sun, the stars, and all that exists in the world." In 1925, she left her mother's house to settle in Moscow.

From 1945 on, she moved often from house to house, evading the communists, who had heard of her piety and fame and wanted to seize her.

APRIL

Matrona lived a life of pain, as well as of asceticism and fasting, praying for the distressed with prophetic foresight and power. Having foretold the day of her death, she died in peace on April 19, 1952. Many miracles were performed at her tomb. Her relics were translated to the women's monastery of the Protecting Veil in 1998, where thousands now come to ask her intercession.

Our Holy Father John of the Ancient Caves

John lived in the eighth century. He traveled to holy places seeking wisdom, then settled in St. Chariton's cave (the so-called Ancient Caves) in Palestine. He lived in godly asceticism and died in peace.

APRIL 20

Our Holy Father Theodore the Hair-Shirt Wearer ("Trichinas")

Theodore was a son of wealthy parents in Constantinople. As a young man he left his home and wealth, living first in a monastery in the capital. Later he settled in a faraway monastic retreat in Thrace. There he devoted himself to ascetic labors: he slept on a stone, did not cover his head from the elements, and wore a hair shirt (hence his name). God gave him the grace of working miracles through prayer. He died in peace in about 400. After his death, a heavenly fragrance spread from his tomb, and many received miracles of healing.

APRIL 21

Hieromartyr Januarius and Companions

Januarius was a native of Naples but was Bishop of Benevento in Italy. He often visited Meseno to see his close friend the deacon Sosius, who was about thirty years old. Under the governor Dracontius, he was arrested and imprisoned along with the deacon and other Christians in the town of Pozzuoli. Januarius suffered martyrdom with the others in 305. It is said that the people of Naples wanted to rush to intervene and save him from execution, but he declined, preferring the crown of martyrdom and assuring them that he would be of greater use to them as their heavenly protector.

❦ APRIL 22 ☙

Our Holy Father Theodore of Sykeon

Theodore was born in Sykeon in Galatia. It is said that when he was six years old, his mother made plans for her son to enter the imperial service, but St. George appeared to her and said, "The heavenly Emperor has need of him." While still a ten-year-old boy, Theodore began fasting and keeping vigils, depending upon the prayers of St. George. He grew in his ascetic exploits, wearing an iron belt and standing in prayer all night. He made a pilgrimage to Jerusalem on foot, visiting the monasteries in the Holy Land and receiving counsel from the desert fathers there. It was in the Holy Land that he became a monk.

Theodore continued with extraordinary works of asceticism, and for such zeal was given the ability to work miracles through his prayers. For his piety he was elected Bishop of Anastasioupolis, consecrated by force against his will in Ancyra. After serving as bishop faithfully for eleven years, he returned to his monastery in his old age. One night, St. George appeared to Theodore and invited him to accompany him on a long journey. After celebrating the services of Holy Week and Pascha, he died in peace on Thomas Sunday, which that year coincided with the feast of his beloved St. George. This was in about the year 617.

❦ APRIL 23 ☙

Holy and Great Martyr and Trophy-Bearer George

George may have been born in Cappadocia and raised, on the death of his father, in Palestine. He became a soldier in the Roman army. Rather than deny Christ and swear by the pagan gods, he declared himself a Christian and was therefore arrested and tortured. He was finally martyred by beheading in Nicomedia. His defiance of the pagan emperor's order and his zeal in confessing Christ brought great courage to others faced with martyrdom. He suffered for his Lord in the early fourth century.

George's life shows us how courage is necessary to overcome evil. As a martyr, he overcame the evil one (whom Scripture describes as a "great dragon"), for the martyrs "overcame him by the blood of the Lamb and the Word of their testimony, and they did not love their lives to the death" (Rev. 12:9, 11). King Richard the Lionheart of England and his crusaders brought back a great devotion to St. George, which they learned in the Holy Land, so that St. George became the patron of England.

APRIL 24

Holy Martyr Sabbas Stratelates ("the General")

Sabbas lived in Rome in the reign of Emperor Aurelian. He was of a Gothic family and was a general in the army. When charged with being a Christian, he did not deny the Faith but boldly confessed it. He was martyred by drowning in the Tiber River in 272.

Holy Mother Elizabeth the Wonderworker

Elizabeth was born in Heraklea in Thrace. She was left an orphan at the age of twelve. Being a pious child, she had her slaves freed, gave away her inheritance, and went to live in the Convent of St. George in Constantinople, governed by her aunt. As a true ascetic, she wore only a single tunic and went about barefoot, even in winter. She would weep with joy during the recitation of the Psalter.

When the abbess of the monastery died, Elizabeth was chosen in her place. Her fame spread throughout the imperial capital, and she healed by her prayers the many sick who approached her. When her time came to die, she received the Holy Mysteries and stretched out her hands to heaven, reciting the Song of Simeon, "Lord, now let Your servant depart in peace." Having recited the holy words, she died in peace. Her body remained incorrupt and was a source of healing for many centuries.

APRIL 25

Holy Apostle and Evangelist Mark

Mark's Hebrew name was John. He was early converted to Christ along with his mother, Mary, who lived in Jerusalem, and he was attached to the twelve apostles. His mother's house was given over for use by the Lord. The Apostles used her house for the Last Supper; to gather after the Lord's Ascension in "the upper room" (Acts 1:13; 2:1) and for worship in Jerusalem (Acts 12:12). Mark accompanied Paul and Barnabas on their first missionary journey but gave up, discouraged by their hardships and difficulties, and left them at Perga to return home (Acts 13:13).

Because of this, Paul was unwilling to let Mark accompany them on their next journey, and he quarreled with Barnabas to the point of splitting up with him. Mark then accompanied Barnabas on a journey to Cyprus (Acts 15:36–40). Paul's quarrel with Mark was later healed, as Mark was with him in Rome during his first imprisonment (Col. 4:10), and he asked to have Mark with him during his second imprisonment (2 Tim. 4:11). It was during Mark's sojourn in Rome that he put the memoirs of his spiritual father Peter into book form as the Gospel of Mark (see 1 Peter 5:13).

After the death of Peter and Paul in Rome, Mark preached the gospel in remote parts such as Libya, settling finally in the great city of Alexandria. The present liturgy of this city (the Liturgy of St. Mark) is tribute to his apostolic labors and spirit. He was martyred in Alexandria by a pagan mob who stoned him. He died for his Lord there, and his relics were gathered by the Church. They were later translated to Venice in 824.

APRIL 26

St. Basil, Bishop of Amasea

Basil became Bishop of Amasea during the persecution of the Church by Diocletian in the early fourth century. He was arrested and brought before the prefect of Nicomedia. When Basil was condemned to die, he burst out in hymns of thanksgiving to the Lord. When the time of his execution came, he embraced his companions and then said to his executioner, "My friend, do what is commanded of you!" After being beheaded, his body was thrown into the sea. After being washed ashore, his body was recovered by the Christians and buried with honor in his church.

St. Stephen of Perm, Enlightener of the Zyrians

Stephen was born in about 1345 in Russia of humble and pious parents. He early served as reader in the cathedral church. He wanted to serve God in monasticism and so moved to faraway Rostov near the Black Sea. He was tonsured a monk in 1365 and served there for ten years, being also ordained priest.

Stephen had a missionary's heart and wanted to preach to those who did not yet know Christ, such as the pagan Zyrians who lived in the east. In 1379 he got the blessing of Metropolitan Gerasim in Moscow and went to preach to the Zyrians. He learned their language, inventing an alphabet for them (using made-up non-Russian letters, lest the Zyrians feel they were being taken over by the Russians), and translated parts of the liturgy and the Scriptures into Zyrian. Some of the Zyrians converted to Christ, though some were hostile.

As a challenge to the power of their gods, Stephen set fire to the sacred tree of the pagan Permiak tribe. His hard, patient, and loving work soon bore fruit—many were converted and churches were built, the second one on the site of the "sacred tree." He opened schools in the churches and trained their men to be priests and deacons. In 1383 Stephen was ordained bishop of the land of Perm to care for his converts.

He cared for his flock as bishop for another thirteen years before dying. His flock grieved for the passing of their father. They wrote, "We have lost our patron and intercessor. He prayed to God for the salvation of our souls and was concerned for our welfare." He passed to the Kingdom in peace in 1396.

ᴧ APRIL 27 ᴥ

Holy Apostle Simeon

Simeon was the son of Cleopas, the brother of Joseph, and was one of the seventy sent out by Christ (Luke 10:1). After the death of St. James, the first Bishop of Jerusalem, he was elected as successor to that see and served the church in Jerusalem with zeal until his old age. When the church in Jerusalem was persecuted, those of the house of David, our Lord's family, were especially singled out. Thus Simeon suffered torture for several days, despite his advanced age. He was crucified for his Lord and endured with joy, inheriting His eternal Kingdom. St. Simeon was succeeded in his episcopate by Justus, another Jewish convert, who himself died in 111.

ᴧ APRIL 28 ᴥ

Holy Apostles Jason and Sosipater

These were Jews, "kinsmen" of St. Paul (Rom. 16:21, RSV). Jason was born in Tarsus. When St. Paul was preaching in Thessalonica, those opposed to him started an uproar and surrounded Jason's house, thinking to find St. Paul there. Not finding him, they dragged Jason before the civil magistrate to accuse him and the Christians of sedition. Jason had to give the assurance of their civic loyalty before he could go free (Acts 17:4–9). He later served as bishop in his native Tarsus.

Sosipater served in Iconium. It is said that the two later traveled to the west, preaching the gospel on the island of Corfu and converting the king's daughter Cercyra. They died in peace in the first century.

ᴧ APRIL 29 ᴥ

The Nine Martyrs at Cyzicus

There were nine Christians, all born in different places. Their names were Theognides, Rufus, Antipater, Theosticus, Artemas, Magnus,

Theodulus, Thaumasius, and Philemon. They were all arrested in the town of Cyzicus in the Hellespont during the pagan persecutions. When they all refused to deny their Faith, they were tortured and beheaded. The place of their burial became a source of healing for those who approached with faith.

St. Basil of Ostrog

Basil was born in the district of Herzegovina of pious parents and became a monk at the monastery of Tribinje. For his ascetic life, he was chosen Bishop of Zahum and Skenderia. He lived at a monastery in Tvrdoš until it was destroyed by the Turks. He then moved to Ostrog. He served as a faithful pastor, defending his flock from the cruelty of the Turks and the guile of the Roman Catholic Church. He died in peace in the sixteenth century. His relics were found to be incorrupt.

APRIL 30

The Holy Apostle James

James was the brother of John and the son of Zebedee. Together with Simon Peter and Andrew, he was a fisherman on the Sea of Galilee. With the others, he heard Christ's call in Galilee and promptly gave up all to follow Him (Matt. 4:18–22). James was appointed to be one of the Twelve and, together with his brother John and Peter, formed a close inner circle of Christ's friends. These three alone witnessed the Transfiguration and the raising of Jairus's daughter (Matt. 17:1–13; Mark 5:35–43). James and his brother were quite hot-blooded and impulsive (he would have called down fire from heaven to destroy a Samaritan town that rejected Christ—Luke 9:51–56), and our Lord nicknamed them Boanerges—"sons of thunder."

James at first shared with the other Twelve a desire for preeminence and had his mother ask Christ that he and John might have the chief places in His Kingdom. Our Lord, however, rejected the ways of ambition and favoritism and said those places were for those for whom the Father had prepared them. He called James and John instead to the self-denial that would lead to martyrdom, this "cup of suffering" they said they were ready to drink (Matt. 20:20–29). James did indeed drink this glorious cup—he was the first of the apostles to suffer martyrdom, being slain with the sword by King Herod in about 44 (Acts 12:2). Thus he fulfilled his service to his Lord and inherited the crown.

❧ MAY 1 ☙

Holy Prophet Jeremiah

Jeremiah was born in the village of Anathoth. The Word of the Lord came to him in 626 BC, while he was still young, and he soon had to flee persecution by his own kinsmen to live in Jerusalem. He encouraged and supported righteous King Josiah in his reforms in Judah and his efforts to restore a purer Yahwism and to fight the idolatrous Baal worship.

Jeremiah prophesied under Jehoiakim (608–597 BC) that Judah should submit to the yoke of being a vassal to Babylon. This was thought to be treasonous by the nationalistic faction, which considered that Yahweh would defend His nation at all costs. Jeremiah prophesied judgment on them for their sins rather than divine defense of the nation in spite of their sins. He worked with his servant Baruch to warn Judah to repent, even up to the end under King Zedekiah, but they refused to repent, and so judgment fell on them. Nebuchadnezzar, King of Babylon, took Jerusalem in 586 BC after a long siege, destroyed the temple, and took many into captivity.

Jeremiah was allowed to stay with the remnant in Jerusalem, but he was taken by some of them who fled to Egypt. He continued his work as a prophet among the people there, and they stoned him to death.

He prophesied not only of judgment for Israel's sins but also of God's restoration of them through Christ, saying God would make a new covenant with His people (Jer. 31). He was one of the greatest of the prophets, one who interceded before God for his people even after his death (2 Macc. 15:12–16).

St. Athanasius the Great, Archbishop of Alexandria

Athanasius was born to Christian parents in Alexandria in 296. In his youth he came to know St. Anthony the Great—whose *Life* he would later write—for he says, "I saw the saint and often poured water on his hands." As a promising lad, he was educated under the Pope of Alexandria himself, with whom he lived "as a son with a father." He was soon made papal secretary and, while yet about twenty years of age, wrote *Oration against the Heathen* and *Concerning the Incarnation of the Word of God*.

Athanasius was ordained deacon in 319 and, as such, accompanied Bishop Alexander to the First Ecumenical Council of Nicea in 325. There he distinguished himself in refuting Arius and securing the triumph of the Faith at the council. After Pope Alexander's death, Athanasius was elected his successor. As Archbishop of Alexandria—a position he held for forty six years—he was tireless in his proclamation of the truth of Nicea—that Christ was true God, of one essence (Gr. *homoousios*) with the Father.

The heresy of Arius, however, was quite virulent, and his Arian foes did all they could to discredit Athanasius. Many times false accusations were leveled at him, and—as the imperial court vacillated between the defenders of Arius and his Orthodox opponents—Athanasius was often deposed and banished as a troublemaker. Indeed, he spent a total of seventeen years in exile in five separate periods. Still, he strove with all his might against Arianism. In his writings he called the heretics (at various times) "devils," "antichrists," "maniacs," "dogs," "chameleons," "gnats," and "leeches."

Athanasius was fearless in his fight for the truth. One time he even seized the bridle of the emperor's horse—much to the emperor's royal astonishment and annoyance!—to demand justice for himself and his cause. He remained a courageous fighter, an immovable rock, holding firm to the truth when it seemed all stood against him—when it was "Athanasius against the world." But though a tenacious and fierce fighter for the truth, he was also, as St. Gregory Nazianzus wrote, "most humble and lowly in mind, most courteous to all, and everyone had easy access to him; he was meek, gentle, and compassionate." After a life of striving for the Faith, he passed to glory in peace in the year 373.

~: MAY 3 :~

Holy Martyrs Timothy and Maura

Timothy was a reader in the local church. During the persecution under Diocletian, Timothy and his wife Maura were arrested a mere twenty days after their wedding and brought before the governor of the Thebaid. When Timothy was interrogated and urged to renounce his faith, the governor asked him, "Do you see these instruments prepared for torture?"

Timothy boldly responded, "But you don't see the angels of God here, which are strengthening me!" During his torture, his ears were pierced with iron rods, and he was hung upside down. His wife Maura was at first afraid to suffer, but Timothy encouraged his bride to be brave for their Lord. When she too confessed that she was a Christian, her hair was torn out and then all her fingers cut off. Finally both spouses were crucified. They endured the cross nine days, exhorting each other to persevere in their faith. They expired on the tenth day, entering the heavenly bridal chamber of their King. This happened in 286.

Our Holy Father Theodosius of the Kiev Caves

Theodosius was born about 1008 in Vasiliev, near Kiev. He spent his boyhood in Kursk and lived in great piety, often giving away his new clothes to the poor—much to his parents' vexation. After his father died, his mother was alarmed at his monastic temperament and tried unsuccessfully to discourage him from this way.

Theodosius left home at age twenty-four, looking for a holy guide for his life. He found an ascetic, Anthony, who lived in a cave, and attached himself to him with devotion, sharing his hard life. He refused to leave the caves in which he lived with the ascetic Anthony, even though his mother, who came looking for him, burst into tears and begged him to return with her. Theodosius worked hard there with the monastic community and was eventually ordained priest.

At length he became the abbot. The community expanded, and Theodosius moved his monks to a larger place in 1062. They adopted the rule of the Studium monastery of Constantinople. They also stressed service to the poor. Theodosius himself was an example to his monks—he was always the first one in church and the last to leave. Even though he was abbot, he worked at the lowest of tasks, such as cleaning out the stables and carrying water. When his monks went astray, he wept over them as a loving father.

Some thought him too lax in discipline, but he continued walking in the way of love. One day, Theodosius was away from his monastery, visiting the prince. The prince arranged for a coach to return him to his monastery. The coachman, not knowing who Theodosius was and thinking him but a poor beggar monk, roughly ordered him to drive while he rested. This Theodosius did without a word of rebuke. The two changed places before they arrived at the monastery. There the coachman was aghast to learn that his "beggar" was the great Theodosius, abbot of the monastery favored by the prince. Theodosius never told anyone of his rough treatment but instead gave orders that the coachman be given a good meal. Such was his humility. The saint died in peace in 1074, a great light for the Russian people.

~: MAY 4 :~

Our Holy Mother Pelagia

Pelagia was a young girl of Tarsus who lived in the reign of Diocletian. Her parents were wealthy, and she was betrothed to the son of a high government official. She saw Christians being martyred and was moved to investigate the Faith that enabled men to die with such joy. She visited her nurse, who was a Christian, and the old woman instructed her in the Faith and brought her to the local bishop. Pelagia was baptized by him and immediately refused to marry her pagan betrothed as had been previously arranged. The young man, who was quite infatuated with her, then committed suicide, and his father, incensed with Pelagia, had her arrested and condemned as a Christian. She died with honor in 287 by being burnt in a bronze bull.

~: MAY 5 :~

Holy Great Martyr Irene

Irene was born in the reign of Emperor Constantine in the Persian city of Magedon, the daughter of Licinius the governor. She studied under Apellian and through him learned of the Christians. She became eager to become a Christian, which upset her father greatly. The more ardent she became in her desire for Christ, the more upset her father became, and he finally, in a fit of rage, attempted to have her trampled by horses. In the confusion of the moment, he himself was trampled, and Irene came to his side, weeping and praying for him. He finally relented of his rage and was reconciled to his daughter. He joined her in her new faith and was soon after removed from office by the Persian King Sedechius. Irene herself suffered persecution and imprisonment as she shared the gospel with her countrymen. She was finally martyred by beheading in 384.

~: MAY 6 :~

Holy and Righteous Job the Longsuffering

Job lived in the land of Uz—that is, in the area of Edom. He was a righteous man and the pride of God's heart. God allowed Satan to send a series of disasters against him (the loss of his livestock, crops, children, and health) to see whether he served God for hope of reward or for love of God Himself. Job maintained his integrity even though harassed by three counselors, who supposed his misfortunes must have been a judgment for secret sins. After a time of testing, God appeared to Job so as to show him that he was no fit judge of God's moral design of the universe. He restored Job's health and fortunes, and Job ended his life in peace and prosperity. Job, in his righteous suffering, was a prophetic image of Christ as well as a model of patient endurance. Some say he is to be identified with Jobab son of Zerah, ruler of Edom (Gen. 36:33).

~: MAY 7 :~

St. Alexis Toth, Confessor and Defender of Orthodoxy

Alexis was born in 1854 in Austro-Hungary to humble Uniate (Byzantine-rite Catholic) parents. His father and brother were Uniate priests and his uncle a bishop. He married and was ordained priest in that church in 1878. His wife and child died soon afterward. In 1879 Alexis was appointed to serve a Uniate parish in America. He arrived there and presented himself to Archbishop John Ireland, the Latin-rite Roman Catholic bishop who was his superior in America. Because the Uniates did not fit his vision of the American Catholic Church, Bishop Ireland refused to recognize Alexis or grant him permission to serve but rather banned all his ministries.

His continued frustration led Alexis to rethink the whole Uniate position, and in 1891 he went with his church warden to seek out the Orthodox bishop in America, Bishop Vladimir of San Francisco. The bishop welcomed Fr. Alexis with open arms so that he and 361 members of his flock were soon reunited with the Orthodox Church. This was encouragement for other Uniates who were enduring the same frustration, and soon Fr. Alexis was able to lead many thousands of Uniates back home to Orthodoxy. He traveled all over, preaching the truth and encouraging the people to return to the Orthodox Church. Despite threats of violence, Alexis remained undeterred in his work of defending the Church.

Though considered for the episcopal office in 1907, he humbly declined, wanting a younger man to fulfill that office. He died in peace in 1909. His relics are preserved at St. Tikhon's Monastery in South Canaan, Pennsylvania.

The Appearance of the Sign of the Cross over Jerusalem

During the reign of Constantine's son Constantius, a great miracle happened. At about 9:00 in the morning on May 7 in the year 357, the Sign of the Cross appeared over the site of Golgotha, shining more brightly than the sun. The whole population, both Christians and unbelievers, saw this sign, left their work, and came to gaze upon it. Many of these unbelievers converted to the Faith. The Bishop of Jerusalem, Bishop Cyril, wrote about it to the emperor, encouraging him to heed this sign and not to incline towards Arianism. The Church commemorates this sign as a reminder that our hope lies not in princes and the sons of men, but in the Cross of Christ and the power of God.

❦ MAY 8 ❧

Holy Apostle and Evangelist John the Theologian

John was born in Galilee of a wealthy and influential family. His father's name was Zebedee. He first followed St. John the Baptizer (John 1:35–39), then began, while a very young man, to accompany Jesus. John was present, with others, at His miracle at the wedding of Cana and His first cleansing of the temple (John 2). With his brother James and their partners Simon Peter and Andrew, John was a fisherman. All four abruptly left everything to become His disciples (Matt. 4:18–22).

John was appointed one of the Twelve and was also one of the inner circle of Christ's close friends, along with his brother James and Peter. As such, he witnessed the Transfiguration, the raising of Jairus's daughter, and the Lord's struggle in Gethsemane (Mark 9:1–13; 5:35–43; 14:32–42). Like his brother James, John was of impulsive and warm temperament. He wanted to call down fire from heaven to destroy a Samaritan village that had rejected Christ (Luke 9:51–56). As a result our Lord nicknamed the brothers Boanerges—"sons of thunder."

John had a special friendship with Peter (see Luke 22:8; John 13:23–25; 18:15–16; 20:2–8; 21:20–24; Acts 4:1f). Along with Peter he was later sent to investigate the state of new Samaritan converts (Acts 8:14). John was our Lord's special close friend (the one "whom [Jesus] loved," John 13:23). With the other apostles he

MAY

remained at Jerusalem after the Lord's Ascension, caring for the Theotokos, whom Christ had committed to his care from the Cross (John 19:26–27).

After her repose, John preached the gospel in Asia Minor, caring especially for the seven churches there (see Rev. 1:11, 2—3). He wrote his apostolic memoirs as the Gospel of St. John, as well as three epistles. When persecution broke out against the Church in the late first century, John was exiled to the island of Patmos (Rev. 1:9). It was from there that he received the vision of Christ's glory and wrote the Apocalypse or Revelation.

John was a man of great zeal for the truth. Once when he found the heretic Cerinthus in the public baths, he abruptly left there, saying, "My friends, let us hurry and go lest the bath should fall in on our heads wherein Cerinthus, the enemy of truth, is!" He was also a man of great love, and love was his special theme. When he was so old and infirm that he could scarcely speak anymore and had to be carried to church, he would simply say to the assembled church, "Little children, love one another." When asked why he said only this, he replied, "Because it is the Lord's command, and if you keep it, it is enough by itself." He lived his whole life in chastity and died in peace about the year 100.

❦ MAY 9 ❧

Holy Prophet Isaiah

Isaiah was born the son of Amoz. He married a woman who shared his prophetic calling and work. By God's command, the two sons she bore him were given prophetic names: Shear-jashub ("a remnant shall return") and Maher-shalal-hashbaz ("the spoil speeds, the prey hastens"). By these names Isaiah meant to proclaim to Judah their spiritual plight and the coming judgment (Is. 7—8).

Isaiah received his prophetic call in the year after the death of prosperous King Uzziah, when he was in the temple (Is. 6). He saw the angelic worship of the seraphim as they cried, "Holy! Holy! Holy!" He was cleansed of his unclean lips by God's grace (imaged in his vision by a burning coal taken with tongs from the altar). When God asked for someone to go and proclaim His message, Isaiah said, "Here I am! Send me!" Thereupon he became a prophet of God with a special mission.

He prophesied in troubled days, warning the kings of Judah through many years. He was the special advisor to righteous King Hezekiah and assured him of God's miraculous victory over Sennacherib when he besieged Judah (Is. 36—37). He prophesied of the coming Kingdom of God and of the Messiah—how He would be manifested by the sign of the virgin's womb (Is. 7:14); how He would be born to bring the people who sat in darkness to a great light (Is. 9:1–7); how He would be a suffering servant who would be despised and rejected, a man of sorrows, as a sheep led to the slaughter (Is. 53). Isaiah prophesied of Christ's glory so wonderfully that he has been called the evangelical or gospel prophet.

Isaiah was martyred under the wicked King Manasseh by being sawn in half (compare Heb. 11:37). He lived in the eighth century BC.

~: MAY 10 :~

Holy Apostle Simon the Zealot
Also called Simon the Cananite (Matt. 10:4), Simon was one of the Zealots (Luke 6:15)—the political group that sought to liberate Israel from Roman domination by military force and uprising. Some say he went to preach in Mauretania and others that he went to Persia. That Simon, a zealot and hater of Rome, shared the apostolate with such a man as Matthew, a tax-collector and collaborator with Rome, is testimony to the power of Christ, who reconciles opposites and makes the lion and the lamb lie down together.

~: MAY 11 :~

Ss. Cyril and Methodius, Equals-to-the-Apostles
Constantine and Methodius were brothers of great wealth, natives of Thessalonica, in which border city Greeks and Slavs mingled together.

MAY

Constantine had a career in the imperial court but forsook it to live as a monk. His older brother Methodius had a career in the army, which he also forsook for monastic discipline. The two retired to a monastery in Mount Olympus in 850.

In 858, the Khazars of southern Russia asked the emperor to send some missionaries to them, and he sent Constantine and Methodius. They worked among the Khazars for about ten years and then went to Constantinople. In 862 the Slavs of Moravia asked the emperor for missionaries, and the brothers were again sent.

The people of Moravia had already been sent Western missionaries, but they had insisted on using Latin, and the Moravians wanted to worship in their own language. Constantine and Methodius therefore translated the Scriptures and liturgy into their own language, inventing an alphabet to do this (the so-called Glagolitic alphabet, which was later replaced by Cyrillic). The Western missionaries in Moravia were quite hostile to Constantine and Methodius's efforts and accused them of interfering with their work. The two were accused and made to go to Rome to explain why they had interfered and used the vernacular in their work instead of Latin.

The brothers went to Rome in 868. The Pope of Rome agreed with them and blessed them to continue using the Slavic vernacular in their mission in those lands. While in Rome, Constantine died, having finally been formally tonsured a monk with the name Cyril. Methodius returned to his mission field, having been ordained by the Pope as Archbishop of Pannonia and Moravia. This added authority did not help him with his Latin opposition there—the Western bishops got him arrested and imprisoned. He was tried and banished to a prison in faraway Swabia. There he remained until a later Pope learned of it in 873 and got him released. Methodius was continually harassed and accused by the Western bishops even though he had the support of Rome.

In 881 he was invited to go to the capital in Constantinople and was received with honor there. The combined support of Constantinople and Rome at last overcame the opposition of the Western bishops, and they left him in peace to do his missionary work. He died in peace in 885. The work of Cyril and Methodius stands as a testimony to the desire of the Church that all the nations of the earth should hear the gospel and worship God in their own vernacular language.

~: MAY 12 :~

St. Epiphanius, Bishop of Cyprus

Epiphanius was born in Palestine of Jewish parents but as a young man, in about 315, converted to the Christian Faith and embraced the monastic way. He visited Egypt and became aware of the various gnostic heresies that abounded there. For his great learning, he was ordained Bishop of Salamis in Cyprus. He traveled to Rome and became friends with St. Jerome. He strove mightily to combat heresy in the Church (writing a volume called *The Medicine Box* to refute them all), especially combating Origenism.

Though zealous for Orthodoxy, Epiphanius was a man of some rigidity. Once when visiting a church in Bethel, he was offended by a curtain that hung across a church door, on which Christ or some saint was painted. Indignant at what he considered an unlawful display, he tore down the curtain and told the people to use it as a shroud to bury the poor.

~: MAY 13 :~

Holy Martyr Glykeria

Glykeria was a young girl of Trajanopolis in Thrace. When attending a pagan feast, she signed her forehead with the holy Cross and openly confessed that she was a Christian. Thus when Christians were arrested, she was arrested with them. She refused to sacrifice to the gods when ordered to do so. She was therefore tortured, by order of the governor Sabinus, by being suspended by her hair and beaten.

Glykeria was taken to Heraklea, where she was welcomed by the bishop of that city and treated with great deference, as a confessor and athlete of Christ. She was subjected to great torture and had her scalp torn off. At length she was executed by being thrown to the wild beasts. This happened in about 177. After her death, she was venerated by the Christians of the city of Heraklea, where some of her relics remain.

✑ MAY 14 ✑

Holy Martyr Isidore
Isidore was a native of the island of Alexandria and a Christian. He was a soldier in the Roman army in the reign of Decius. He went to the island of Chios with his fellow soldiers but was denounced as a Christian by a centurion named Julius. When ordered to renounce his faith, Isidore steadfastly confessed Christ. For this he was tied to the ground by four stakes and beaten with a knuckled whip by his men. Despite his sufferings, he refused to disavow Christ and swear by the gods. For this he was beheaded, after being further tortured, in the year 251.

✑ MAY 15 ✑

Our Holy Father Pachomius the Great
Pachomius was born of pagan parents in Upper Egypt and was converted to the Faith by the love and compassion some Christians showed him when he was in distress. After his release from the army, he was baptized and, coming under the influence of the ascetic Palamon, he joined him as a disciple. He built a monastic dwelling at Tabennisi, where Palamon joined him. The rule for his community was simple: each monk lived separately in his cell, fasting as much or as little as he wished, though they ate and worshipped together. Many joined Pachomius in his monastery, so that he soon had to found six other monasteries to accommodate the growing numbers. As many as seven thousand monks inhabited these monasteries.

Pachomius was a man of great humility and patience, and he had a great gift of discretion. The monks made plaited mats to support themselves. One time a monk made two plaited mats in a day instead of the usual one. He hung them up in front of his cell so that all the others might admire him for his zeal. Pachomius merely said to him, "Take the mats with you into the dining hall and into the church so that no one will miss seeing how industrious and zealous you are." The monk was then ashamed, for he knew that he had given place to vanity.

Pachomius was the father of cenobitic or common-life monasticism. He died in peace in 346.

~: MAY 16 :~

Our Holy Father Theodore the Sanctified

Theodore was born to a noble Christian family in southern Egypt and lived a devout life from his childhood. On the Feast of Theophany, during the festive family meal, he was pierced with compunction and a desire to embrace the ascetic life. From that time on, he fasted every day until evening and abstained from all luxurious foods.

Two years later, Theodore was received into the monastery of Latopolis. There he learned about the ascetic Pachomius and went to live in his monastery in Tabennisi as his disciple. So great was his zeal that after Pachomius's death, Theodore succeeded him as abbot, ruling all his monasteries. He was devoted to his spiritual father, passing long nights in prayer to God at his tomb. When challenged by philosophers regarding his faith in Christ, he answered them, and then cautioned, "Take note: shun useless questions and scholastic syllogisms. Draw near to Christ and you will receive the remission of sins." He died in peace in 368.

~: MAY 17 :~

Holy Apostles Andronicus and Junia

Andronicus was a Jew like St. Paul, his kinsman (Rom. 16:7, RSV), and was converted to Christ before him. With his wife Junia, he was distinguished among the other apostles for his great service. It is said he preached among the Pannonians near Moravia. The couple were arrested and taken to Rome, where it appears they suffered martyrdom, thus receiving the crown of glory Christ promises to all who steadfastly love Him.

~: MAY 18 :~

Holy Martyr Peter and Companions
In the year 250, a number of Christians were arrested for their Faith, among whom were a young man named Peter, a nobleman called Dionysius, two soldiers named Andrew and Paul, a young sixteen-year-old girl named Christina, and a believer named Nicomachus. Nicomachus broke under torture and denied Christ. All the others courageously confessed Christ and refused to deny Him, even when tortured. They endured until the end and victoriously entered the Kingdom.

~: MAY 19 :~

Hieromartyr Patrick, Bishop of Brussa, and Companions
Patrick was a Bishop of Asian Brussa in Bithynia in the time of Emperor Julian the Apostate. The local magistrate attempted to force Patrick to acknowledge that the healing properties of the local hot water spring could be attributed to the pagan gods Aesculapius and Hygeia. When asked to acknowledge and sacrifice to the pagan gods, Patrick refused, saying that the pagan gods were simply demons and that all healing came from the one true God of the Christians. In his final words, he gave thanks to God, who created the hot springs for the salvation of the righteous. After his prayer, he bowed his head to the executioner's blow and was beheaded with axes, along with three of his presbyters, Acacius, Menander, and Polyenus.

~: MAY 20 :~

Holy Martyr Thaleleus
Thaleleus was a physician in Anazarbus in Cilicia. During the persecution under Emperor Numerian he tried to hide, but was apprehended,

taken to Aegae, and brought before Theodorus, the governor. The governor ordered that a hole be bored through the bones of his ankles and a rope passed through the holes, so that Thaleleus would be suspended upside down. The executioners tried to evade carrying out such a barbaric order but were executed themselves for their compassionate refusal. The governor ordered Thaleleus cast into the sea to drown. When Thaleleus succeeded in scrambling ashore, he was executed by beheading. He suffered for his Lord with honor in 284.

᛭ MAY 21 ᛭

Emperor Constantine, Equal-to-the-Apostles, and his mother, Helen

Constantine was born in 272 in Naissus but was raised in his mother Helen's town of Drepanum in the East. When his father, Constantius, became one of the four co-emperors over the Roman Empire (he ruled over Britain and Gaul), Constantine was taken to the court of co-emperor Diocletian to be educated. He entered a military career and saw the persecution of Christians firsthand. In 306 Constantius was dying, and Constantine escaped westward to Britain to bid him farewell and to succeed him as an emperor of the West. With Constantius's death, Constantine ruled the West along with the evil and cruel Maxentius.

In 312, Constantine decided to overthrow Maxentius and end his cruelties. He marched against Maxentius toward Rome and met him by the Tiber River. It was a crucial time. Before the battle, Constantine prayed to the Supreme God, and at midday he had a vision—a cross of fire appeared to him in the sky along with the words, "In this sign, conquer." He consulted with some Christian priests in his camp and concluded that Christ was calling him to faith and victory. Constantine adopted this sign instead of the Roman eagles as his banner, and with this sign he won the battle against Maxentius at the bridge across the Tiber.

Constantine entered Rome in triumph and began a liberation of the Christian Faith. Persecutions of the Christians ceased; it became

MAY

possible for the Church to own property; Christian exiles were recalled. Constantine himself funded church buildings. He made the Christian day of worship, Sunday, a legal day of rest from all official business. He gave generously to support the poor and orphans.

Constantine wanted to build a Christian empire, united under one God and (after his defeat of co-emperor Licinius in the East in 324) under one emperor. He founded his own capital in the East—the New Rome, Constantinople ("Constantine City")—a city never stained by pagan worship as the Old Rome had been. Taking concern for the unity and peace of the Church, he called and paid for the First Ecumenical Council in Nicea in 325.

His mother, Helen, also converted, and she desired to glorify the Holy Land. Thus churches were built there: the Church of the Nativity above the place of Christ's birth in Bethlehem, and the Church of the Resurrection above Golgotha and the Empty Tomb in Jerusalem. The True Cross was recovered and set up in the church for all to venerate.

Constantine's path was difficult and, as emperor in the troubled days, he had to make many hard decisions. He did not always decide correctly. He exiled St. Athanasius in exasperation, believing the Arian slanders that Athanasius was trying to prevent corn supplies being shipped from Alexandria to Rome. But he always tried to be true to the vision he had seen and to shepherd an empire he wanted to convert to Christ.

In 337 Constantine fell ill and prepared for baptism (which, like many other Christians in those days, he had delayed until the end). His old friend Bishop Eusebius officiated. The emperor laid aside the imperial purple and was clothed in the white robe of the neophyte. Despite the urging of Arians, he recalled Athanasius from exile. He entered the sacred baptismal waters and fulfilled his long-delayed desire. He died soon after and was buried in his new Church of the Apostles in Constantinople.

In glorifying Constantine (with his pious mother, Helen) as a saint, the Church shows its gratitude to him for giving it life and enabling it to fulfill its work of converting all nations. As one equal to the apostles in his effects on the empire, Constantine tried his best to serve his Lord and conquer by the Sign of the Cross.

~: MAY 22 :~

Holy Martyr Basiliscus

Basiliscus was a friend of Eutropius and his brother Cleonicus (whose feast day is March 3). In the town of Amasea, many were arrested, including Basiliscus, Eutropius, and Cleonicus. These three were the closest of friends and said they would stand firm together for Christ. They declared themselves to be as inseparable in faith and love as the Holy Trinity were one from another.

When Eutropius and Cleonicus were martyred, Basiliscus feared he would not have the courage to go it alone. He prayed, "O Lord Jesus Christ, remember me, even to the end, that I may not be separated from these holy men who have been taken from me and who now are crowned!" The time came for Basiliscus to appear before the governor. He too refused to offer sacrifice to the gods and, after suffering terribly, was also martyred by beheading and so joined his friends in the heavenly Kingdom. This happened in 308.

Holy Martyr John-Vladimir, King of Serbia

John was born near the end of the tenth century to pious parents of the royal house of Serbia, which ruled in Ochrid. He married Kosara, the daughter of King Samuel, and ruled Serbia after his father's death. He was a true Christian and was more attached to piety than to power. He was himself merciful, meek, and chaste. He zealously supported the church in Serbia, building churches, monasteries, hospitals, schools, and seminaries. His love for prayer grew, and he increasingly left the business of court to go to a church and monastery he had built in the forests in order to pray and meditate.

His wife conspired with others at court to have John assassinated and herself made sole ruler. Thus it was that he was traitorously struck down by his brother-in-law while on a military campaign in 1015. Miracles were wrought in answer to prayer over his grave. In

1925, a church was built to him near the monastery he founded. He abides as a testimony to true royal piety.

~: MAY 23 :~

St. Michael, Bishop of Synnada

Born in Synnada in Phrygia, Michael left home early for Constantinople, where he became a friend of St. Theophylact of Nicomedia. They were such close friends that they were inseparable. When Tarasius became Bishop of Constantinople, the two friends became monks, one after the other, in the monastery Tarasius founded on the Bosphorus. When Tarasius learned of their zeal for holiness, he arranged to have them consecrated bishops—Theophylact as Bishop of Nicomedia, and Michael as Bishop of his hometown, Synnada. As such they took part in the Seventh Ecumenical Council in 787.

When persecution against the defenders of icons again broke out under the Emperor Leo, Michael was exiled, though even then he continued to preach the truth and to work miracles of healing through his prayers. He was further exiled to many places, in each place praying for the faithful and witnessing to the truth. He eventually died in want and poverty, a true confessor for his Lord, entering the Kingdom in about 826.

~: MAY 24 :~

St. Simeon the Younger

Simeon was born in Antioch in 522. His father perished in an earthquake, and he was cared for by his mother, Martha. When he was six years old, his mother decided to give him over to the care of some monks. He was raised in the ways of the desert by a monk named John.

As a young man, Simeon was greatly influenced by the example of St. Simeon the Stylite, who had died about a hundred years earlier and whose relics were in Antioch (his feast day is September 1). Inspired by his elder namesake, the younger Simeon also built a pillar outside Antioch and adopted the asceticism of living there as a stylite.

It is said he was ordained priest on top of the pillar and lived there on a platform large enough to celebrate the liturgy. The people who flocked to him to hear his wisdom would ascend the pillar by a ladder to receive Holy Communion from his hands. He died in peace in the year 596 at the age of seventy-five.

St. Vincent of Lérins

Vincent was born in Gaul and followed a military career but at length renounced the world to embrace monasticism on the island of Lérins, which was a busy center of monastic spirituality for the surrounding area. He was ordained priest. He strove for Orthodox truth in the matter of grace and free will, along with his Gallic countryman St. John Cassian. He opposed Blessed Augustine's opinion that man was predestined to enter salvation or damnation, so that his free will was not truly free. In opposition to this, Vincent asserted that man's will was important in his cooperating with God's grace. St. Vincent, in his work *Commonitory*, stated the principle that Scripture must be interpreted according to the catholic consensus—as it was interpreted "everywhere, always, and by all." He died in about 445.

~: MAY 25 :~

Third Discovery of the Head of St. John the Baptizer

During the iconoclastic troubles of the eighth century, the relic of St. John's head was taken to Comana in Armenia. In 850, when the persecution subsided, it was again returned to Constantinople with great pomp and joy and placed in the church there. Its translation is testimony to the abiding love of Christians for St. John, the Forerunner of the Lord.

~: MAY 26 :~

Holy Apostle Carpus

Carpus was a close friend of St. Paul and probably traveled with him throughout Greece. He was in Troas when St. Paul parted from him and left his heavy cloak there with him. In prison, Paul requested Timothy to fetch this cloak from his friend Carpus to help him endure the cold of prison (2 Tim. 4:13). Carpus became the Bishop of Berea in Thrace, working miracles and leading many to baptism. He died in peace, and his relics worked miracles among the faithful.

MAY 27

Hieromartyr Therapon of Sardis

Therapon was a devout presbyter in the town of Sardis in Lydia. He was arrested in the time of Emperor Valerian and was cruelly tortured, being bound to four posts and beaten until the flesh was stripped from his bones. He was taken from place to place, being imprisoned in Sinaos and Ancyra and Satala. After further torture, he was beheaded, suffering for Christ in about 259.

MAY 28

St. Nicetas the Confessor, Bishop of Chalcedon

Embracing monasticism as a youth, Nicetas was at length ordained Bishop of Chalcedon. As bishop, he took special care of the needy orphans, widows, and beggars. When Emperor Leo the Armenian persecuted those who defended the holy icons, Nicetas was exiled from his see. He died after much hardship and trial, a true confessor for the truth.

Holy Hieromartyr Eutyches

Eutyches was born in the first century and was a disciple of the apostles, being acquainted with both Paul and John. He traveled widely, sharing the gospel with all and suffering many hardships. He ended his days as a martyr (some say by being drowned) and inherited the Kingdom.

MAY 29

St. Theodosia of Tyre

Theodosia was a virgin of Tyre who was not yet eighteen years old. When some martyrs of her church who had been arrested were brought before the magistrate in Caesarea, she went to them to encourage them to be steadfast and to ask for their prayers. While doing so, she herself was arrested with them. The commander had her tortured, digging into her sides and breasts to the very bone. Still alive, she was cast into the sea. She suffered with cheerfulness and joy and inherited the heavenly glory in 300.

MAY 30

The Venerable Isaac the Confessor

Isaac lived as a hermit in the East and came to Constantinople in the fourth century. He possessed prophetic gifts and warned the emperor of danger from the invading Goths. The citizens of the imperial city were impressed by his holiness and his prophetic gifts, and a certain one of them, Saturnius, urged him to stay in the capital. He even built him a monastery there. Before his death, Isaac appointed a disciple of his named Dalmatus as his successor. Thus the monastery was later known as the Dalmatian Monastery. Isaac died in peace in 383.

St. Macrina the Elder

Macrina was a disciple of St. Gregory the Wonderworker of Neocaesarea. She was also a woman of outstanding piety and a great influence for godliness in her family. Her grandchildren were St. Basil the Great, St. Gregory of Nyssa, and St. Macrina the Younger. In the persecution of Galerius in 304, Macrina and her husband had to hide in the mountain forests in Pontus for seven years. They suffered from cold and hunger, managing to keep alive by catching and killing wild deer. They died in peace in the fourth century. St. Macrina is a testimony to the great power of godliness in a family.

MAY 31

Holy Apostle Hermas

Hermas was a friend of St. Paul. A Greek by birth, he sojourned for a while in Rome, and while he was there St. Paul wrote him greetings (Rom. 16:14). He is said to have served as a bishop and finished his life as a martyr. It is possible that he is the author of the so-called *Shepherd of Hermas*, which contains many prophetic visions and revelations.

JUNE 1

Holy Martyr Justin the Philosopher

Justin was born of Greek parents in the Samaritan town of Shechem (called Flavian Neapolis) about 105. Being wealthy, he had a good education and was drawn to study philosophy. He passed through the philosophies of the stoics, the peripatetics, and the Pythagoreans and became at length a Platonist. Musing one day on a beach, Justin met an old man, and they spoke of philosophy and the quest for truth. The old man sowed doubts as to the sufficiency of philosophy and told Justin truth was to be found in Jesus Christ. Justin said that his words kindled a fire in his soul, and he began to study the Christian Faith.

He was at length baptized in 133 when he was thirty years old. He felt that philosophy was fulfilled in the gospel and so continued to wear the distinctive garb of a philosopher. A layman, he nonetheless traveled abroad, preaching the gospel: "It is our duty," he said, "to make our teaching known." He opened a school of philosophy in Rome. He wrote two *Apologies*, defending the Christian Faith from pagan slanders, and the *Dialogue with Trypho*, in which he debates with a Jew.

Another philosopher, Crescens, a Cynic, took a dislike to Justin and denounced him to the government as a Christian. He was brought to trial and commanded to sacrifice to the gods. "No right-minded man forsakes truth for falsehood," replied the philosopher. "Do with us as you will. We are Christians and cannot sacrifice to idols." With others, he was martyred in about 166.

JUNE 2

St. Nicephorus, Patriarch of Constantinople

Nicephorus was born in 758, son of a prosperous government official. He advanced in a career in the world, becoming imperial secretary. Seeking a life of quiet and holiness, he renounced the world and returned to a monastery in the province of Marmara. When the Patriarch of Constantinople died, it was decided that talented Nicephorus should succeed him, and he was elected to that office in 806.

When the iconoclastic Emperor Leo ascended the throne, he waged war against the holy icons and commanded that they be removed. He was opposed by his patriarch, who firmly replied, "We cannot change the ancient traditions: we respect holy icons as we do the cross and the book of the gospels." For this Nicephorus was banished in 813. Even in exile he was harassed until he died in 828. After the iconoclastic storm had passed and icons were again restored, his incorrupt relics were returned with honor to Constantinople on March 13.

JUNE 3

Holy Martyr Lucillian and Companions

Lucillian was a pagan priest who was converted to Christ in his old age, when he was living in Nicomedia. He was baptized, and when a persecution broke out, he was arrested and imprisoned with other, younger Christians—Claudius, Hypatius, Paul, and Dionysius. They spent their time in prison singing psalms and encouraging one another in the Faith. Finally they were further tortured and executed in Byzantium, suffering with honor for their Lord. A young Christian girl, Paula, openly retrieved the martyrs' bodies for Christian burial and was herself arrested. After torture, she also suffered martyrdom, being beheaded for her Faith. They all suffered in about 275.

~: JUNE 4 :~

St. Metrophanes of Constantinople

Metrophanes' father, Dometius, was bishop of the little town of Byzantium (before the reign of Constantine), and Metrophanes at length succeeded him to that see after Dometius had died. He was quite aged at the time of the First Ecumenical Council of Nicea in 325 and was unable to attend, though he did send a representative. Emperor Constantine greatly admired and praised him. He asked the bishops of the council to visit Metrophanes in his final sickness and to bless his see, the new capital, with their presence. Metrophanes lived to see his quiet little town transformed by Constantine into his new capital of Constantinople. He died right after the council in 325. He was, in an honorary way, the first Patriarch of Constantinople.

~: JUNE 5 :~

Hieromartyr Dorotheus, Bishop of Tyre

Dorotheus suffered greatly in the persecution of Diocletian. He was a great scholar, knowing Greek, Latin, and Hebrew, and wrote many books. During the persecution of Licinius in 320, Dorotheus fled to Odyssopolis on the Black Sea (modern-day Varna) until the storm blew over. He took his part in the First Ecumenical Council of Nicea in 325. When Emperor Julian the Apostate reigned and opposed the Christians once more in 361, the elderly bishop fled to Odyssopolis again. There he was arrested and tortured, despite his advanced age. He died of his sufferings and inherited the Kingdom of God.

~: JUNE 6 :~

Our Holy Father Bessarion

Bessarion served God from his youth and lived as a hermit. Unlike other hermits who lived in a hut or cave, he had no fixed residence but moved throughout the mountain forests. All he possessed was his tunic, his cloak, and a gospel book. Finding a naked man one day, he gave him his outer cloak to cover him, and so had nothing but the gospel book left as a possession. A local government official met him afterwards and asked him, "Bessarion, who robbed you of your clothes?" "This book," he answered, meaning the gospel. (The official, greatly edified, gave him some clothes.)

Another time, Bessarion met a man who had fallen into debt and was about to be sold as a slave to pay the debt. Bessarion then sold his gospel book to pay the man's debt and save him. At length monks came to look to him for leadership as abbot. At a Sunday liturgy, a priest asked one of the monks to leave because of some sin. "I also am a sinner," said Bessarion the abbot, and he rose and left with the priest. He was given grace to work miracles through his prayers. He died in peace in 466.

The Venerable Hilarion the New

Hilarion was born in the eighth century. He was a disciple of St. Gregory of Decapolis and an imitator of St. Hilarion the Great (feast day October 21), whose name he took. He became abbot of the Dalmatian Monastery in Constantinople. Hilarion stood firm in defense of the holy icons during the iconoclastic persecution of the Church. He was imprisoned and tortured in prison, only finding release with the reign of the Empress Theodora. He entered into rest in 845 at the age of 70.

༜ JUNE 7 ༜

Hieromartyr Theodotus of Ancyra

Theodotus was an innkeeper near Ancyra in Galatia. He sheltered his fellow Christians in his house during persecutions. His aunt Tecusa and six other virgins were accused of being Christians and were arrested. They remained steadfast in the Faith even when insulted and badgered. To break their spirit, the magistrate ordered that the seven be stripped and forced to bathe with the idol of Diana, thus making them priestesses of Diana, though against their will. (Each year at that time the idol of Diana was solemnly taken down to a pond and washed, and those women who wished to be her priestesses bathed with the idol, thereby consecrating themselves to her.)

The seven Christian virgins were taken, each in a cart, down to the pond amid a roaring, jeering crowd. The virgins refused the consecration and threw away the pagan priestess vestments with which they were adorned. The governor in rage ordered them drowned. Theodotus, on learning this, was greatly grieved and wanted to recover their bodies for honorable burial. His aunt Tecusa appeared to him in a dream and told him where their bodies might be found. Theodotus and his friends went and recovered the bodies from the water after the soldiers guarding them departed from their posts, taking shelter in a storm. Theodotus's deed was discovered, and the governor learned that it was he who had violated his order and honorably buried the Christians.

When they searched for him, Theodotus boldly gave himself up. He was racked and horribly tortured. His jaws and teeth were smashed in and, after languishing in prison for five days, he was further tortured. At the place of his final execution, he prayed, "O Lord Jesus Christ, I thank You that You have given me strength to crush the head of the old dragon. Give peace to Your Church and save it from the tyranny of the Evil One." He was beheaded and entered into the Kingdom in 303.

Hieromartyr Marcellinus, Pope of Rome

Under the persecution of Diocletian, Pope Marcellinus was ordered to surrender the Scriptures, to sacrifice to the gods, and to offer incense—and he did so. After his apostasy, his conscience struck him mightily. He repented of his sin and confessed himself a Christian before the authorities. For this he was executed and crowned with the glory of martyrdom. His lapse and recovery show how God accepts repentance and how He exalts those who humble themselves before Him. Pope Marcellinus suffered in 304.

June 8

St. John of Kronstadt

John was born in 1829 in the village of Sura, in the Archangelsky province in Russia, the son of a poor church reader. He was a compassionate and pious boy, and some of his fellow villagers often asked him to pray for them. As a boy from a clerical family, he went to a parochial school and later to a theological academy. As a youth he was subject to depression, which he fought with prayer. He wanted to be a missionary to China, but he was ordained priest in 1855 and assigned to a local parish in the naval town of Kronstadt, which had much immorality and much poverty.

John undertook to be a pastor to Kronstadt. He extended kindness and care to the poor and to children and remonstrated with the drunkards, encouraging them to sobriety. Not content to merely celebrate the services, he worked hard to further the social work of the church in Kronstadt. At times he would return home barefoot because he had given away his shoes to the needy. He mobilized the local population to build a Home for Constructive Labor so the poor could work and feed themselves. He also created a monastery in Pskov and a women's monastery in Poland. As people gave him money, he would pass it along to the churches.

Fr. John lived with his wife as brother and sister. Unlike many in that time, he encouraged frequent reception of Holy Communion, himself celebrating the liturgy every day. He served with great fervor, often receiving Holy Communion with tears. He held general confession to accommodate the thousands who responded to him and came to him for help. During these services, people openly wept and sobbed loudly as Fr. John enumerated sins to be repented of, so great was the outpouring of God's grace. At Holy Communion, he would have sometimes as many as five thousand prosphoras.

John's fame grew and grew, and he would travel far to minister to those who requested his prayers, so that he was called "the pastor of all Russia." God worked great miracles of healing through his prayers—including instantly healing the lame, blind, and deaf. His fame and popularity brought great controversy and opposition for him, but he endured and carried on with this work.

John fell ill with an inflammation of the bladder and, against his doctor's advice, continued to fast and to serve Divine Liturgy every day. He died in peace in 1908. All Russia mourned his passing, knowing they had in their midst a true wonderworker and a pastor who loved their souls. His relics are preserved in St. Petersburg.

~: JUNE 9 :~

St. Cyril, Archbishop of Alexandria

Cyril was born about 380 in Alexandria. When his uncle, the haughty Patriarch Theophilus of Alexandria, died in 412, Cyril not only succeeded to his office of Patriarch of Alexandria but also inherited his prejudice and opposition to St. John Chrysostom, who was then Patriarch of Constantinople. Though he at first refused to commemorate John in the list of Orthodox patriarchs, Cyril later regretted his prejudice, relented at the urging of a monk in his diocese, St. Isidore of Pelusium, and was reconciled to the cause of John.

Cyril, like his flock in Alexandria (which was known for its unruliness and excitability), was also a fiery and impulsive spirit in his zeal for the truth. Once when the powerful Jewish community procured the disgrace and punishment of one of Cyril's admirers, he opposed them. In retaliation, they massacred a number of his flock. Cyril was incensed and sought redress: he organized a force that attacked the synagogue and drove the Jews from the city. Another time a mob of Cyril's flock, angry that a certain lady philosopher, Hypatia, was harassing their patriarch, dragged her off and tore her to pieces. Cyril himself was aghast, having had nothing to do with this deed, but the event darkened his reputation.

In 428, Nestorius was made Patriarch of Constantinople. He avowed a heretical doctrine of Christ, denying that Mary was the Mother of God. Nestorius said she should be called rather "the Mother of Christ," as her child Jesus was not God but merely one in whom God dwelt. Cyril wrote to his brother bishop, urging him to avoid heresy. Nestorius responded with haughty contempt. Cyril wrote him again, and still Nestorius would not leave his errors. Cyril was adamant: "I care not for distress or insult or bitterest revilings—only let the Faith be kept safe!" he said.

Cyril again wrote Nestorius, but he was more obstinate than ever. Rome joined Alexandria in condemning Nestorius's teaching. The emperor summoned a church council at Ephesus in 431 to resolve the matter—the Third Ecumenical Council. At the council, Nestorius, though present in Ephesus, refused to come to the council despite repeated summons inviting him. He was therefore condemned for his teaching and was deposed. The Patriarch of Antioch, though favoring Nestorius personally, gave an orthodox confession of his faith and was reconciled to Cyril and the Church. Cyril's steadfastness for the truth had been vindicated by the council.

In the years following the council, Cyril patiently and tirelessly strove to explain the true teaching to opponents of it and to win them back to the Church. Cyril died in peace in 444. His contemporary, Pope Celestine of Rome, praised him as "a generous defender of the Church and Faith and an apostolic man." The Church has called him "the Seal of the Fathers."

~: JUNE 10 :~

Holy Martyrs Alexander and Antonina

Alexander was a soldier; Antonina was a young girl. Both were Christians in Alexandria, though they did not know each other. During the persecution of the Church in that day, Antonina was arrested and imprisoned. Alexander, as a soldier with opportunity to help, felt compelled to rescue her. He visited her in prison, wrapped her in his military cloak, and told her to keep her head lowered. She went out through the guardhouse in front of the gates, and he took her place in prison. Thus the young girl was able to escape. Alexander, however, was at length discovered and brought before the judges to be interrogated as a Christian.

Antonina could not endure to be free at such a cost, and she turned herself in. Both of these athletes for Christ were put to torture—their hands were cut off and their naked bodies flayed and burnt with torches. They were finally executed and entered the heavenly courts with joy in the year 313.

~: JUNE 11 :~

Holy Apostles Bartholomew and Barnabas

Bartholomew was also known as Nathanael. He was a native of Cana in Galilee and a companion of Philip, who introduced him to Christ (John 1:43–51). He was a man of integrity, a true Israelite, without guile. After our Lord's Ascension, it is said that Bartholomew preached the gospel in Armenia. There he encountered opposition from a local prince. (It is possible that he converted the prince's daughter to the Faith and this was the cause of the opposition.) The prince had Bartholomew flayed alive, suspended on a cross, and left to be eaten by flies. He suffered with honor in about the year 50.

Barnabas was a Levite from Cyprus. His actual name was Joseph, Barnabas being a nickname which meant "son of encouragement" (Acts 4:36). He was a man of some wealth and gave it all up to the common fund of the apostles to feed the poor. When Paul was converted to Christ, it was Barnabas who believed in the sincerity of his conversion and introduced him to the other apostles, taking Paul with him on their first missionary journey. He quarreled with Paul later over the issue of whether to take Mark along with them, when he had deserted them on a previous missionary journey. The two separated, Barnabas going with Mark to preach in Cyprus and Paul going with Silas. It is said that Barnabas's remaining mission work was done in his native Cyprus, and that he was martyred by Jewish opposition in Salamis. He suffered for his Lord in about 53.

❧ JUNE 12 ☙

Our Holy Father Onuphrius the Great

In about the fourth century, Onuphrius lived in the Egyptian desert as a hermit. He had a long white beard that reached almost to the ground. He lived in his monastery in the Thebaid, but left to seek a more solitary existence, "dwelling in the desert" (as he said) "for the love of God." He lived near a large date-palm tree, which, along with herbs and other fruit, provided him with sustenance. Onuphrius lived among the rocks in ascetic holiness for sixty years, at the end of which time he was found by a monk named Paphnutius. They spoke together before he died, and Paphnutius buried him. He lived alone with God. "My food and drink," he said, "are the sweet words of God."

❧ JUNE 13 ☙

Holy Martyr Aquilina

Aquilina was a native of Biblos in Palestine and a Christian. When a girl of only twelve years, she suffered under the persecution of Diocletian. The magistrate Volusian ordered that small daggers be heated until they were red-hot. As they were being heated, she prayed for strength to be steadfast, saying, "O Lord Jesus Christ, You have made me strong with Your ready help that I may fight against the enemy, Satan: finish the course of my contest that I may be worthy to enter Your heavenly marriage-chamber!" The red-hot daggers were thrust into her ears, and the pain was so great that she fainted and was taken for dead. She was thrown out but the next morning was found to be still (though barely) moving. She was then executed by beheading. The young girl suffered valiantly for her Lord in 293.

❧ JUNE 14 ☙

Holy Prophet Elisha

Elisha was the son of Shaphet, and he lived in Abel-meholah in the Jordan Valley. He was a farmer when Elijah the prophet called him to join him as a prophet and as his successor in about 856 BC. After Elijah's ascension, Elisha dwelt in Jericho with the community of prophets. He assisted Jehoram, King of Israel, in his military campaign against Moab. Elisha was a wonderworker, turning bitter waters to sweet drinkability, raising a boy from the dead, curing the foreign general Naaman of his leprosy, and striking Syrian soldiers with blindness. He lived for a time in Gigal. He went to Damascus to anoint the foreign king Hazael as king over Syria, and he anointed the firebrand Jehu the next king over Israel.

Elisha was a man of healing, intimately involved with the spiritual politics of his day. Through him God worked His purposes for the political fortunes of His people, for salvation and judgment. Even after Elisha's death, God continued to work wonders through his relics—a dead man, coming into contact with his bones, was immediately revived. Elisha died in about 800 BC.

~: JUNE 15 :~

Holy Prophet Amos

Amos was a shepherd by trade, living in Tekoa, about six miles south of Bethlehem in the kingdom of Judah, in the eighth century BC. Yahweh called him from tending his flock to be His prophet. The southern kingdom under Uzziah and the northern kingdom under Jereboam were at the height of their power, prosperity, and decadence. Amos was sent from Judah into the northern kingdom to denounce the luxury and sin of the ruling classes and call them to repentance. He announced the impending judgment of God upon the impenitent and prophesied of the coming Kingdom of God, when He would reconstitute Israel and make all things new, raising up the booth of David that had fallen (Amos 9:11; Acts 15:16).

Blessed Augustine of Hippo

Augustine was born in Thagaste in Numidia, North Africa, in 354. He was the son of a pagan father and a devout Christian mother (St. Monica). He was raised a Christian, though unbaptized. His skin was a dark bronze, his eyes black, and he was tall and long-limbed. He was easily hurt and of quarrelsome temperament. He detested the Greek language and mathematics and was often thrashed as a schoolboy for impudence and for playing around in class. He loved poetry. He had a rather wild youth: he later wrote, "I wandered further from You, Lord, and You left me to myself. The torrent of my fornications tossed and swelled and boiled over. Lord, how loathsome I was in Your sight!"

When Augustine was sixteen, his father died, and he went to Carthage. It was there he became a Manichaean. He also began to live with a girl who had a son by him, Adeodatus. One day his closest friend died and, overcome with grief, Augustine fled to Rome. When a teaching job became available in Milan, he went there to take it, and there fell under the spell of Milan's popular bishop, Ambrose. His mother Monica had followed him from home and was with him now in Milan. She constantly urged him to become a Christian. Augustine was rapidly reaching a crisis—he knew he should convert but did not want to. He would pray in his heart, "O Lord, make me chaste—but not yet!"

Finally, the moment of truth arrived. Augustine spoke with a friend about godly chastity and was reading Athanasius's *Life of Anthony*. Seeking peace from his internal struggle with lust, he went to rest in a garden. There he heard a child's voice from somewhere, chanting, "Take up and read!"—possibly as part of a child's game. He ran to his friend, who was then reading St. Paul's Epistle to the Romans, and took up and read at random, "not in revelry and drunkenness, not in lewdness and lust . . . But put on the Lord Jesus Christ, and make no provision for the flesh, to fulfill its lusts." (Rom. 13:13–14, RSV).

The decision was made, and Augustine's heart was at peace. He accepted the Faith and was baptized with his friend and his son in 387. He at length returned to North Africa and was ordained priest (against his will) in the town of Hippo. Five years later, he was elevated to succeed the bishop there. He threw himself into his episcopal work, tending his flock, aiding the needy, and writing commentaries, sermons, and letters. His works fill fifty large volumes, including his great work *The City of God*, which defended the Church against the slanders of the city of man. He strove against Pelagian and Donatist heresies and also against the Manicheans. His works were later to form the theological basis for the medieval Western church, over which he would tower above all others as its foremost theologian.

In 430 the Vandals were besieging Hippo. Augustine, an old man of seventy-six and worn out from work, fell ill and died in peace. In his famous memoirs, his *Confessions*, he wrote, "Lord, You made us for Yourself, and our heart is restless until it finds rest in You." Augustine was a man who rested in God, a true lover and seeker of God. He wrote that in the Kingdom "we shall rest and we shall see; we shall see and we shall love; we shall love and we shall praise. Behold what will be in the end, without end! For what is our end but to reach that Kingdom which has no end?" Blessed Augustine entered the Kingdom in 430.

~: JUNE 16 :~

St. Tikhon, Bishop of Amathus

Tikhon was the son of simple Christians who lived in Amathus, a town in southern Cyprus. His father was a baker, and Tikhon would often give bread to the poor free of charge (to his father's great distress). After the death of his father, Tikhon gave away all his possessions and presented himself to the local bishop, Mnemonius, who recognized the zealous young man's sanctity and ordained him deacon, thus putting him in charge of the church's charitable work. After the death of Mnemonius, Tikhon was elected Bishop of Amathus in his place and consecrated by St. Epiphanius for his work. He toiled long in Cyprus to convert the pagans there, mightily opposing the pagan worship and calling all to serve Christ. St. Tikhon had prophetic knowledge of his approaching death and consoled those who grieved at the thought of losing him, reminding them of the hope of the resurrection. He died in peace in 425, a vigorous pastor and a man of God.

~ JUNE 17 ~

Holy Martyrs Manuel, Sabel, and Ishmael

These were three brothers and educated men of Persia. They were sent as political ambassadors of the Persian official Balanos, as part of a delegation to negotiate a treaty between the Romans and the Persians. They were received by the Roman Emperor Julian, who had himself relapsed into the pagan worship of the Roman gods.

The emperor was looking for a pretext to make war on Persia. He invited the brothers to a sumptuous feast in Chalcedon, which included making sacrifices to the gods. As devout Christians, the brothers naturally refused to take part. When challenged to renounce their Christian Faith, the three replied, "Why are you bothering with all this? It is useless to try to separate us; we are all three united by faith in the Holy Trinity, and whatever one of us declares will be echoed by the other two. Nothing can make us change." For this they were executed, possibly partly as a diplomatic confrontation with Persia. They suffered for the Lord in 362.

~ JUNE 18 ~

Holy Martyr Leontius

Leontius was a native of Yelada and a soldier at Tripoli in Phoenicia, where he distinguished himself by his bravery. He healed his fellow soldier Hypatius of a fever by his prayers and thereby converted him and another soldier, Theodulus. While garrisoned at Tripoli, Leontius used the army provisions to help the poor, hiding from others neither his Christian Faith nor his disdain for the pagan gods. When persecution broke out, he refused to sacrifice to the gods and, by order of Hadrian, was tortured along with his two friends, being stretched out between four stakes and beaten. His tormentors said, "This is how those who rebel against the emperor and our gods are punished!"

Leontius retorted, "You can destroy my body, but you will never conquer my soul!" He died as he was being beaten, surrendering his brave soul to his heavenly King. This happened in about 135. A magnificent church was later built in his honor in Tripoli.

~: JUNE 19 :~

Holy Apostle Jude

Jude was the brother of James, our Lord's "brother" or kinsman (Mark 6:3), being (probably) the son of Clopas, the brother-in-law of the Theotokos. He wrote the Epistle of Jude in the New Testament, not referring to himself as "the brother of Jesus," but in pious humility identifying himself merely as "the brother of James," the Bishop of Jerusalem. He wrote probably from Palestine in about 67. It is said that he preached also in Edessa and was martyred there.

~: JUNE 20 :~

St. Methodius of Olympus

Methodius was an ascetic from his youth, famous for his philosophical learning. Some say that he was elected a bishop, though to which see is disputed. He once traveled from Milet to Patara to participate in a discussion on the truth of the Resurrection (from which event some refer to him as the Bishop of Patara). He wrote a defense of consecrated virginity, entitled *The Banquet of the Ten Virgins*, in the style of a Platonic dialogue. In this allegorical work, the Lady Virtue, the sister of Philosophy, gives a banquet, and each of the virgins invited in turn gives a speech praising virginity.

Methodius continued to travel, discoursing and debating with pagans, heretics, and gnostics, advancing the claims of the Christian gospel. He was arrested, tortured, and martyred for Christ in Chalcis, Syria, under Licinius. This happened in about 311.

~ JUNE 21 ~

Holy Martyr Julian of Cilicia

Julian was born to a noble and wealthy family in Anazarbus in Cilicia Secundus. His father was a pagan senator, but his mother, Asclepiodora, was a devout Christian. It was from her that he learned the Christian Faith and became mighty in the Scriptures.

Julian was arrested for his Faith when only eighteen. When threatened with terrible torture for refusing to obey the emperor's law, he responded, "I'm not afraid. Nothing will make me deny the law given me in my childhood." He was compelled to eat food that had been offered to idols as a way of forcing him to commit idolatry and sacrifice to the gods, but he remained unmoved, saying that sacrifices like this made under duress did not count as sacrifice. His mother was brought to him in prison, as the authorities felt sure she would persuade him to save his life by sacrificing to the gods, but instead she encouraged him to persevere in his faith in Christ. At length he was martyred by being put into a sack with scorpions and snakes and then thrown into the sea. He suffered with honor in the persecution of Diocletian.

~ JUNE 22 ~

Hieromartyr Eusebius, Bishop of Samosata

As bishop, Eusebius was a pillar of strength and constancy in the struggle against Arianism. The Arian Emperor Constantius, wanting to further the cause of the Arians, demanded that Eusebius surrender a document he had in his possession. Eusebius defied his emperor and declined to give it up. The emperor demanded it, saying if Eusebius refused, he would cut off his right hand. Eusebius said, "Cut them both off—I will not surrender the document!" The emperor backed down.

Eusebius traveled throughout Asia Minor, strengthening the cause of Nicene Orthodoxy. He was able to help secure the elevation of St.

Basil the Great to the important see of Caesarea. He was exiled for a time under the Arian Emperor Valens. He was killed when an Arian woman threw a tile down from a roof which struck him on the head. Before he died, he made his friends promise they would not search for the woman. He died in about 380, a martyr for the gospel.

St. Alban, Protomartyr of Britain

Alban was born a pagan. In the persecution of Diocletian, he compassionately sheltered a Christian priest in his house at Verulam and was converted by him. When the authorities came to arrest the priest, Alban pretended to be him and took his place while the priest escaped. When his cloak was removed and they saw it was Alban, they were furious. Alban refused to sacrifice to the gods as they demanded. He said, "I am a Christian and bound by Christian obligations." He was scourged and led away to execution. He was beheaded and inherited the Kingdom in about 304.

JUNE 23

Holy Martyr Agrippina

Agrippina was born in Rome to a noble family and lived as a virgin, refusing to marry. So powerful was her life's witness that she persuaded many other girls to embrace the way of Christian virginity and forgo marriage. During the persecution in the time of Valerian in 257, Agrippina was denounced to the authorities as a Christian and arrested. She remained defiant in her faith, which enraged the authorities all the more. She was stripped and flogged with rods until her blood soaked the ground and she died. Her holy body was left in a field to be eaten by dogs, but some of her brave friends, Paula, Bassa, and Agathonica, quietly recovered her relics at great risk to themselves. The holy relics were then taken to Sicily, where a church was built in her honor. Agrippina suffered for her heavenly Bridegroom in about 260.

JUNE 24

Nativity of St. John the Forerunner and Baptizer

The righteous Zachariah and his wife Elizabeth, of the house of Aaron in the tribe of Levi, long prayed for a son, but they had none, as Elizabeth was barren. One day, Zachariah's once-in-a-lifetime turn came to burn incense as priest in the temple at Jerusalem. The Archangel Gabriel was sent to him when he was in the inner court, burning the incense before God. Gabriel announced that Zachariah's prayer was heard and that Elizabeth would conceive a son even now in her old age, whom he should name John. Zachariah was initially incredulous and unbelieving in the miracle, for which he was made unable to speak until the child's birth.

In fulfillment of God's word, Elizabeth conceived and gave birth to a son. At his circumcision, Zachariah's mouth was opened, and he spoke in praise to God. John was born to be the Forerunner to the Messiah, a "prophet of the Most High [who] will go before the Lord to prepare his ways" (Luke 1:76, RSV). In obedience to the angelic instructions, John was raised as a dedicated Nazirite from birth, drinking no wine or strong drink. As the Forerunner who would baptize and reveal Jesus as the Christ to Israel, he went in the spirit and power of Elijah to prepare the people for the Lord. The child, filled with the Holy Spirit from the womb, grew in strength and frequented the Judean desert until his manhood, when the Word of the Lord came to him in the fifteenth year of the reign of Tiberius Caesar.

JUNE 25

Our Holy Mother the Martyr Febronia

Febronia lived from her infancy in a community of fifty virgins in Syria. At eighteen years old she was very beautiful and of great piety. When the local government official Selenus enforced the imperial decree against the Christians, the women of the community wanted to flee the impending persecution. Febronia, however, was very ill and unable to move. The women at length fled, and Febronia was forced to remain behind, awaiting the arrival of the soldiers to arrest her. They apprehended her and brought her to the governor before a large crowd of spectators. She was stripped (clothed only in a tattered cloak) and remained serene, saying, "Do I seem lost to shame? No, but I am stripped as a wrestler in the games is stripped to strive for victory."

She was tied down over a slow fire and scourged. She was racked and her sides torn with iron combs. Seventeen of her teeth were torn out. When her right breast was cut off, she cried out, "My Lord! My God! See what I suffer and receive my soul into Your hands!" Her other breast was cut off and, when unbound, she fell to the ground in a heap. Her hands, her feet, and finally her head were cut off. Her terrible suffering moved an attending magistrate, Lysimachus, to tears, and he later became a Christian. She suffered with honor for her heavenly Bridegroom in about 304. Her relics were translated to Constantinople in 363.

~: JUNE 26 :~

Our Holy Father David of Thessalonica

This holy man renounced the world, leaving his earthly land in Mesopotamia, and entered a monastery of Ss. Theodore and Mercurius. The monks there were known as "the cowled ones" for the monastic cowls they wore. This monastery was situated just outside the city of Thessalonica, near the ramparts. There David lived as a hermit, imitating the famous stylites (such as Simeon, who lived atop a pillar) by climbing atop an almond tree and living there. He remained in this extraordinary dwelling, being battered by wind, sun, rain, and snow, enduring the harsh weather of all the seasons.

For his great asceticism and holiness, God granted David prophetic insight and the grace to work miracles. At length, at the entreaties of others who wanted him as their guide, he descended from his location atop the tree and went to live in a more conventional cell on the ground, guiding his disciples from there. His fame spread, and many came to visit him.

At the entreaties of many, David went to Constantinople to bring to the emperor their request that the seat of the prefect of Illyricum be transferred to Thessalonica. Impressed by David's sanctity, the emperor granted the request. David died on the voyage home, as he had prophesied before beginning his journey to Byzantium. His blessed soul ascended to his Lord in about 540. He was buried in his monastery in accordance with his last wish.

~: JUNE 27 :~

St. Sampson the Hospitable

Sampson was born in Rome of wealthy parents. He received a good education and became a physician, compassionately tending the sick and praying for them, urging all his patients to serve Christ. He moved to Constantinople, where he continued his medical ministry. When the emperor became ill with an incurable disease, Sampson was brought to court to tend to him. Sampson simply laid hands upon the emperor's afflicted part, and he was healed. The emperor tried to reward him with wealth, but he replied, "I had silver and gold, but I left it all for Christ that I might gain heavenly and eternal wealth." When the emperor insisted on rewarding him, he bade him use the money to build a home for the poor (which he did). Sampson died in peace, a true physician of Christ, in 530.

~: JUNE 28 :~

Translation of the Relics of Ss. Cyrus and John

The feast day of the two holy unmercenary physicians Cyrus and John is January 31. They were martyred in 311 in Canopus.

In the early fifth century, Cyril, Bishop of Alexandria, was striving against the pagan cults in Egypt, such as the worship of Isis. Led by God, he decided to have the relics of the holy martyrs translated from Canopus to the city of Menuthis, which was a pagan cultic center. He did this in 412, and many turned from worshipping the pagan gods to serve the God of the Christians, so great was His power through

His saints. Many found healing through the relics and prayers of Cyrus and John: Ammonius, son of the governor of Alexandria, was healed, as was a certain Theodore, who was healed of his blindness. The Church keeps this feast of the transfer of the saints' relics as a witness to the saving grace of God, which He manifests through His chosen ones.

Ss. Sergius and Herman of Valaam

It seems that Sergius, a Greek monk, went to the northern reaches of Lake Ladoga in the twelfth century to begin a small hermitage there. He converted a local Karelian, Herman, to the Faith. This Herman succeeded Sergius in the leadership of the small monastic community that clustered about him. From these small beginnings the great monastery of Valaam arose. It was a spiritual center for evangelism among the Karelians of Finland and a great light of ascetic holiness in Russia.

~: JUNE 29 :~

Holy Apostles Peter and Paul

These two great apostles, who had very different lives and callings, were united in Christ in their deaths, both being martyred for Christ under Nero's persecution in Rome and, by their blood, glorifying the Church in that unity.

Peter, born Simon, was the son of John and was a fisherman in Galilee with Andrew, his brother. He was called by Christ to be a fisher of men and the first of the apostles. He first confessed the apostolic truth, "You are the Christ, the Son of the living God," at Caesarea Philippi (Matt. 16:16). For this, Christ gave the Church through him the keys of the Kingdom of heaven, that it should have authority with God to save men. Peter, as a confessor of Christ, showed himself to be the rock of the truth, and he was given the name Peter (Cephas), which means "Rock."

Peter was a generous, loyal, and impulsive man. At the Lord's arrest, he thrice denied his Lord and afterwards wept bitterly over it. After His Resurrection, Christ restored him to his apostolate, as

JUNE

Peter thrice confessed his love for the Lord and was thrice told to once again feed His sheep. Peter was the spokesman for all the apostles—such as on the Day of Pentecost, when his preaching converted three thousand. His special role of apostle to the Jews led him to travel all over—to Antioch and eventually to Rome. He first took the step of preaching to and baptizing Gentile converts after God prepared his heart with a vision telling him to call no faithful man—even a Gentile—unworthy of baptism (Acts 10). He wrote two New Testament epistles and remained to the end the chief of the apostles.

Paul (or Saul) was born of the tribe of Benjamin and a Roman citizen. He received a good education under the famous Rabbi Gamaliel in Jerusalem. He was a Pharisee and so zealous for his ancestral Law that he at first persecuted the Christians. Christ revealed Himself to Paul in a blinding vision when he was on his way to Damascus, and after that Paul served his Lord as a Christian. After his conversion he went away to Arabia to pray and then returned again to the church in Damascus. Barnabas took him with him on his missionary journey, and with Barnabas (and later with Silas), Paul went all over the Mediterranean preaching to Jews and Gentiles. Though harassed by Judaizers, who asserted that one must be a Jew and circumcised to be saved, Paul stood firm for the truth that Christ accepts repentant sinners as they are, without the self-justifying works of the Jewish Law.

Paul was the Apostle to the Gentiles and championed their cause before the rest of the Church. He wrote many New Testament epistles. He was a man of fervent love for his churches and zealous for the truth. He was arrested by his fellow Jews in Jerusalem and brought to Rome on a charge of treason. He was later released and traveled, some say, as far as Spain. He was arrested in Rome again when persecution broke out under Nero.

Thus were the two apostles united in their deaths in Rome. Peter was crucified upside down (requesting this position himself, saying he was not worthy of suffering in the same way as his Lord). Paul, being a Roman citizen, was beheaded. They live forever in the memory of the Church, two witnesses for their Lord (compare Rev. 11:3) whose blood is the seed of the Church. In their icons, they are often shown upholding together the single Church of Christ.

~: JUNE 30 :~

Synaxis of the Holy Apostles

This day commemorates all the Twelve Holy Apostles. All were equally called by Christ to serve Him in their own unique ways. All shared together the authority as His ambassadors, so that whoever received them received Christ (Matt. 10:40). All were given authority to heal the sick, cast out demons, and work miracles. They went their own ways, teaching the one Faith, proclaiming the one Lord. Thus they served Him faithfully and all received the one reward. The Lord promised to all that they would join Him in the age to come and sit on twelve thrones, judging the twelve tribes of Israel.

~ JULY 1 ~

Holy Unmercenaries Cosmas and Damian

These two brothers came from the region of Ephesus in Syria and were raised as Christians. God gave them gifts of healing, so that they were able to heal many who came to them by the laying on of hands. They refused to take money for this ministry, but simply urged those whom they helped to trust in the Lord. Though the brothers inherited great wealth, they gave much of it away to the poor and needy. Their other feast day is November 1. This day reflects their connection with the city of Rome, where a church was dedicated to the holy unmercenary physicians by Pope Symmachus in about 500.

Holy Martyr Potitus

Potitus was a boy from Sardinia. His father and mother harassed him for his faith in Christ, and he suffered also from the government authorities. In the time of Emperor Antonius he was arrested and beheaded at the age of thirteen.

~ JULY 2 ~

St. Juvenal, Archbishop of Jerusalem

Juvenal was a vigorous defender of Orthodoxy in a critical time. He ruled as Patriarch of Jerusalem in the years 420–460, making his contribution at the Third Ecumenical Council. Seeing the importance of Jerusalem as the Holy City, he strove mightily to have it elevated to the status of a patriarchate, freeing it from dependence upon the Metropolitanate of Caesarea and the Patriarchate of Antioch.

Juvenal supported Cyril of Alexandria in his struggle against

JULY

Nestorius and for a time supported Cyril's successor, the Monophysite heretic Dioscurus. When Dioscurus was condemned at the Fourth Ecumenical Council of Chalcedon, Juvenal also condemned the heretic. Perhaps as a reward, his see was given the long-awaited status of a patriarchate with authority over Palestine. After the council, some Monophysite supporters of Dioscurus began a revolt, and Juvenal had to remain in exile from his see until the emperor put down the revolt and assured his safe return home. Upon returning home, Juvenal strengthened the work of the monks, especially of Ss. Euthymius, Theodosius, and Gerasim. He died in peace in 458 after ruling the Holy City as hierarch for thirty-eight years.

The Deposition of the Robe of the Theotokos

In the fifth century, two nobles of Constantinople, Galbius and Candidus, were traveling in Palestine to venerate the holy places. While in Nazareth, they stayed in the home of a Jewish girl who knew the whereabouts of a robe worn by the Mother of God, which had been treasured by the local church down through the years. The two noblemen persuaded the Christians there to part with the precious relic and brought it back to Constantinople, where it could be more widely known and venerated. After they informed the emperor and the patriarch, the robe was ceremonially placed, with much rejoicing, in the Blachernae church in the imperial city. Today's feast commemorates the transfer of this precious relic to the capital city (which looked upon her as its patron) and the protecting prayers of the Mother of God for all those who ask her intercession.

St. John of Shanghai and San Francisco

St. John was born in southern Russia in 1896 with the name Michael. He went to Kharkov University and, at the time of war, moved to Belgrade in Serbia. Around 1926 he was tonsured a monk with the name John, was ordained a priest, and served the church in Ochrid. John was a true ascetic, never sleeping in a bed and eating only once a day at eleven PM. In Great Lent, he ate only prosphora. He received Holy Communion every day, which was a rare piety in those days. He was ordained bishop in 1934 and went to serve the Russian faithful in Shanghai, China. He arranged for relief work for the poor and the orphans. He often would give his shoes away to the poor and would arrive at the church barefoot.

When the communists took over, he evacuated his flock to the Philippines for over two years. In 1951 he was sent to care for a diocese in Western Europe, serving there in the Western Rite and using, as well as Slavonic, the local vernaculars of French and Dutch (and later, English, when he was in the U.S.). In 1962 he was sent to San Francisco. He served the Russian flock there until 1966, when he died in peace.

St. John was truly humble and a man of prayer. He prayed until he fell asleep from exhaustion each night. He was a wonderworker even in his lifetime, healing the sick and having prophetic insight, and he has worked countless miracles since his repose. He was glorified in 1994, and his relics were found to be incorrupt.

~ JULY 3 ~

Holy Martyr Hyacinthus the Chamberlain

Hyancinthus was born in Caesarea in Cappadocia and served as chamberlain to Emperor Trajan at the age of eighteen. One day, when a feast was being celebrated in honor of the pagan gods, Hyacinthus went aside to pray and avoid the pagan festivities. One of his colleagues noticed this and denounced him as a Christian. He was commanded to eat the food that had been offered to the idols, thus participating in the idolatrous worship. He refused to do so, making the sign of the Cross and confessing himself a Christian. For this he was beaten repeatedly with kicks as the soldiers tried to shove the food into his mouth. The noble servant of Christ refused to eat voluntarily and continued to spurn the worship of the gods. After being tortured, he was thrown into a prison cell and only given food that had been offered to idols in order to break his spirit and make him relent. He refused to eat it and gradually starved to death. He suffered for Christ in about 108.

❦ JULY 4 ❧

St. Andrew of Crete

Andrew was born in Damascus in about 660. At a young age he went to Jerusalem, where he was tonsured a monk at the monastery of St. Sava. He stayed there for ten years, serving as secretary to the patriarch. He was sent as his representative to Constantinople for the Sixth Ecumenical Council. Later, in about 700, he was chosen Archbishop of Gortyna in Crete. Andrew was not distinguished for his theological ability or dogmatic steadfastness. Rather, his gifts were devotional and mystical. He composed many hymns for the Church, including his *Great Canon of Repentance*, which has 250 verses and is sung by the Church in Great Lent. He wrote many other hymns, each with its own melody (called *idiomela*). He was a great preacher. He died in peace in about 740.

❦ JULY 5 ❧

Our Holy Father Athanasius of Athos

Athanasius was born at Trebizond in about 920. He was an orphan, cared for first by a relative who was a nun and later by an army officer of Constantinople. He formed a friendship with Nicephorus, a general who would later become emperor, and taught at the capital. His soul longed for monastic holiness, and he joined the monastery at Mount Kyminas in Bithynia.

In 958 he went to Mount Athos, then peopled only with hermits. He wanted to build a monastery there, but the hermits opposed such an innovation. Athos had no cenobitic monasticism before, and the hermits resented the interference of a stranger who wanted to introduce a new disciplined order in their domain. Athanasius's friend Nicephorus (now emperor) was able to intervene so that the hermits accepted his work. He built the first monastery (or lavra), which was simply called the Lavra, and other monasteries were to follow.

Athanasius's vision was that Athos and monasticism should play a leading role in the Church, and that Athos should be a holy mountain where men might come from all over the world to seek God. Athanasius died in an accident on his beloved Athos, when he was struck by falling masonry of a church being built. He went to his Lord in 1003.

❦ JULY 6 ❧

Our Holy Father Sisoes the Great

Sisoes renounced the world when still a young man and lived in the desert monastery of Scetis in Lower Egypt. Later he moved further out to the Mountain of St. Anthony, after that great saint had died. He was a man of great gentleness. Once three hermits came to visit him and ask his counsel. They told him they were tormented by fearful thoughts of the future judgment and of going to hell. After a pause, Sisoes replied, "I've never given judgment and hell a thought. I think of how good my Lord is, and I know He will have pity on me." The three were not happy and left still disturbed. When he saw they were still upset despite his answer, he cried after them, "Alas, my brothers! I should be a better man if I had thought as you do!"

Another time a hermit came to him and confessed a sin. Sisoes told him to rise and go forward and not be discouraged. He said to Sisoes, "My father! Is there to be no end to this? How often am I to be told to rise after a sinful fall?"

Sisoes replied, "Always—until death catches you fallen or struggling to rise."

Another time a monk sinned and the brethren asked him how long he should abstain from the daily Holy Communion as a punishment. They suggested a year. "Oh no!" Sisoes said. "That is a long time."

"Well," said they again, "what about six months?"

"That's too long too."

"Well then, forty days," they offered again.

"Forty days! That is too long."

"What!" they said at last, "should he have Holy Communion immediately after sinning?"

"I don't say that," Sisoes replied, "but I think God is so loving and merciful that one bitter pang of conscience may avail for Him without abstaining from Holy Communion for more than—say three days."

He was a man of true humility. "For thirty years," he once said, "I have been asking my Lord Jesus Christ to give me power to control my tongue, yet every day that tongue of mine is tripping me."

When he died, he saw St. Anthony and the prophets and apostles coming to him along with the angels. Then, with a thrill of agitated trembling, his face lit up with joy and he cried, "My Lord! My Lord comes to me!" He sank back on his pallet dead. He died with joy at the age of 88 in 420.

JULY 7

Our Holy Father Thomas of Malea
Thomas was born to a noble and wealthy family and began a career in the military. His courage and zeal were rewarded, and he became a famous general. He was large and physically strong and was famed for his victories over the barbarians. In his heart, however, he secretly desired the life of solitude lived by the prophet Elijah. He renounced the world and went to live in the solitude of the desert on a mountain called Malea near Mount Athos. The zeal he had showed in the service of the earthly emperor he continued to show in the service of the heavenly King, and God rewarded his ascetic fervor by granting him gifts of healing. When he stood in prayer, he seemed to be a pillar of fire. His holy solitude was discovered, and many came to him to seek his wisdom and his prayers. He died in peace in the tenth century.

JULY 8

Holy Great Martyr Procopius
Procopius was born in Jerusalem and was a reader in the church in Scythopolis in Palestine. He was sent to Caesarea, where he was arrested and brought to the governor, Flavian. When urged to sacrifice to the gods, Procopius refused, crying out that there was but one God, the Creator of all. He was beheaded. The story is told of how he was converted to Christ as a young man, had a cross made of gold,

and bowed down, venerating it. This story was quoted at the Seventh Ecumenical Council to show how ancient was the veneration of the Cross and icons. Procopius suffered for Christ in 303.

~: JULY 9 :~

Hieromartyr Pancratius, Bishop of Taormina

Pancratius was born in Antioch in the first century. During his travels, he met the apostle Peter, who installed him as pastor of the church in Taormina, Sicily. On the sea voyage to Sicily, Pancratius shared the gospel with the ship's crew, converting many of them to the Lord. He worked tirelessly as a good shepherd of his flock there, even converting Boniface, the head of the city. The saint finally suffered martyrdom by stoning. His relics are preserved in Rome.

~: JULY 10 :~

Our Holy Father Anthony of the Kiev Caves

Anthony was born in 983 in Liubech in the province of Chernigov, at about the time Russia converted to the Faith through Prince Vladimir. He was therefore raised as a Christian. He traveled south to Mount Athos and was tonsured a monk. There were no other Russian monks on Mount Athos then, and after living a life of exemplary holiness, he was given the blessing by his abbot to return to Russia to transplant monasticism in his native land. Anthony returned to Kiev and settled in a cave outside the city.

During the bloody upheaval that followed the murder of Vladimir's sons Boris and Gleb, Anthony went back once more to the safety of Mount Athos for another fifteen years. When he returned to Kiev in a time of restored peace, others soon joined him in his monastic enterprise. When twelve joined him and wanted to enlarge their quarters, Anthony blessed this endeavor and appointed one of them, Theodosius, to be their abbot. They lived there as in a northern Athos, and Anthony retired to live in the solitude of a hermitage nearby, guiding the community he had founded and blessing them with his prayers and counsel. He lived forty years in solitude and died in peace in 1073.

The Forty-Five Martyrs of Nicopolis in Armenia

During the pagan persecution that swept over the Church, Christians at Nicopolis in Armenia also were arrested. Among these were Leontius, Maurice, Alexander, Sisinius, and others. Refusing to worship the gods, they were whipped and thrown into prison, where they languished for many days. During their trial, two of the soldiers guarding them also declared themselves to be Christians. All were condemned for their obstinacy of faith, and their limbs were chopped off. Then the holy confessors, now numbering forty-five, were thrown into the flames, where they perished. They suffered for their heavenly Lord in the early years of the fourth century.

~: JULY 11 :~

Translation of the Relics of the Holy Great Martyr Euphemia

Euphemia's feast day is September 16, the day on which she suffered; this day commemorates her wonderworking relics. These relics were brought to Chalcedon (the city where the Fourth Ecumenical Council was held), where their presence comforted and confirmed the faith of the Orthodox. The relics then were translated to Constantinople and placed in the Church of St. Euphemia. During the iconoclastic persecution of the Church, Euphemia's relics were brought for a time to the island of Lemnos for safekeeping and placed in the church of the holy martyr Glykeria. Finally they were returned to her church in Constantinople. The care taken by the Church of the saint's relics witnesses to the love the faithful have for the martyr and to the power of her heavenly intercession.

St. Olga

Olga was the grandmother of St. Vladimir, enlightener of the Rus. Her husband, Igor, was murdered by a rebellious Russian tribe. She was a strong and valiant woman and carried on her husband's military plans. She was known, for her fierce shrewdness, as Olga the Wise. Olga made a visit to Constantinople, where she converted to the Christian Faith and was baptized by the patriarch with the name Helen. Her influence and prayers helped to convert her grandson Vladimir to the Faith. She died in 969.

~: JULY 12 :~

Holy Martyrs Proclus and Hilary

These two were born in Kallippi in Asia Minor. Hilary was Proclus's uncle. They were arrested as Christians during Trajan's reign. They refused to sacrifice to the gods, and when threatened with torture, Proclus said, "If you are afraid to disobey the emperor's commands and be punished for it, how much more do we Christians fear to disobey God's commands and suffer eternal punishment!" After torture, they were executed and inherited the Kingdom.

~: JULY 13 :~

The Holy Archangel Gabriel

Gabriel's name means "mighty one of God," and he is included in the intertestamental Book of Enoch as one of the four great angels along with Michael, Raphael, and Uriel (Enoch 9:1). (The names of the three other archangels are traditionally given as Selaphiel, Jegudiel, and Barachiel.) Gabriel seems to be especially charged with revelation. It was he who delivered the vision to Daniel the Prophet (Dan. 8:16, 9:21), and he described himself as one "who stands in the presence of God"—that is, to hear His counsel and to speak it to whom God wills (Luke 1:19). His greatest revelation for our salvation was his greeting and message to our Lady Mary, announcing her call to be the Theotokos.

Our Holy Mother Sarah the Egyptian

Sarah was abbess of a women's monastery in Scetis. For thirteen years she was plagued by thoughts of impurity. She prayed constantly against it, saying, "Lord, strengthen me!"—not asking that the temptation be removed but that she be made strong.

At last, she had a vision of the demonic spirit of impurity fleeing and saying, "You have conquered me, Sarah!"

She said, "Not I, but Christ who works in me!" She died in peace after sixty years as a nun, entering into the Kingdom in 370.

JULY 14

Holy Apostle Aquila

Aquila was born in Pontus and, with his wife, Priscilla, was made to leave Rome when Emperor Claudius expelled all the Jews. They moved to Corinth, and Aquila worked as a tentmaker along with St. Paul when Paul came to Corinth in about 54. Aquila and his wife did apostolic work together, instructing Apollos in the fullness of the Faith and baptizing him when he came to Ephesus. They worked as Paul's fellow workers, risking their lives to help him (Rom. 16:3–4). They went to Rome and thence to Ephesus, and they always opened their home to meetings of the church. It is said they were martyred.

JULY 15

Holy Martyr Cyricus and his mother, Julitta of Tarsus

Julitta was born of noble parents in Iconium. She married but was widowed early, left with her newborn child, Cyricus. Several years later, when Diocletian began to persecute the Church, she fled with her young son to Seleucid but was found and arrested. When she was taken to be interrogated, her son was taken by the interrogating judge. The young boy refused to be separated from his mother. He cried out, "I am a Christian! Let me go to my mother!" and began to scratch the judge. In anger the judge threw the child onto the ground and kicked him savagely, so that he rolled down the stairs and died. After many tortures, the mother, Julitta, also died by beheading and gave up her soul to God, thus joining her son in the Kingdom. This happened in the year 304.

Holy Prince Vladimir, Equal-to-the-Apostles

JULY

Vladimir learned of the Christian Faith from his grandmother Olga but continued a pagan. In 980 he became prince of Kievan Rus. He had to decide how best to rule his people and guide them among the other nations. His ambassadors went abroad to examine the religions of the other nations, and those who went to Constantinople brought back word that the worship there was so overwhelming that they "did not know whether they were on earth or in heaven." "There," among the Christians, they said, "we know God dwells among men. We cannot forget that beauty." They pointed out too the Christian faith of Vladimir's grandmother Olga.

This counsel worked in his heart, and in 988 he decided to convert. He proposed to the emperor of Constantinople that he marry the emperor's sister Anna and that Russia be allied with Byzantium. Thus Vladimir was baptized by the Bishop of Kherson, and when he returned home, he announced to his people that all should join him as Christians. He cut down their idols, including the dreaded idol Perun, which he threw into the Dnieper River. This greatly impressed the people, and the hold of the old religion was broken. They joined Vladimir in baptism in the Dnieper.

Vladimir began the task of converting his country. He furthered literacy and sent clergy throughout the country to preach to all. He himself changed from a fierce warrior to one concerned also for the poor and needy. He died in peace in 1015, the enlightener of the land of the Rus.

~: JULY 16 :~

Hieromartyr Athenogenes, Bishop of Sebaste

In the reign of Diocletian, the governor came to Sebaste. Athenogenes was arrested with ten men who lived the ascetic life. They refused to sacrifice to the gods, and the governor threatened them with death, saying he would kill them like the other Christians whom he had caused to die. "Those whom you describe as having died are in heaven and rejoice with the angels!" Athenogenes replied. For his steadfast refusal to sacrifice, he was tortured with his companions and was executed in the year 311.

❦ JULY 17 ❧

Holy Martyr Marina (Margaret)

Marina was born in Antioch during the reign of Emperor Claudius II. Her mother died giving birth to her, and her father, a pagan priest, gave her into the care of another who, as it turned out, was a Christian. Thus Marina became a Christian too. When she was eighteen it was thought to marry her to Olymbrius, a government official who was, of course, a pagan. When she refused to marry him because he was not a Christian, she was denounced and arrested. She was stripped, flogged, and tortured by fire. She was finally executed by beheading, suffering for her heavenly Bridegroom in about 289.

❦ JULY 18 ❧

New Martyr Elizabeth

The future new martyr was born in 1864 as a daughter of a German prince. After her mother died when she was fourteen, she was partly raised by her grandmother, Queen Victoria of England, and considered English to be her mother tongue. Her sister Alexandra married the Russian tsar, so that Elizabeth ("Ella" to her family) became part of the Russian royal family. She married the Grand Duke Sergius, the governor of Moscow. She later converted from Protestantism to Orthodoxy of her own free will and was received by chrismation on Lazarus Saturday in 1891. Her pious spirit could not hide in a life of privilege but worked tirelessly to serve the sick in hospitals. When her husband was killed by an assassin's bomb in 1905, Elizabeth visited the assassin in prison, forgiving him, giving him a gospel book to read, and urging him to repent.

After this she fled the social life of her rank even more. She sold her jewelry and opened the Martha and Mary Home in Moscow to minister to the poor. She took monastic vows in 1909 with seventeen other women, as the Sisters of Love and Mercy. They also opened a hospital. Elizabeth moved out of the palace into a building she purchased in Ordinka. There she worked for the poor to the point of exhaustion. Her own life combined service with asceticism, as she slept in a modestly furnished room on a bed without a mattress. She would only sleep a few hours a night, rising at midnight to pray.

After Paschal Vespers of 1918, the communists forced Elizabeth to leave Moscow and join the royal family near Ekaterinburg. She was housed in a monastery there with other arrested nobility. She was later moved to nearby Alopaevsk, to a schoolhouse where she was kept under guard. On the night of July 5, Elizabeth was taken with others to a place twelve miles away and executed. The prisoners were thrown down a mineshaft, then grenades were tossed in after them. Elizabeth lived for several hours and could be heard singing hymns. The last thing she did as she lay dying in the mineshaft was to bandage the wounds of Prince Ioann with her handkerchief.

Her body was taken to Jerusalem in 1920 and buried in the church of St. Mary Magdalene. The Russian Orthodox Church glorified her as a new martyr in 1992. She abides in the Church as a radiant soul, shining with divine beauty in a time of darkness.

Holy Martyr Emilian

During a persecution of the church in the town of Dorostolon in Thrace, a Christian named Emilian went through the town at night and smashed all the idols he could find. An innocent villager seen passing by was arrested and condemned for the crime. Emilian did not want an innocent man to suffer and so gave himself up to the authorities. When asked on whose orders he had done the deed, he replied, "God and my conscience ordered me to destroy these dead pillars you call gods." He was then condemned, flogged, and tortured. He was executed and entered the Kingdom in 362.

JULY 19

Our Holy Mother Macrina the Younger

Macrina the Younger was born in Caesarea in Cappadocia in about 327. Her grandmother Macrina the Elder was a heroine for the Faith under the persecution of Galerius. Younger Macrina was engaged to a young lawyer, but he died, and she devoted herself to the spiritual life, acting as head (after her mother's death) of her small ascetic community at the estate at Annesi. She lived in poverty of spirit, owning only a simple cloak, a hood, a pair of worn-out shoes, an iron cross she wore at her breast, and a ring that contained a fragment of the True Cross. She slept on the ground and spent her life caring for her nuns. She exercised a strong influence on her younger brothers, St. Basil the Great and St. Gregory of Nyssa.

Nine months after her brother Basil died, Macrina also fell ill. Gregory went to visit her and found her on her deathbed, choking with asthma. She tried to hide her pain, and they spoke of the hope of the soul and of resurrection. At the end she made the sign of the Cross and tried to sing the customary hymn at the lighting of the lamps. Soon she died in peace, and her brother closed her eyes. He referred to her in some of his writings as "the Teacher." She died in peace in 379.

JULY 20

Holy Prophet Elijah/Elias

Elijah was born in Tishbeh in the region of Gilead in the ninth century BC. He prophesied at a time of great apostasy in Israel, when King Ahab and his wife Jezebel were furthering a syncretistic Baal worship. Some, like Elijah, rejected this as apostasy and worthy of death, and these were persecuted by the king. Many of the devotees of Yahweh were slain. Elijah warned Ahab that God would bring a drought on the land as a judgment on Israel's apostasy. So saying, he fled for his life to the brook Cherith, where he hid, being fed by God through a raven. (He is often so pictured in his icon.) He later went to help a foreign woman of Zarephath miraculously survive the drought and famine.

After the horrors of famine in Israel, the crisis came to a head when Elijah publicly challenged the prophets of Baal on Mount Carmel. Altars were set up to Yahweh and to Baal. Sacrifices were laid out on both altars but were not burned. Elijah proposed that whichever deity miraculously sent fire from heaven to consume his sacrifice would be shown to be the true God whom Israel would follow. The prophets of Baal proved unable to bring fire, but with a word Elijah brought down Yahweh's fire on the sacrifice—fire so powerful it burned up the altar along with the sacrifice. The apostate Baal priests were slain, and the restoration of Yahwism in Israel began.

Elijah went south to Mount Horeb to pray and was there commissioned by the still, small voice of God to further the work of restoration (which included taking Elisha as his successor). After more work and striving for the pure worship of Yahweh, Elijah ascended alive to heaven in a chariot of fire. He was a man of tender heart but also of fiery and uncompromising spirit. He was the greatest of the prophets and an embodiment of them all. As such, he, with Moses, spoke in glory with Christ at His Transfiguration.

Mother Maria of Paris

Born into privilege in Latvia in 1891 with the name Elizabeth Pilenko, the future confessor became an atheist as a teenager. Her family moved to St. Petersburg, where she married a Bolshevik. The marriage lasted three years and produced a daughter, Gaiana. Elizabeth then began to draw closer to the Christian Faith, moving to the south of Russia.

The year 1918 found her in Anapa in southern Russia. There she married again, a former teacher named Daniel Skobtsov. With her husband, child, and mother, she fled the country to Georgia and then to Yugoslavia. She bore two other children, Yuri and Anastasia. Finally in 1923 they arrived in Paris, where Elizabeth studied theology and began doing social work. Times were hard, and there was much heartbreak. Their daughter Anastasia died of influenza three

JULY

years after they arrived in Paris, and Gaiana was sent to a boarding school in Belgium. These stresses took their toll, and the marriage broke up, with Daniel going to live with his father. Elizabeth threw herself into her social work, ministering to the destitute.

Her bishop encouraged her to embrace monasticism, but her heart was with the city's poor. Eventually, after getting a church divorce with her husband's permission, she took monastic vows, but only with the assurance that she could continue to live in the world and continue her work there. Her new name was Maria. Her rented house in Paris became a haven for the needy, lonely, and refugees. It was also a center for intellectual theological debate. The nun Maria continued to serve God and His poor, using both head and hand. For her, true service required both.

Part of that service in Nazi-occupied Paris involved providing aid to persecuted Jews. For her part in this, she was arrested and taken to Ravensbrück concentration camp in Germany. On Holy Saturday 1945 Maria was taken to the gas chamber, where she offered her soul to the Lord she had served so well. It is said that she voluntarily took the place of another who had been selected for execution. Mother Maria Skobtsova of Paris was glorified by the ecumenical patriarchate in 2004.

※ JULY 21 ※

Holy Prophet Ezekiel

Ezekiel was the son of Buzi and a priest in the temple. He was taken captive from Jerusalem to Babylon in the reign of King Jehoiachin in 597 BC. He formed the center of a group of Jewish exiles by the River Chebar. Ezekiel had visions of the divine glory as God's chariot-throne—showing that the divine glory dwelt not just in the Jerusalem temple but, like a chariot, could be present anywhere, even in exile. He prophesied judgment on Judah and the surrounding nations as well as their restoration under the Messiah. He spoke also of Christ, the Son of David, as their Good Shepherd (Ezek. 34:23), of God washing them with water and giving them a new heart (Ezek. 36:25–26), and of the resurrection of the nation to new life (Ezek. 37).

St. Simeon of Emessa, Fool-for-Christ, and his companion, St. John

Both Simeon and John left their families to pursue a life of holiness, Simeon leaving his aged mother and John his wife. They became monks in the monastery of St. Gerasim and then left for the desert. At length, Simeon felt led by God to return to the world of society as a fool-for-Christ, to guide men to holiness through the "folly" of speaking the truth few men dared to speak. John advised him to keep his heart separate from the temptations of the world and to remain anchored in God: "Keep your heart from all that you see in the world. Whatever there may be that touches your hand, let it not take hold of your heart. And pray for me, that God may not part us from each other in the age to come." The two friends embraced each other and parted for the love of God. John remained in the desert, while Simeon returned to the world to guide men there to salvation. Their feast shows how God calls His children along different paths of holiness to the same goal of eternal life.

JULY 22

St. Mary Magdalene, Equal-to-the-Apostles

Mary was a woman "out of whom [Christ cast] seven demons" (Luke 8:2)—a severely troubled and tormented young woman. (There is no evidence she was a prostitute.) After being healed by Christ, she followed the other women who ministered to Him (Luke 8:1–3), listening to His words and sharing His work.

Mary was with His Mother and the others at our Lord's Cross and was one of the myrrh-bearing women who went to anoint our Lord's dead Body. As such, she was greeted with them by the angel, who told them He was risen. Mary was sent by the angel to tell the apostles (an "apostle to the apostles") and afterwards returned to weep at the Tomb. There she met the risen Lord, who greeted her by name and sent her again to announce the Resurrection to her brethren.

Mary was undoubtedly a woman of spirit and determination. She greatly loved the Lord who had forgiven her sins and given her new life. It is said she later went to Ephesus to proclaim the gospel there.

❦ JULY 23 ❧

Holy Martyrs Trophimus and Theophilus

These two suffered in the reign of Diocletian in Lycia with thirteen others because they would not obey the emperor's edict and offer sacrifice to the pagan gods. They were horribly tortured and mutilated before their final execution. They were stoned, flayed with iron flails, and their knees were broken. After many such tortures, they were executed by beheading. They suffered for Christ and attained their heavenly rest in the beginning of the fourth century.

❦ JULY 24 ❧

Holy Great Martyr Christina

Christina was born in Tyre to pagan parents. She converted to Christ at the age of eleven, rebelling against the paganism of her family and having nothing to do with idols. She was arrested as a Christian. She was tortured to induce her to deny the faith: her breasts were cut off and her tongue cut out. Defiantly, she picked up her bloody tongue and threw it the face of her torturer. At length she was executed by beheading and inherited the Kingdom. Christina suffered for her Lord in the early third century.

Holy Passion-Bearers Boris and Gleb

These were sons of Prince Vladimir, equal-to-the-apostles and baptizer of the land of the Rus. They were meek and compassionate, living in a time of brutality and barbarity. Before Vladimir's death in 1015, the kingdom was divided among all his sons, including Boris and Gleb. Svyatopolk, the oldest son, wanted to possess the lands given to Boris and Gleb and sent assassins to kill them. He went first to kill Boris. Boris knew of the danger but refused armed protection because he did not want bloodshed to ensue in a civil war. He merely waited, reciting the six psalms of Matins. He prayed, "O Lord Jesus Christ, You accepted Your Passion for our sins. Give me strength to accept my passion. Lord, lay not this sin to my brother's charge." He and Gleb were slain by their brother and buried in Vishgorod, being immediately venerated as martyrs to the spirit of peace in the gospel. They were the first saints glorified in the land of the Rus.

~: JULY 25 :~

The Dormition of St. Anna, Mother of the Theotokos
The feast of St. Anna's life is celebrated on September 9; this day is the commemoration of her falling asleep. St. Anna, with her husband St. Joachim, was called by God to raise her daughter, Mary, in the ways of holiness, so that the child might fulfill her calling to be the Mother of God. After a long life of coping with the shame of barrenness, and then the joy of raising her daughter, Mary, St. Anna fell asleep, having served God in her generation.

St. Olympias the Deaconess
Olympias was born in about 368 and was orphaned early, being then cared for by her uncle. She married the wealthy Nebridius, the emperor's treasurer, but was widowed after only twenty days of marriage. She then decided to live as a celibate in ascetic holiness for the rest of her life. Since she was charming as well as wealthy, many wanted to marry her, and she had to use much determination to remain single. Olympia prayed, lived in simplicity, and fasted so much that she ruined her health and suffered intestinal disorders ever after. She gave away such huge sums of money to so many that St. John Chrysostom had to urge her to be more careful with her money.

Olympia was ordained deaconess in the church of Constantinople in 391. She supported her close friend John Chrysostom even after his condemnation and exile, which cost her dearly. She herself became a target of persecution and slander. Because she would not recognize as valid John's condemnation or the legitimacy of his successor, she was driven from the city for a while. All her goods were sold at public auction, her clothes were torn off by soldiers, her farm was plundered by a mob, and her community of nuns were forced to disperse. She still had money, however, and supported John in his exile. Olympia died in 408, harassed until death. She was a true confessor for the truth and a heroine for Christ.

~: JULY 26 :~

St. Jacob Netsvetov

Jacob was born in 1802 of pious parents in Atka Island, Alaska. His father was a Russian and his mother an Aleut. In 1823 the family moved to Irkutsk in Siberia, and Jacob enrolled in seminary. He married a Russian woman and was ordained priest in 1828. He yearned to return to his native Alaska to do missionary work, and so, with the blessing of his bishop, he was sent back to Atka. His missionary parish was over a thousand miles long, as it included a whole string of islands.

On Atka, there was no church built, so Fr. Jacob erected a tent for services which he would take with him on his missionary journeys around his "parish." After six months, he had baptized 16 people and chrismated 442. He built a church and a school to teach both Russian and the vernacular Aleut. He continued Bishop (later Saint) Innocent Veniaminov's work and served his Atka flock until 1844. Then, sent by Bishop Innocent, he went to preach to the people of the Yukon. He worked in southwest Alaska for twenty years until his health failed. Fr. Jacob died in 1864 at the age of sixty, a true evangelizer of his people and a light of Christ to those in darkness.

Our Holy Mother Paraskeva

Paraskeva was born of Christian parents and lived an ascetic life in poverty and simplicity. She was arrested during a persecution of the Church and tortured horribly, suffering and dying for her Lord in the second century. Her relics were later taken to Constantinople.

~ JULY 27 ~

Holy Great Martyr Panteleimon

Panteleimon was born to a pagan father and a Christian mother, Euboulia, and was given the name Pantoleon. His parents placed him under a well-known physician for his education. He became a physician in turn and won great fame for his medical skill. He was converted to Christ by Hermolaus, a presbyter who was hiding in Nicomedia to escape persecution. Pantoleon was at length baptized and gave away his family inheritance to help feed the poor. His heart burned with love for those who suffered, and he often treated the poor for free, healing them with his prayers as well as his medical expertise.

Pantoleon was denounced as a Christian during the persecution of the Church under Diocletian and refused to recant his faith despite terrible suffering. He was finally executed by beheading, submissively bowing his neck to the stroke that would send him to God. He was called by the Church not Pantoleon but Panteleimon, which means "all-merciful," for he was a truly merciful and compassionate physician of souls as well as bodies.

~ JULY 28 ~

Holy Apostles Prochorus, Nicanor, Timon, and Parmenas

These men were some of the seven deacons ordained by the apostles in Jerusalem (Acts 6). They are considered by the Church to be among the Seventy.

It is said that Prochorus served in Nicomedia and was finally martyred in Antioch. Possibly he served as secretary to St. John the Theologian.

Nicanor returned to his native Cyprus and was there also martyred under Vespasian.

Timon served his Lord, reaching Arabia and preaching in the city of Bostra. He also was martyred by the pagans, who put him to death by fire.

Parmenas died in Jerusalem after an illness and was buried by the apostles there. As true servants of Christ, they all received the reward of eternal life.

~: JULY 29 :~

Holy Martyr Callinicus

Callinicus was born in Cilicia and raised as a Christian. He traveled through many towns preaching the gospel. He was arrested in Ancyra, and when examined and threatened with torture if he would not deny Christ, he replied, "Every torture for my God is as welcome to me as bread is to a hungry man." They thrashed him with ox sinews and lacerated his flesh with iron nails. He was dragged to Gangra, about eighty miles away, to face execution there. He suffered by burning and died for his God in about 250. The Christians of Gangra received the martyr's relics as a precious treasure, and a church was later dedicated to him there.

~: JULY 30 :~

Holy Apostles Silas, Crescens, Epaenetus, and Andronicus

Silas (sometimes called Silvanus) went with Paul and Barnabas from Jerusalem to the churches, bringing word of the decision of the Apostolic Council of Jerusalem that Gentile converts need not be circumcised. Being a prophet, he exhorted the Christians of Antioch to remain true to the Lord. He accompanied Paul on his missionary journey after Paul broke up with Barnabas, and did much work with him. He served as bishop in Corinth.

Crescens also worked with Paul and went to Galatia when Paul was in Rome (2 Tim. 4:10).

Epaenetus was a friend of Paul in Rome and was one of Paul's first converts in Asia (Rom. 16:5). It is said that he served as bishop in Carthage.

Andronicus was a Jew, St. Paul's "kinsman," and was converted to Christ before Paul was. It is said he preached among the Pannonians near Moravia.

❦ JULY 31 ❧

St. Eudokimus

Eudokimus was born of noble and pious parents in Cappadocia. He was a soldier in the time of Emperor Theophilus in the ninth century and was made military governor of Cappadocia. Eudokimus, however, did not value the passing pomp of the world but sought the glory of the age to come, dedicating himself to chastity and the pursuit of holiness. He avoided the society of women, gave abundant alms to the poor, prayed, and read spiritual books. He said that everyone must learn to listen rather than speak, and so he spoke as little as he could.

Eudokimus fell gravely ill at the age of about thirty and died shortly thereafter. The saint had prayed that he would rest in obscurity, but God willed that his sanctity should be known, and so miracles accrued around his tomb. When his grave was opened eighteen months after his repose, his relics were found to be incorrupt and were translated to Constantinople, where they were laid in a church built by his parents.

~: AUGUST I :~

Holy Maccabean Martyrs

When the Syrian king Antiochus ruled Palestine in the second century BC, he advanced a program of Hellenization, making the Greek culture, language, and vision of the world the unifying factor that would meld his domains into one single and stable whole. When he tried to Hellenize Palestine, however, he was confronted with a group of Jews who refused to cooperate with his program of syncretism.

Antiochus proposed the Jews could worship Yahweh under the name Jupiter and that all gods were really the same. The pious in Israel said the gods of the nations were idols. This, with other factors, led Antiochus to make a savage attempt to stamp out ancestral Judaism in Palestine. The Law was to be burned, circumcision and Sabbath observance were outlawed, and Jews were forced to eat unclean food. Some in Israel refused to obey the royal decrees—even at the cost of their lives.

Such were the seven Maccabean brothers, their aged mother, and an old man named Eleazar. They were arrested and taken to Antioch and tortured horribly, each in turn, to make them apostatize, deny the Law of their God, and eat unclean food. First, aged Eleazar was killed, then the seven brothers in turn, their horrified mother watching each of her sons being tortured and killed. Then the mother threw herself into the flames prepared for her sons and died, lest anyone abuse her. They all suffered for the Lord God of their fathers in about 167 BC.

AUGUST 2

Translation of the Relics of the Protomartyr Stephen

After St. Stephen's stoning in Jerusalem in the first century, his body was buried in a cave in Caphargamala by one who sympathized with the young Christian movement. Centuries passed, and the place of St. Stephen's burial remained unknown by the Church. In 415, a certain Lucian, who was a priest in that area, had a dream in which the one who buried the body of the protomartyr appeared to him and told him the place where the relics were buried. Lucian obtained the blessing of the local bishop and, taking a group of Christians with him, went to the place he had seen in his dream and dug there. There he discovered the relics, which gave off a strong, sweet fragrance. The relics were buried with honor in Jerusalem, and, much later, taken to Constantinople.

Blessed Basil, Fool-for-Christ

Basil lived in Russia. When he was sixteen he began a life of ascetic labors and lived in that state for seventy-two years. He went barefoot and dressed in tatters, having no fixed residence and suffering from hunger and cold. Though many insulted him as a madman, he lived in truth as a fool-for-Christ, speaking the truth that other men could not. His true worth and holiness at length became known, and even the tsar, Ivan the Terrible, sought his blessing and counsel.

Once when that tsar came to a town during his reign of political terror to massacre its inhabitants, Basil rebuked him for his sins. It was in Great Lent, and Basil offered Ivan a piece of raw meat. The tsar expressed his surprise at this breach of the Great Fast. Basil replied, "Ivasko, Ivasko [a disrespectful diminutive of Ivan], do you think it unlawful to eat a piece of beast's flesh and not unlawful to eat so much human flesh by your massacres?" The tsar accepted the rebuke and spared that town. Later, when Basil died, the tsar even attended his funeral. He was buried in the tsar's great Moscow Church of the Mother of God—later renamed for this humble and holy fool-for-Christ. (This is the famous Cathedral of St. Basil with the multifaceted, multicolored domes that stands in Red Square.)

⁓ AUGUST 3 ⁓

Our Holy Fathers Isaac, Dalmatus, and Faustus

In the reign of the Arian Emperor Valens, the humble hermit Isaac came from his hermitage to Constantinople to plead with the emperor to cease supporting the Arian heresy and establish the Orthodox Faith, saying that God would bless him if he did so. The emperor refused to hear. Isaac continued boldly to badger the emperor, repeatedly warning him that God would bless him and the empire only if he followed the truth, and that divine punishment would overtake him if he refused to hearken. Valens refused to hear him, and on a military campaign against the Goths, Valens was captured and killed.

When Orthodox Emperor Theodosius came to the throne, he heard of Isaac's boldness for the truth and his prophecy of Valens's punishment. He greatly honored Isaac and persuaded him to stay in Constantinople in a monastery built for him. The monastery became a great spiritual center. Theodosius's officer Dalmatus, moved by a desire for holiness, renounced the world and took himself and his only son Faustus to live in Isaac's monastery. He lived in great holiness there, and when Isaac died, he succeeded him (at Isaac's request) as head of the monastery. Dalmatus took part in the Third Ecumenical Council in 431. He and his son, Faustus, lived in holiness and died in peace in the fifth century.

⁓ AUGUST 4 ⁓

Our Holy Mother Eudoxia

Eudoxia was originally from Asia Minor, where she was captured by the Persians and carried away to Persia. Being devout, she shared her faith with her Persian women friends. For this she was arrested, beaten with ox sinews, and thrown into prison. At her trial two months later, Eudoxia boldly confessed Christ. For this they beat her with thorn branches until her torn flesh fell to the ground. After another six months in prison, she was again brought before the judge. Since she continued her bold confession of Christ, they again beat her.

After much torture, she was executed by beheading. Though dying in a foreign land, she finally entered her heavenly homeland and inherited the martyr's crown of glory. This happened in about 364.

❦ AUGUST 5 ❧

St. Eusignius

Eusignius was a soldier under Maximian. After a life of military service, he retired in his hometown of Antioch, where he lived a pious life of fasting, prayer, and good works. During the time of the Emperor Julian the Apostate, Eusignius was denounced as a Christian. When he was interrogated, he rebuked the emperor for his apostasy from the Faith and was beheaded, despite his old age and life of service. He suffered for his true King in 362.

St. Nonna the Righteous

Nonna's husband belonged to the heretical cult of the Hypsistarians (which seems to have been influenced by Persian Zoroastrianism, as they placed the symbols of light and fire on their altars). Through her prayers and urging, he was won back to the Faith, later becoming Bishop of Nazianzus. Her son was St. Gregory of Nazianzus. Nonna was a strong and determined woman with a great zeal for holiness and reform. She never spat in church (an unusual thing in her time), never attended the theater (which was a place of lewdness), never embraced pagan women in greeting or socialized with them, and always averted her eyes from pagan temples. When her son Gregory was born, she dedicated him to God by placing his hands on the gospel in church. She eventually became a deaconess and died in peace in 374.

❦ AUGUST 6 ❧

The Transfiguration of Our Lord, God, and Savior Jesus Christ

Before our Lord's Passion, He took Peter, James, and John with Him up onto a mountain to pray. During the night, He was transfigured before them, even His garments shining with brilliant white light.

Moses (embodying the Law) and Elijah (embodying the Prophets) appeared with Him and spoke of the Passion He would accomplish. Peter, wanting to preserve the glory as God's glory was preserved in the Tabernacle, offered to build three tabernacles for them as for three co-equal prophets.

The cloud of the Father's glory overshadowed them, and they heard His voice saying, "This is My Beloved Son—listen to Him." Then the apostles looked around and saw the Lawgiver and the Prophet no longer, but only Jesus. Thus they were taught that the Old Testament Law and the Prophets were to give way before the permanent New Testament glory of Jesus and that His Passion was not an unexpected defeat but Christ's goal, predicted by the Law and the Prophets. In order not to excite messianic hysteria among the people, the three apostles were commanded to tell no one of the vision until after the Resurrection. Thus was the true messianic glory of Jesus revealed to the apostles as far as they could bear it.

☙ AUGUST 7 ❧

Our Holy Father Dometius

Dometius was born in Persia in the fourth century and was attracted to the Christian Faith from a young age. When he grew older, he left home and traveled to Nisibis, on the border of the Roman and Persian Empires, and there received baptism. He immediately embraced a life of monastic asceticism, immersing himself in the study of the Scriptures. He was so zealous in his study that often he forgot to go to the refectory with the other monks but remained bent over his studies. Many were jealous of him, and to avoid difficulties, he left the monastery and traveled to the monastery of St. Sergius.

After eighteen years, the abbot had him ordained deacon (though much against his will). Later, when he discovered that they wanted to honor him further for his holiness and ordain him priest, he fled to the town of Cyrrhus in Syria, some way away, and lived there. He later withdrew further into solitude, living as a hermit in the wilderness. Through his prayers and holiness, sick people coming to him were healed. It is said that he was martyred, dying for his Lord in 363.

~: AUGUST 8 :~

St. Emilian the Confessor, Bishop of Cyzicus

Emilian was a monk in the monastery founded by Bishop Tarasius. After a while, he was made Bishop of Cyzicus in the time of the iconoclastic controversy. The iconoclastic emperor Leo ordered the destruction of the icons, but Emilian challenged him, asserting that he had no right to dictate to the Church. For his refusal to destroy the holy icons and for challenging the emperor, he was banished. He spent five years in exile, enduring hardship and trial. He died in 820, apparently assassinated by agents of the emperor. Emilian entered the Kingdom as a faithful servant and confessor of the Lord in dark times.

~: AUGUST 9 :~

Our Holy Father Herman, Wonderworker of Alaska

This day commemorates the glorification of St. Herman as a saint in the Church in 1970; the feast of his repose is celebrated on December 13. St. Herman, though born in Russia, traveled as an apostle of Christ to shine the light of the Orthodox way in the new land of America. It was in this new land that he labored and reposed, finding a new home far from his native Russia. In the same way, many Orthodox have come from other faraway lands to find a home in North America, and it is the Church's destiny, through the prayers of St. Herman and all his fellow saints, to take root here and to shine the light of Christ to all.

Holy Apostle Matthias

After the defection of the traitor Judas Iscariot, another man had to be found to complete the number of the Twelve Apostles. This man was to be chosen from the seventy who had been with Christ from the beginning of His ministry. Matthias's name, along with that of Joseph Barsabbas, was put forward to be chosen by lot. Matthias was chosen and enrolled into the apostolate. He seems to have returned to Jerusalem, where it is said he was martyred by the unbelieving Jews.

❦ AUGUST 10 ☙

Holy Martyr Lawrence the Archdeacon and Pope Sixtus

During the persecution under Valerian, Sixtus, Pope of Rome, was arrested to be martyred. Lawrence, as his deacon and constant assistant, wanted to join him in his martyrdom and called after him, "Father, where are you going without your son? Bishop, where are you going without your deacon?"—as bishops were always accompanied by their deacons.

Sixtus bade him stay, and said, "My son, you will follow me soon enough—after three days."

Soon Lawrence was arrested also. As archdeacon, his task was to keep the church's money and distribute it as needed—such as to the poor. His captors told him to produce and hand over the great wealth of the Roman church. He asked for a day to produce it and was allowed a day to gather all the money.

Lawrence spent the time going throughout Rome spending the wealth on the poor for whom the money was originally intended. He then gathered these poor, blind, and lame into one place, and when the emperor demanded that he produce the church's treasures, he showed his poor charges and said, "These are the treasures of the church!"

The authorities were not impressed and in fury took Lawrence to be tortured. He was stripped and put on a red-hot gridiron to be slowly roasted to death. God strengthened him so that after suffering a while, to show they could not break his spirit, he called out, "You can turn me over—I'm done on this side!" Thus Lawrence died for Christ and joined his beloved Bishop Sixtus, inheriting the crown with him. This happened in 258.

~: AUGUST 11 :~

Holy Martyr Euplus the Deacon

Euplus was a deacon in the city of Catana, Sicily. He was arrested for being a Christian and, when brought in for examination, came with the gospel book. The examining judge in curiosity bade him read from it, and he read, "Blessed are they who are persecuted for righteousness' sake, / For theirs is the Kingdom of heaven" (Matt. 5:10). When asked what it meant, Euplus replied that it was the Lord's law and that he followed this Lord, Jesus Christ. For thus confessing himself a Christian, he was put on the rack.

After some torture, Euplus was asked if he still persisted in his way. With his free hand, he signed himself with the Cross and said, "What I said before, I say again—I am a Christian and read the Holy Scriptures." He was ordered to lay aside his foolishness and adore the gods. He replied, "I adore Jesus Christ—I detest the demons. Do what you want—add new tortures, but I am a Christian." They told him to adore Mars, Apollo, and Aesclepius. He said, "I adore the Father, the Son, and the Holy Spirit, besides whom there is no God." They told him to sacrifice to the gods if he would be delivered. He said, "I sacrifice myself, now, to Jesus Christ my God." When the tortures increased, he kept repeating, "I thank you, my God. Jesus Christ, help me. It is for Your Name's sake I endure these agonies!" He prayed, moving his lips even when he could no longer speak. Finally he was led out and beheaded. As he was led out, Euplus kept crying out with joy, "Thanks be to Christ my God!" He suffered with honor and died for the Lord in 304.

~: AUGUST 12 :~

Holy Martyrs Anicetus and Photius

Anicetus and his nephew Photius lived in Nicomedia. In the persecution under Diocletian, Anicetus loudly defied the emperor's edicts. He was arrested and taken to the arena to be thrown to the lion. The lion, however, refused to attack him but merely came up to him and licked his face. Anicetus's nephew Photius was present in the crowd, and he leaped over the barrier and joined his uncle, confessing himself to be a Christian too. The two were then taken back to prison, where they languished for three years. Then another governor took them from prison and slew them, burning them in the furnace used for heating the public baths. They suffered for Christ in about 305.

~: AUGUST 13 :~

St. Tikhon of Zadonsk

Tikhon was born in 1724 in Korotsk in the region of Novgorod and baptized with the name Timothy. His father was church caretaker. The family lived in great poverty. The Russian church at that time was split by the Old Believer schism. Timothy at length succeeded in going to school and eventually to seminary. A quiet and studious boy, he was teased at school by the other boys for being poor.

Timothy was eventually tonsured a monk with the name Tikhon. He was later ordained priest and, later still, named assistant bishop to the Archbishop of Novgorod. In 1763 he was appointed Bishop of Voronezh. When he arrived in his diocese of Voronezh, Tikhon was in poor health—his hands shook, and he had fainting spells. His work was challenging: drunkenness and impiety were rampant, Old Believers slandered the Church for its laxity, his cathedral had burned down in a fire that ravaged the town, and his own residence was a wreck. There was no seminary, and the clergy were lax, drunken, and quarrelsome.

Still, Tikhon threw himself into his work, upbraiding his clergy and trying to teach his flock by example and by word. He tried to defend his clergy from government punishment. He wrote many spiritual works to educate and edify his people. He stressed to his clergy that preaching and teaching were among the first duties of the Church. He tried to win back Old Believers to the Orthodox Church.

Tikhon was young, in poor health, and perhaps too idealistically impatient, and his health suffered further. He asked to be allowed to resign his episcopal duties and retire to a monastery. At last in 1768 he moved to Tolshevo monastery, but the superior there, being of Old Believer sympathies, was not welcoming to him. So Tikhon moved to Zadonsk monastery, where he lived in simplicity and prayer.

He was a friend of the simple peasants and children. He would listen to the Scriptures read to him, especially Isaiah, his favorite prophet, and often be in tears. He became a true center of spirituality in his early retirement, giving a great amount to charity. He loved to meditate on the Passion of his Lord and how we should imitate Him. He died in peace in 1783. Much loved by the people, he was glorified as a saint in 1861.

AUGUST 14

Holy Prophet Micah
Micah was of the tribe of Judah and the village of Moresheth, southwest of Jerusalem. He was born in about 739 BC and prophesied after the prosperous reign of King Uzziah, during the reigns of Jotham, Ahaz, and Hezekiah. Micah rebuked the selfish and luxurious materialism of the people, threatening divine judgment if they did not repent. He prophesied the final restoration of God's people through Christ, whose birth in Bethlehem he foretold (Mic. 5:2–5). He died in about 687 BC.

AUGUST 15

The Dormition of the Most Holy Mother of God
After the Ascension of her Son, the Theotokos stayed in Jerusalem, being cared for by St. John the Theologian, into whose care Christ committed her from the Cross. When the time for her to die drew near, she called to the Apostolic Church her Son had founded, and all gathered around her to say farewell. She died in their midst in glorious peace. Her funeral was disturbed by Jewish opposition so that in death as in life, she and her Son were a sign to be spoken against (Luke 2:34).

Thomas was not present for her burial and went to her tomb

to venerate her holy body. Upon arriving there, he found the tomb empty. The Church thus concluded that her divine Son had raised and translated His Mother to life with Him in the Kingdom. She is the first to share, in advance, the resurrection glory, even as she was the first to believe. In her falling asleep she was not abandoned to the grave, and even now has not forsaken the world but assists us by her invincible intercession.

AUGUST 16

Holy Martyr Diomedes

Diomedes was born in Tarsus in Cilicia and was a physician at Nicea. As a Christian he was arrested and taken in chains in a chariot to Nicomedia. On the way he had a heart attack and, feeling ill, asked the soldiers to stop that he might rest for a while on the grass. Out of compassion they did as he asked. He had just strength enough to kneel down on the grass before he died. The soldiers still cut off his head and brought it to Nicomedia to show they had not let their prisoner escape. Diomedes suffered for Christ in about 304.

AUGUST 17

Holy Martyr Myron the Priest

Myron was a priest of Achaia, of a gentle and noble spirit, beloved by his flock, who served God during the persecution under Decius in about 250. He had been a friend to the governor, Antipater, but when Antipater invaded a church with his soldiers during the liturgy with the intention of arresting some of the prominent Christians there, Myron turned on his former friend. He then exhorted the flock to stand firm and endure for the sake of Christ. Antipater withdrew but had Myron arrested. When Myron was called upon by the magistrate to sacrifice to the gods, he resolutely refused. They stretched him on the rack to flay him alive, but he still repeated over and again, "I am Christian; I will not offer sacrifice!" He was tortured by fire and finally executed by beheading. He suffered for Christ in about 250.

~ AUGUST 18 ~

Holy Martyrs Florus and Laurus

Florus and Laurus were twin brothers who worked as stonemasons in Illyria. They were commissioned to build a structure that was to be used as a pagan temple. The brothers took the money given them for their work but gave away the sum to the poor. The temple was built and the statues of the pagan gods duly installed. The brothers, however, were grieved that their efforts would be used to further the worship of idols. They entered the site at night and pulled down the statues with ropes. When the sacrilege against the pagan gods was discovered, the authorities were enraged, and Florus and Laurus and all the poor who had helped them were arrested. The brothers were martyred by being thrown down a well. They suffered in the second century. Their relics, discovered to be incorrupt, were later taken to Constantinople.

~ AUGUST 19 ~

Holy Martyr Andrew the General

Andrew was born in Syria and served as an army officer in the time of Emperor Maximian. Though yet unbaptized, he sympathized with the Christians. At the moment of engaging in battle, he exhorted his men to put their trust that day in Christ and not in the false gods of the pagans. When Andrew and his men proved victorious, they converted to Christ, who had given them His protection and victory. For this they were denounced as Christians by one of their pagan fellow soldiers and threatened with death.

Since Andrew remained steadfast in his faith, and since he was so popular as a war hero, the authorities at length released him and his men, fearing mutiny and rebellion among the other soldiers. Andrew and his men went to Tarsus and asked for baptism from the bishop there, and so became Christians in truth. The authorities, however, were not content to leave Andrew to spread the outlawed Faith among others in the army and so moved to have them all arrested in Tarsus.

Andrew and his men fled towards Melitene in Armenia. They were apprehended in a defile on Mount Taurus.

Rather than meet armed force with force, Andrew exhorted his companions to lift up their hands in prayer rather than in conflict. They offered their prayer, and immediately the soldiers fell on them, slaughtering them like unresisting lambs. Thus did Andrew and his companions enter the heavenly courts as soldiers in the army of Christ and inherit the eternal reward. This happened at the end of the third century.

~: AUGUST 20 :~

Holy Prophet Samuel

Samuel was the last and greatest of the Judges. Born in about 1080 BC, he was the son of Elkanah and Hannah. Though Hannah was barren, yet in answer to prayer she received the gift of conception and bore Samuel. Thereafter she devoted him to God, and he was raised by Eli, the high priest at the tabernacle at Shiloh.

While still a child, Samuel heard God's call to be a prophet and seer. After Israel's defeat and the loss of the Ark of the Covenant to their Philistine foes, Samuel functioned as the center of unity for the tribes of Israel. He traveled throughout the land, judging causes, calling the people to prayer, blessing, and offering their sacrifices. He rallied Israel against the Philistines, and through his prayer, God sent a thunderstorm against their foes, which routed them. Samuel erected a stone memorial to God's help, calling the place Ebenezer ("stone of help").

When Israel demanded a dynastic king with a standing army to defend them from the continuous Philistine threat, Samuel first opposed this, realizing the people were putting their trust in armed might and in princes rather than in God. But at their insistence, Samuel gave them a king, anointing Saul to be their leader. Saul was a great military leader but was not zealous in obeying God and leading the people in covenant holiness. Thus Samuel withdrew his support from him and secretly anointed David, Saul's officer, as Saul's successor and replacement. Samuel grieved for his old friend Saul's disobedience and remained in his home in Ramah. He died in peace in about 1017 BC. Samuel was a great prophet, leading God's people through dark and troubled days to the greater stability of the Davidic monarchy.

~: AUGUST 21 :~

Holy Apostle Thaddaeus

The apostle Thaddaeus, after the Lord's Resurrection, went to Edessa and preached the gospel, making friends with King Abgar and exercising a ministry of healing. It is also said that Thaddaeus preached in Syria and Armenia, completing his earthly course in Beirut. A story is told about how, during Christ's earthly ministry, King Abgar heard of the power of Christ and asked for Him to come and heal him of his leprosy. In response, Christ miraculously imprinted an image of His face upon a cloth and sent it to the king for his healing. It is thought that this story is a vestigial echo of the presence in Edessa of the wonderful relic of the burial shroud of Christ, in which His image was imprinted (which shroud later found its way to Turin). This story witnesses to Christ's concern for Edessa, which traces its Christian roots to the earliest days of the apostles.

~: AUGUST 22 :~

Holy Martyrs Agathonicus and Zoticus

Zoticus was a Christian of Carpus in Bithynia. He was arrested and brought before Count Eutolmius, who had been charged by the emperor to force the Christians to sacrifice to the pagan gods. The count asked Zoticus why he had been teaching others in the town not to offer sacrifice to the gods. He replied, "Christ desires me as a sacrifice, that His Name may be glorified to the ends of the earth." For this Zoticus was summarily executed along with some other Christians.

The count then returned to Nicomedia. It was reported to him that Agathonicus, son of the prefect Asclepiadus and a member of one of the noble families, had been converting others to Christ. The count therefore had Agathonicus arrested and brought to him at Nicomedia. He had the saint whipped and imprisoned, intending to take him to stand before the emperor. After further torture, since Agathonicus remained steadfast in his Christian confession, he was executed by beheading along with others.

~: AUGUST 23 :~

Hieromartyr Irenaeus, Bishop of Lyons

Irenaeus may have been born in Smyrna. In youth he learned the Faith from St. Polycarp, and he says he treasured his teaching "not on paper but in my heart." He went to Gaul, where he was ordained priest by Bishop Pothinus and was sent by his bishop to Rome. While he was away, a persecution broke out against the Church there, and the bishop was martyred. Irenaeus was ordained in his place. He wrote *A Refutation of Knowledge Falsely So-Called*, which particularly refuted the varieties of gnosticism. When the Bishop of Rome wanted to break communion with the churches of Asia over differing dates for celebrating Pascha, Irenaeus (with others) wrote to him urging him to peace, despite such differences of calendar. By this a reconciliation of the quarreling parties was effected. It is said by some that Irenaeus suffered martyrdom, dying for the Lord in about 202.

~: AUGUST 24 :~

St. Cosmas the Aitolian, Equal-to-the-Apostles

Cosmas was born in Aitolia in Megadendron in 1714. He went to Mount Athos and was tonsured a monk but decided to return to his native land to preach the gospel and strengthen the faith of his people. Though nominally Orthodox, the people were living in great ignorance of the Faith. Cosmas obtained the blessing of the Patriarch of Constantinople Seraphim II for his mission and then traveled all over. He was a true apostle of Christ, preaching and teaching the people, especially in Albania.

Cosmas received the gift of prophetic foresight. He was tireless in his work, establishing four hundred schools, charitable institutions, and churches. Whenever he came to a village, he planted a cross as a proclamation of the gospel. His work attracted the notice of the Turks, and he was taken and strangled, his holy body being thrown into a river. He suffered, a true martyr for Christ, in 1779 at the age of sixty-five. When the Turkish Pasha announced to Cosmas that he was to be killed, he fell to his knees in joy and thanked God for the gift of a martyr's crown. He was glorified as a saint in 1961.

Hieromartyr Eutyches

Eutyches is said to have been born in Sebastopol and to have accompanied St. Paul and (after Paul's death) St. John the Theologian. He was perhaps the same young man who, when Paul preached at Philippi, fell down from a window, died, and was restored by the apostle (Acts 20:9–12). It is said that Eutyches died a martyr in his hometown.

AUGUST 25

Holy Apostle Titus

Titus was born in Crete of pagan parents and converted to Christ by St. Paul, who called him "my true child in a common faith" (Titus 1:4, RSV). He accompanied Paul and Barnabas when they went up to Jerusalem for the apostolic council, which decided that the Gentiles did not have to be circumcised when they became disciples of Jesus. Titus worked with Paul in Antioch and accompanied him on some of his apostolic journeys, laboring with him in his work with the Corinthians.

Paul left Titus in Crete to minister and set the churches in order, appointing those who were worthy as pastors. Paul wrote a letter to him (the Epistle to Titus), giving him instructions and encouragement, for there were many pastoral challenges in working with new converts in Crete, and Titus would have to teach them with great authority. From Crete Titus traveled to Dalmatia and joined Paul in Rome during his final imprisonment. Later he returned to Crete and died there in peace at a great age. He was laid to rest in the church at Gortyna.

~ AUGUST 26 ~

Holy Martyr Adrian and his wife, Natalia

Adrian was a pagan, though his wife, Natalia, had converted to the Christian Faith. During Emperor Maximian's persecution of the Church, Adrian was present as a young officer when twenty-three Christians of Nicomedia were being tortured. His heart was moved, and springing into the midst of the Christians, he cried aloud, "Write me down a Christian also that I may be numbered with these soldiers of Christ." The emperor was exasperated and arrested Adrian. He imprisoned him with the other twenty-three. Adrian's servant saw this and ran to tell Natalia what had happened and how her husband had at last converted to Christ. Natalia joyfully ran to her husband in prison, fell at his feet, and kissed his chains.

When the day of the trial had come and all were in court, Adrian was ordered to be beaten by four men. He was then thrown on the ground and lashed until he was a bloody mass of wounds. He was then dragged back to prison with the others. Natalia, with the deaconesses, ministered to their wounds in prison. When orders were given that women were no longer allowed to minister to the confessors, she and the others cut their hair and dressed as men, bribing the guards in order to gain entrance and minister to the men.

Orders then came for the prisoners' execution, so that Natalia was present when her beloved husband died. They wheeled an anvil into the cell, laid Adrian's feet on the block, smashed his legs with a hammer, and cut off his feet. She tenderly took his hand as he feebly stretched it out to hers, and held it as the executioners cut it off. She closed her martyr husband's eyes as he died for Christ.

The other twenty-three were also killed. Their bodies were to be burnt, but a heavy rain overnight impeded the fire, and the Church recovered some of their precious relics. Adrian's relics were buried in Byzantium. Natalia went to his grave and died there in peace. The young couple, aged twenty-three years, had been married only thirteen months when Adrian suffered for his Lord. They joined each other in Christ's Kingdom in about the year 304.

~: AUGUST 27 :~

Our Holy Father Pimen the Great

Pimen was born in Egypt and, with his six young brothers, fled to the desert of Scetis when he was only fifteen. He was a great ascetic. He had the wisdom of moderation. He said, "Let a monk eat once a day. That is better than severe fasting, for he who fasts long is often proud of his achievement. We do not fast to kill our bodies but our passions."

A desert tribe caused the brothers to move to Terenuth, where they lived in an old deserted pagan temple. The seven brothers lived together in monastic solitude and harmony. Pimen became a wise shepherd indeed (*pimen* is Greek for "shepherd"), and others came to join him.

Once a monk complained to him that the younger novices were falling asleep during the midnight vigil and asked Pimen if he should shake them awake. Pimen replied, "Poor fellows! Do nothing of the kind! When I see their sleepy heads droop, I want to spread out my lap for their heads so that they might sleep in peace."

Another time one came to him complaining that he could not overcome his hard heart. Pimen advised him, "Read the Word of God. The drip of a fountain pierces stone, and the gentle Word falling softly day by day on the dead hard heart after a while melts it." Pimen lived in the fifth century and died in peace at a great age.

~: AUGUST 28 :~

Our Holy Father Moses the Black

Moses lived in the fourth century. He was a huge man of great physical strength and was a ferocious robber until he was converted to Christ. Even after his conversion, as a monk, he was greatly troubled by lust. Near despair over this, he went to see the monk Isidore. It was night, and Isidore took him to show him the sun arising at dawn. "See," Isidore said, "as the light comes, the darkness flies away, not all at once but gradually. So it is with your soul." Thus Moses was encouraged and returned home to his monastic cell.

Moses was later ordained priest by the Patriarch of Alexandria. "See," said the patriarch to the priest, now clothed in white priestly robes, "the black man is made white!"

"Only the outer man," replied Moses. "The inner one is still dark enough, God knows!"

To overcome lust, Moses used physical exercise to tire himself out, carrying water five miles to aged hermits who were too infirm to get their own. He did this despite suffering from back pain.

As his fame grew, Moses became leader of a monastic community. He was finally killed by a group of Bedouins. Though he was warned of their approach, he refused to defend himself (though he told his monks to flee), accepting this fate as a judgment on him for the violence of his previous life. He said, "All who take the sword shall die by the sword." Some of his monks refused to leave him and so were killed along with him.

❧ AUGUST 29 ☙

The Beheading of St. John the Baptizer

John, preaching a baptism of repentance to Israel, also rebuked the ruler Herod for his sins, saying it was not lawful for him to marry his brother's wife, Herodias, while his brother Philip still lived. Herodias hated John for this, and when Herod arrested John and imprisoned him, she plotted to have him killed.

When her daughter Salome pleased Herod and his dinner guests by performing an erotic dance at a great banquet feast, Herod promised to give the girl whatever she asked for as a reward. At the instigation of her mother, she asked for John's head on a platter. Sorrowing, but fearing to lose face before his guests, Herod had John beheaded. John's disciples came and buried his body. His head was later recovered. Thus did John, the great Forerunner of the Kingdom, suffer for righteousness and receive his reward. While he lived, he was a burning lamp shining in the darkness.

AUGUST 30

Ss. Alexander, John, and Paul, Patriarchs of Constantinople

Alexander was Patriarch of Constantinople during the time of the Arian controversy, succeeding the aged Metrophanes (feast day June 4), who ruled the see before Constantine turned the quiet town of Byzantium into the capital city of Constantinople. Alexander died in 340.

John the Faster ruled the see and defended the Church when the heretical Anastasius was emperor. He died in 595.

Paul ruled the see for only five years before repenting of his initial support of iconoclasm, secretly taking the great schema, and becoming a hermit. He died in 784.

Today commemorates these three great men who, in various ages, served the church of Constantinople by their holiness.

AUGUST 31

Hieromartyr Cyprian, Bishop of Carthage

Cyprian was probably born in Carthage. He was a very popular lawyer and teacher of rhetoric. When he was about forty-six he was converted to Christ through an aged priest (whose name, Caecilian, he took and added to his own names, Thascius Cyprian). So great was Cyprian's zeal for God that two years later in 277 he was elected Bishop of Carthage by the people. Some priests hotly resented him and throughout his episcopate did all they could to oppose him, fomenting rebellion and causing schisms.

When the persecution under Decius broke out in 249, Cyprian, like others, fled from the city to hide out in safety, being motivated by concern for his flock, because his visible presence in the city ("which was offensive to the pagans," he wrote) was causing the tumult against the Christians to increase. Still he cared for his flock from his place of refuge, providing relief for the confessors in prison and encouraging all. He wrote many treatises, including one *On the Unity of the Church*. Nonetheless, his opponents criticized him for fleeing.

Cyprian returned to the city in 251 and was involved in a controversy concerning the lapsed. He opposed those who said the ones who lapsed and denied Christ in the persecution could be restored to the Church even without the bishop's blessing. Cyprian said the bishop's blessing was necessary for anyone to be restored to the Church.

In 252, a plague broke out that took a heavy toll on all in the city. Cyprian was tireless in caring for these victims, Christian and pagan alike. At another time, he, with the other African bishops, was involved in a controversy with the Bishop of Rome over the rebaptism of heretics returning to the Church. Rome received such by chrismation only, while Cyprian and the African bishops received them by baptism as well. The African church held three local councils, which upheld the practice of receiving non-Orthodox by baptism and chrismation together.

Cyprian wrote concerning Pope Stephen's arrogance in demanding that all submit to his practice, "None of us makes himself a bishop of bishops or tyrannically tries to frighten his colleagues into obeying, since every bishop is incapable of being judged by another. Let us wait for the universal judgment of Christ."

The controversy was cut short by a new persecution under Emperor Valerian in 257. Cyprian was arrested and banished to Curubis, a pleasant small town 50 miles from Carthage. In 258 the persecution increased, and clergy were threatened with death, not just banishment. Cyprian returned voluntarily to Carthage and was arrested. At his trial, the governor asked, "Are you Thascius Cyprian, the bishop of so many impious men? The emperor commands you to sacrifice to the gods."

Cyprian replied, "I will not sacrifice."

"Consider well," the governor said.

"Fulfill your orders," Cyprian rejoined, "the case admits of no consideration." When Cyprian was condemned to death, he simply said, "Thanks be to God!" He was led to the place of execution, was stripped, and knelt in prayer. He gave a generous gift to his executioner and himself tied on his blindfold. He was beheaded and entered into eternal joy. The faithful took his relics and buried them with honor. He suffered for Christ in 258.

The Feast of the Cincture of the Most Holy Theotokos

At her death in Palestine, the cincture (or belt) of the Most Holy Theotokos was left with the Christian community there. Eventually, her clothes were taken as precious relics to Constantinople. In the late ninth century, the Empress Zoe was sick in soul and asked that the relics be placed upon her for her healing. The sash was removed from its reliquary and placed upon the sick empress, whereupon she was healed. The feast today commemorates this healing power of the relic and the effectual intercession of the Most Holy Mother of God.

~: SEPTEMBER 1 :~

Our Holy Father Simeon the Stylite

Simeon was born in Gesa in Cilicia, the son of a shepherd. When he was eighteen he entered a monastery nearby. He fasted greatly, eating only once a week and giving away the rest of his food to the poor. After about a year there, he left and lived in various places in Syria. In 423 he began to live in a cell built upon a pillar in Telanissus. The cell was about twelve square feet—so small he could stand or sit but not stretch out to lie down. Thus he sought not only to discipline himself by asceticism but also to witness to others about Christ.

Indeed, many came to admire and seek counsel from the holy man, including some Bedouin Arabs, and many were converted through him. Simeon wished to avoid being continually pestered and to have time to pray. To avoid the increasing crowds, he lengthened his pillar throughout the years from its original ten feet to a final height of sixty feet. Yet he did give counsel to inquirers when necessary, being at their disposal every afternoon.

Simeon was full of kindness and sympathy, and his advice was practical, free of any fanaticism. He himself was no fanatic but only sought, by his dramatic witness, to direct men's attention away from the vanity of the world. Once he was sent an order in the name of the local bishops to come down from his pillar-cell and give up his extraordinary asceticism. Humbly, he prepared to obey. The messenger, however, was only testing his humility and, when he saw his willingness to obey, blessed him to continue as he was. Simeon remained thirty-six years on his style, serving God faithfully until he died in 459. His relics were taken to Antioch and buried with honor.

SEPTEMBER 2

Holy Martyr Mamas

Mamas was a shepherd boy who was arrested as a Christian at Caesarea in Cappadocia. He was about fifteen years old when he suffered for his Lord. Seeing that he was but a youth, the authorities spoke kindly to him, trying to persuade him to deny his Faith. They said to him, "Simply say that you have sacrificed to the gods and we will release you."

Mamas boldly replied, "Neither in my heart nor with my lips will I ever deny Christ my Savior!" After being tortured, the young man died for his King in about 275.

SEPTEMBER 3

Hieromartyr Anthimus

Anthimus was the Bishop of Nicomedia in Bithynia. When the place where the Christians met for worship was torched (with great loss of life), a number of the faithful escaped to the surrounding mountains. Among these was the bishop. He was arrested not long after and subjected to terrible torture. He was beaten with rods and burnt with fire, and yet the torturers could not break his spirit or cause him to recant his faith in Christ. At length Anthimus was beheaded and entered the heavenly courts along with other Christians of his flock. They suffered for Christ in about 303.

SEPTEMBER 4

Hieromartyr Babylas

Babylas was elected Bishop of Antioch in about 237. One day the emperor (some say it was not the emperor himself but a governor) attempted to enter the church in his opposition to the Christians. Bishop Babylas boldly withstood him, forbidding him entry. Taken by surprise, the intruder withdrew but had Babylas arrested the next day. Loaded with chains, the bishop remained defiant: "These bonds that you think my shame are to me an adornment more splendid than your purple robe and diadem."

Along with Babylas, there were arrested three young boys (ages seven, nine, and twelve) who had been brought up in his house. The boys were flogged, despite their young age, and Babylas was thrown into prison. According to the church historian Eusebius, Babylas died in prison of ill treatment. He was buried in Antioch, a shining martyr and glory of the Antiochene church. St. John Chrysostom, a presbyter in that church, sang his praises in his sermons. Speaking of Bishop Babylas, Chrysostom said, "Who else in the world would Babylas fear, having withstood the emperor? By this he taught kings not to spread their power further than the measure given them by God."

∾ SEPTEMBER 5 ∾

Holy Prophet Zachariah and the Righteous Elizabeth
Zachariah and Elizabeth were called to be the parents of St. John the Forerunner, and they were both blameless in all God's Law. They were both of the priestly family of Aaron. Elizabeth was barren and to her old age had no child, even though they long prayed for one. When Zachariah was fulfilling by lot his once-in-a-lifetime ministry of burning incense before God in the inner temple, the Archangel Gabriel appeared to him to tell him that his prayer was heard and that Elizabeth would conceive and bear a son, whom he should name John. Initially incredulous that his barren wife Elizabeth should give birth in her old age, Zachariah was struck mute as a judgment for his unbelief until the child was born and named John.

Elizabeth did indeed conceive soon after. When she was six months pregnant, she was visited by her kinswoman, the Theotokos, who told her of her own Annunciation by the archangel. When her greeting reached Elizabeth's ears, John leaped for joy in her womb. Thus Elizabeth recognized Mary as the Mother of the Messiah and rejoiced with her. John was born, and at his circumcision, Zachariah's tongue was loosed and he praised God, being filled with the Holy Spirit and prophesying of John's future greatness as the Forerunner.

~ SEPTEMBER 6 ~

Holy Archangel Michael

Michael's name means, "Who is like God?" Michael is one of the seven archangels—the others being traditionally named as Gabriel, Raphael, Uriel, Selaphiel, Jegudiel, and Barachiel. Michael seems to have been specially charged with protecting the people of God, serving as a warrior. He served as "the great prince who has charge of [Israel]" (Dan. 12:1, RSV) and, as such, he warred in the heavenly places against the satanic angelic prince over Persia (Dan. 10:13). At the Ascension of Christ, Michael and his angels warred against Satan and cast him out of heaven to earth (Rev. 12:7–12). As a guardian and advocate of God's people, Michael contended with Satan when the devil contested Moses' burial (Jude 9). He thus remains the champion of God's people, protecting us by his angelic strength.

~ SEPTEMBER 7 ~

Holy Martyr Sozon

Sozon was a shepherd boy in the village of Midarze in Lycaonia. He was born with the name Tarasius but took the name Sozon at his baptism. During a time of persecution, he went to the city of Pompeiopolis and chopped off the hand of an idol with his shepherd's crook. He then went boldly into court and confessed that he had done the deed. The governor asked, "What made you do that?"

He replied, "I wanted to show you that I was a Christian and that I thought you to be impious."

The governor said, "Come, adore the gods and we'll overlook it."

He retorted, "What god—that one-handed fellow? I should be ashamed to venerate such a god, who can't even defend himself against my shepherd's crook."

Sozon was put on the rack and cried out, "Lord Jesus! Help Your servant!" He was given the chance for release if he would sacrifice to the god. He replied, "Fool! Don't you see that I did it to show I was a Christian? I don't fear your torture, and I hate that filthy idol!"

Nails were driven into his shoes, and blood spurted from his torn feet as he was made to walk. He still refused to do as they ordered and so was burnt to death, "to silence," as the governor said, "his accursed tongue." Up to the end he audaciously answered his torturers back defiantly. The humble shepherd boy suffered with honor for his Lord in about 304.

~: SEPTEMBER 8 :~

The Nativity of the Most Holy Mother of God

The Theotokos was born to Joachim and Anna in response to their faith and prayers. Anna was barren, and she could not conceive. After much prayer, God gave her conception, and she gave birth to a daughter who, as God foreknew, would become the Mother of Jesus. For Mary was to be the true daughter of Zion into whose midst God would come to dwell (Zeph. 3:14–15). From her birth God watched over her to prepare her for the work to which He would call her at the Annunciation—that of being the Most Holy Theotokos. As St. John the Forerunner was filled with the Holy Spirit from the womb and cared for by God for his mission, so was Mary from her birth also prepared for her holy vocation. Thus her birth proclaims joy to the whole universe, for from her would be born Christ our God, who grants us eternal life.

~: SEPTEMBER 9 :~

Ss. Joachim and Anna

These are the parents of Mary the Theotokos. They were pious and quiet people. Anna was barren—she could not conceive. But after years of prayer, she conceived (like Hannah, her biblical namesake) and gave birth to a girl, Mary. The couple's piety and faith summed up and embodied all the piety and faith of Israel so that in their daughter, the hopes of Israel would be fulfilled. As parents of the Theotokos, they are the crown and final fruit of the long years of Israel's preparation to bring forth the Messiah in the flesh.

New Martyr Alexander Men

Alexander was born in Moscow in 1935, when the communists were grievously oppressing the Russian church. Of Jewish parentage, Alexander was baptized secretly when seven months old and was later expelled from college due to his religious beliefs. He was ordained a priest in 1960. He baptized many hundreds of converts. His popularity in preaching and his success led to constant harassment from the KGB. He preached to packed lecture halls, opened a university, was active in Christian ecumenism, and helped found a Bible Society. Fr. Alexander was killed on September 9, 1990, by an axe-wielding assassin while on his way to serve Divine Liturgy. Fr. Alexander shone as a light in a dark place, fearlessly serving his Lord throughout the long night of communist persecution.

❦ SEPTEMBER 10 ❦

Holy Martyrs Menodora, Metrodora, and Nymphodora

These were three virgin Christian sisters of Bithynia who lived together. During a persecution they were arrested and brought to the governor, Fronto. Moved by their beauty and modesty, he spoke gently to them, trying to persuade them to sacrifice to the gods. They politely declined. The eldest, Menodora, was tortured first. Her back was bared, and she was strung up to a post and beaten with rods. When urged to apostatize, she answered so firmly that the governor lost patience and ordered her jaw to be broken with a cudgel. They did so, and she soon died under the torture.

After four days, Metrodora was brought into court and offered her freedom and other bribes if she would apostatize. She replied, "Sir, we are three branches sprung from one root. We cannot accept what you offer." She was also hung up and her skin was burnt with torches. She cried out to Christ in prayer all the time. After two hours of torture she was dead.

Nymphodora was next, and she also refused to apostatize. She was hung up like her sisters and her sides were torn with iron hooks. She did not utter a word, though some saw her lips moving soundlessly in prayer. Angry, the governor ordered her killed with clubs. Thus they beat her, and she died, joining her sisters as three noble and holy souls in the Kingdom. They suffered with honor in about 305.

~: SEPTEMBER 11 :~

Our Holy Mother Theodora

Theodora was a woman of Egypt who committed adultery. Her conscience smote her, and she determined to live in monastic holiness. In order to be safe from harassment and to secure entrance in the men's monastery she knew of, she cut her hair, wore men's clothes, and ran off to the monastery in the Thebaid under the name of Theodore. She kept her feminine gender a secret and lived in solitude. Even when falsely slandered by a prostitute who claimed she was a man who had fathered her child, she did not reply or disclose the truth about herself but accepted the untruth and cared for the prostitute's illegitimate child. After she died, the monks discovered she was a woman. She lived in truly heroic penitence and holiness, dying in the peace of Christ in about 490.

St. Paphnutius the Confessor

Paphnutius lived in ascetic holiness from his youth and suffered under Firmilian in Egypt. His eye was gouged out and his leg hamstrung so that he could not walk properly. He was sent, mutilated, to work in the deadly mines in about 311.

After his release, he went to be with St. Anthony the Great to learn greater holiness. He was ordained bishop and as such was present at the First Ecumenical Council in 325. Constantine heard him with great reverence, venerating his eyeless socket and embracing him.

When the Fathers at that council considered mandating celibacy for all clergy, the celibate Paphnutius stood up and said with roaring emotion, "Lay not this heavy yoke on the clergy. Marriage is honorable among all, as the Apostle said. By exaggerated strictness you will do the Church more harm than good. All cannot bear such an ascetic rule. The wives themselves will suffer for it. Marriage itself is continence. It is enough for a man to be forbidden marriage after ordination according to the ancient custom." All were greatly impressed, and his counsel was hearkened to and became the norm for the Church. He died in peace in the fourth century.

❦ SEPTEMBER 12 ☙

Holy Martyr Autonomus

Autonomus was a bishop of Italy. When persecution broke out there, he fled to Asia Minor and traveled throughout the region, encouraging believers and preaching to unbelievers. When the emperor reached Nicomedia, Autonomus moved to Pontus to avoid persecution. When things were quieter in Asia Minor, he returned there to continue his evangelical work. Some of the locals, however, burst into his chapel while he was standing in prayer at the altar and killed him. Thus the martyr inherited the Kingdom according to the merciful divine will in the fourth century.

❦ SEPTEMBER 13 ☙

Consecration of the Church of the Resurrection in Zion

Empress Helen, mother of Emperor Constantine, recovered the Lord's True Cross in Jerusalem and built churches in the Holy Land, such as the Church of the Nativity in Bethlehem. She also built a large church in Jerusalem to house the True Cross, the site enclosing both Golgotha and the Empty Tomb nearby. The church happened to be completed and ready for consecration on the thirtieth anniversary of Constantine's ascent to the throne, so both were celebrated on this day together. A local council of bishops meeting in Tyre came down for the consecration. The church became the spiritual center of Christendom, the holy Zion, mother of all the churches and a place of international pilgrimage. The consecration took place in 335.

St. Cornelius the Centurion

Cornelius was a centurion and a "God-fearer"—a Gentile who worshipped only the Jewish God, but who had not yet taken the step of accepting circumcision and becoming a Jew. He lived at Caesarea, giving alms liberally and praying with faith to the true and living God. For his piety, God sent him an angel, who instructed him to send men to nearby Joppa, to the house of Simon the tanner, and ask that his guest Simon Peter be sent to bring him a message from God.

Cornelius obeyed the angelic counsel, and Simon Peter came to his home and preached the gospel. He and his household listened with open and receptive hearts, and God responded to their faith by pouring out the Holy Spirit upon them, so that they all spoke with tongues. Seeing such irrefutable evidence that God had accepted Gentiles even without circumcision, Peter baptized them. Cornelius continued a life of faith, speaking about Christ to all he met. It is said that he traveled to Phoenicia, Cyprus, Antioch, and even as far as Ephesus, sharing the Good News which had so transformed his own life. He died in peace in the first century.

~: SEPTEMBER 14 :~

Elevation of the Holy and Life-Giving Cross

This day commemorates two events: the finding of the True Cross by St. Helen in Jerusalem, and the returning of the holy relic to Jerusalem after it had been taken by the Persians when they captured Jerusalem in the seventh century.

According to the story, the Cross was discovered under the temple of Venus that Emperor Hadrian had built over the original Golgotha. Its location was attested to by local residents who had guarded the tradition from the first century. Digging there, they found three crosses—our Lord's and the ones for the two thieves who were crucified with Him. A man who had recently died came back to life when placed on one of the crosses. The Patriarch Macarius thus identified this one as the True Cross. He lifted it up and cried in prayer, "Lord, have mercy!"—which chant all the people echoed with joy. Today's feast witnesses to the true life-giving nature of Christ's Cross and Death—for on it He destroyed death and brought joy into the entire world.

~: SEPTEMBER 15 :~

Holy Martyr Nicetas

Nicetas was a Goth born near the Danube River who converted to Christ in his youth. The Gothic kingdom was divided and at war, and in 370 King Athenarik of the eastern kingdom began to persecute the Christians in his region. Nicetas was one of those seized. He was beaten and thrown alive into the fire. He sang hymns from the midst of the flames until he perished. Though nominally Arian (as were all the Goths after 376), he no doubt held this belief through ignorance, not understanding the philosophical subtleties of the Arians but loving Christ our God in simplicity of heart. He died for his Lord as a true martyr in about 378.

~: SEPTEMBER 16 :~

Holy Great Martyr Euphemia

Euphemia was a young girl of Chalcedon, the child of rich and devout parents. When Priseus, governor of Bithynia, a devotee of the pagan god Ares (or Mars), held a feast for the god, the Christians fled in small groups in an attempt to escape notice. Euphemia was among them, but as she was from a noble household, her absence could not be hidden. She was brought to the governor, who tried to persuade her to sacrifice to the idol. "Don't waste your time," she replied. "We Christians are people of reason, and it would be a disgrace for us to abandon the one true God to worship senseless idols." Such bold defiance enraged the governor, and Euphemia was imprisoned and tortured, along with others. At length she was thrown to the wild beasts and killed by a bear. She bore her testimony for Christ and inherited the martyric crown in about the year 303.

～ SEPTEMBER 17 ～

Faith, Hope, Love, and their mother, Sophia

A woman named Sophia (Greek for "wisdom") lived, it is said, in Rome in the second century. She was a widow with three daughters, whom she had named Faith, Hope, and Love. When they were twelve, ten, and nine years old respectively, a persecution broke out. The children were martyred, and their mother, who also suffered, died afterwards. The martyrs show us how true faith, hope, and love are fulfilled in the act of persevering in serving Christ to the end, no matter what the cost. This is the true wisdom that leads to eternal life.

～ SEPTEMBER 18 ～

St. Eumenius, Bishop of Gortyna

In his youth Eumenius gave away his wealth to the poor and practiced a life of ascetic severity. His face was often bathed in tears, and no one ever heard him criticize another or listen to others criticize. Seeing such holiness, the people of Gortyna in Crete chose him to be their bishop. He cared for his flock as a true shepherd, and by his prayers worked wonders, healing the sick and driving out demons. He went to visit the Thebaid, and it was there that he died in peace. The faithful sent his holy body back to Rhaxos in his homeland, where the body of his predecessor also lay. Eumenius lived in the seventh century.

～ SEPTEMBER 19 ～

Holy Martyrs Trophimus, Sabbatius, and Dorymedon

In the third century, two eminent Christians, Trophimus and Sabbatius, were taken during a persecution of the Church as they refused to take part in a pagan celebration of Apollo. They were tortured horribly but would not deny Christ. Sabbatius died under the torture. Trophimus continued to suffer tortures and then languished in prison. Dorymedon was also a Christian and came to minister to Trophimus in prison, though secretly, as he was a government official. He was discovered so doing, however, and perished with the martyrs. The three suffered for Christ in the third century.

~: SEPTEMBER 20 :~

Holy Great Martyr Eustace (Placidus)

Placidus was a pagan army officer who took part in the persecution of Christians. Later he and his family converted and, being baptized, received new names: Placidus was renamed Eustace, his wife Tatiana was renamed Theopista, and his children were renamed Theopistus and Agapinus. During a persecution of the Christians, Eustace, his wife, and their two sons were arrested. They were all martyred together and inherited the Kingdom. They suffered in about 118.

It is said Placidus was converted when hunting a stag. The stag came to him with a cross in his antlers and a voice saying, "Placidus, Placidus, why do you persecute me? I am Jesus Christ." The story tells us how, when as a pagan Placidus was seeking to hunt and conquer Christians, Christ the hunted was Himself hunting and seeking him.

~: SEPTEMBER 21 :~

Holy Apostle Quadratus

Quadratus was a disciple of the Twelve and one of the Seventy. Eusebius of Caesarea, writing in his famous *History of the Church*, says that he was known for his prophetic gifts, much like the daughters of Philip the Evangelist. Quadratus preached the gospel with power and was a shining light, illumining the darkness with the Word of Christ.

~: SEPTEMBER 22 :~

Hieromartyr Phocas, Bishop of Sinope

Phocas was born in the city of Sinope on the coast of the Black Sea, the son of a shipbuilder. He converted from paganism to the Christian Faith, and God gave him the gift of working miracles. Phocas labored hard as Bishop of Sinope, bringing many pagans to Christ.

Refusing to deny his faith when arrested for being a Christian, he died for Christ in the reign of Trajan at the turn of the second century.

❦ SEPTEMBER 23 ❧

The Conception of St. John the Baptizer

The parents of John, Zachariah and Elizabeth, had long wanted a child, but Elizabeth was not able to conceive. Finally after years of prayer, God miraculously granted her conception in her old age, and John was conceived in her womb to be the Forerunner. As one called to such a vocation, John was filled with the Holy Spirit from his mother's womb. Today's feast shows God's love in granting life and conception to all, such as these righteous women under the Law: Sarah, wife of Abraham and mother of Isaac; the mother of Samson; and Hannah, the mother of Samuel. God cares for His children even from their conception and watches over them in the womb, even as He watched over Holy John.

❦ SEPTEMBER 24 ❧

Holy Martyr Thekla, Equal-to-the-Apostles

Thekla was born in Iconium in Asia Minor of humble parents. She was converted through the preaching of St. Paul when she was a girl of eighteen. Rather than marrying, she traveled all over, preaching the gospel, preserving her virginity, and suffering hardship and persecution for Christ. She became an image and inspiration for young Christian girls about to suffer for their Faith. For her labors in preaching, Thekla is honored with the title equal-to-the-apostles.

Holy North American Martyrs Juvenaly the Priest and St. Peter the Aleut

Juvenaly came with his fellow Russian missionaries from Valaam to North America in 1794, along with St. Herman of Alaska. He was a priest-monk and desired greatly to preach to the native Alaskans. Herman described Juvenaly, along with his missionary colleague

Macarius, as "so energetic, almost like madmen wanting to rush off in all directions." Juvenaly went to mainland Alaska and baptized more than seven hundred Sugpiaq natives, then continued northwest to Cook Inlet. While on his preaching expedition, he was martyred by a hunting party of coastal Yupiks. As he was a foreigner, the natives were frightened, thinking him a rival shaman, and killed the priest with arrows and spears. As they attacked him, he stood up in his boat to bless them with the sign of the Cross.

Peter was another martyr on North American soil. He was an Aleut converted to Orthodoxy by the Russian missionaries. He was trapping furs with some friends. There was a Spanish Roman Catholic colony in northern California which was quite hostile to the Russian presence. The governor there ordered all Russian trapping to cease. When Peter and his men were there, they were arrested by the Spanish colonists. Peter and his thirteen friends were taken to San Francisco and locked up. Peter was brought out, and each finger was cut from his hands, one joint at a time. With each cut, he was ordered to convert to Roman Catholicism. Peter refused, saying he was a Christian, and said, "I will not betray my faith." After much torture, he died from loss of blood. The order came the next morning for the others to be released. They brought news of their comrade to the Russian mission in Alaska, where Peter was immediately recognized as a martyred saint. Juvenaly was martyred in 1796, Peter in 1815. Their blood and dedication were the seeds of the Church in the new land of North America.

~: SEPTEMBER 25 :~

St. Sergius of Radonezh

Sergius was born in Rostov in about 1314 of pious parents and given the name Bartholomew. He was a thoughtful and pious boy. After the death of his parents in 1334, Bartholomew, not yet twenty years old, decided to live as a hermit with his brother Stephen, who had become a monk. They received the blessing of the metropolitan and began to build a hermitage. They lived in the midst of the forests of Radonezh, in a place they dedicated to the Holy Trinity. Stephen later left to join a monastery in the city, while Sergius remained alone in the forest, struggling against the demons, living amidst the bears and wolves. He tamed a bear, who came every day to him to be fed.

Soon other men joined him in his retreat. Reluctantly, he allowed them to elect him abbot of the now-growing community. He said, "I would rather obey than command, but fearing the judgment of God, I submit to His will." He lived in humility and gentleness, doing the humblest of tasks himself. The monastery was extremely poor, and some monks grumbled, but God supplied their needs.

The monastery grew, and Sergius became famous for his sanctity. He received the gift of prophetic insight and was granted visions. He was once offered the office of patriarch but declined it. Through his influence, other monasteries were founded. Many sought his counsel, including Prince Dmitri, who, supported by Sergius's prayers, liberated Russia from Tartar tyranny at the battle of Kulikovo in 1380. Sergius continued to serve God and was the father of Russian monasticism. He died in peace at the age of seventy in 1392.

Our Holy Mother Euphrosyne

A wealthy widower named Paphnutius had a daughter, Euphrosyne, whom he loved dearly. When she was eighteen, he intended to marry her to some pious man. She did not want such a life but had a heart only for monastic solitude and prayer. So, without telling her father, she cut her hair, dressed in men's clothes, and presented herself to the nearby monastery as a palace eunuch seeking entry to the monastery. She said her name was Smaragdus (Greek for "emerald"). The abbot did not suspect her of being a woman and so admitted her to the monastery. There she lived in peace and solitude, praying with the monks but keeping to herself, lost among the other 352 monks.

Her father, seeing her gone, was frantic to find her and searched everywhere. He asked the prayers of the monks too, and even came to know Smaragdus, without, however, recognizing her as his daughter. It was only when she was about to die that she revealed herself to her father. Euphrosyne died in peace after thirty-eight years in the monastery. Her father became a monk there too after her death and was buried beside his daughter. Euphrosyne entered into rest in about 470.

⁕ SEPTEMBER 26 ⁕

Repose of St. John the Theologian

St. John reposed after a long life of serving his Lord. He died finally in Ephesus and was buried there. While he lived, a rumor began that he would never really die but would remain until the Lord returned. But John himself, in his gospel, took care to refute this notion, pointing out that the Savior did not say to St. Peter that John would remain until He came but only, "If I will that he remain till I come, what is that to you?" (John 21:20–23).

⁕ SEPTEMBER 27 ⁕

Holy Martyr Callistratus

Callistratus was born in Chalcedon and became a soldier of the Calandon cohort of the army. As a Christian, he avoided the dissolute life often associated with the military of that day, as well as the customary worship of the pagan gods. Some of his fellow soldiers became suspicious and followed him when he left the camp to find the solitude to pray undisturbed, as was his custom. There they heard him repeating the name of Jesus Christ, and they denounced him as a Christian to their superiors. Until then Callistratus had kept his faith hidden, but now he boldly confessed that he was a Christian. For this he was beaten, sewn into a sack, and thrown into the river. He perished in the water, a martyr for his heavenly Lord, in about 304.

⁕ SEPTEMBER 28 ⁕

Our Holy Father Chariton

Chariton was an eminent citizen of Iconium. During a persecution, he was arrested and spoke boldly against the gods and for Christ. He was tortured savagely and thrown into prison with his flesh torn to shreds. Later, he was released and fled to Egypt until the persecution had ended. He continued in ascetic holiness, showing the same zeal for fasting that he had shown in boldly confessing Christ before his persecutors. Chariton became famous for his holiness and founded an ascetic community in the wilderness of Pharan, as well as two other such communities. He died in peace as he lay on his bed in about 350.

SEPTEMBER 29

Our Holy Father Cyriacus the Hermit

Cyriacus was born in Corinth and was made a reader in the church there while still a young man. He went to Jerusalem at the age of eighteen and visited many holy monks in Palestine—St. Euthymius, St. Gerasim, and St. Chariton. He was very ascetic, living for years eating only raw vegetables. It is said of him that the sun never saw him eat (for he ate only once a day in the evening) and never saw him angry at anyone. He died in peace in 557.

SEPTEMBER 30

St. Gregory, Enlightener of Armenia

Gregory was born in Armenia in about 240, during a time of great political upheaval. His father was hired to assassinate Khosrov, the king of the country. After the assassination, his mother gave her baby Gregory to fellow townsmen for safety when they fled the country. They fled to Caesarea with the child and raised him as if he were their own. Thus Gregory was raised a Christian.

As an adult, Gregory returned to Armenia and entered into government service under King Tiridates, son of the murdered Khosrov. When Tiridates discovered that Gregory not only was a Christian who refused to honor the national idol, Anahit, but also was the son of the man who had assassinated his father, he threw him into prison and treated him with some brutality. Tiridates also harassed other Christians as well, torturing and killing some young Christian virgins, including Rhipsimia, Gaiane, and their companions. Tiridates at length became convinced that he should embrace the Christian Faith. Gregory was released and became advisor to his king, convincing him to cease from his ferocity and further the Church's work. Gregory was sent back to Caesarea to be ordained bishop.

The Metropolitan of Caesarea was overjoyed and ordained Gregory missionary bishop for Armenia. Gregory returned to his native Armenia and baptized Tiridates, the royal family, and subsequently the majority of his people, laying the foundation for Christian Armenia. He persuaded Tiridates to build a great church at the base of Mount Ararat, Holy Etchmiadzin (which means church "of the descent of the Only-begotten Son"—i.e., "of the Incarnation"). This was to be the mother church of the nation.

Gregory also built other churches to the martyred virgins Rhipsimia, Gaiane, and their companions. He worked as enlightener of his land for many years and, having built a secure foundation, retired to a monastery in Mount Sebuh, letting the work continue in the hands of his clergy and fellow bishops. King Tiridates sent to Caesarea for Gregory's son Aristanes to come and join in the work. Aristanes was consecrated patriarch and catholicos by his father and the other bishops. He attended the First Ecumenical Council in Nicea in 325. Gregory died in peace in about 335, a true father to Christian Armenia.

OCTOBER 1

The Veil of Protection of the Most Holy Theotokos

In 911, Constantinople was under military threat, and the people were praying for God's help in the Blachernae church in the suburbs of the city. It was in this church that the omophor or veil of the Mother of God was preserved as a most precious relic. The church was crowded for an all-night vigil. St. Andrew, a fool-for-Christ, was there along with his disciple Epiphanius.

At about four in the morning, St. Andrew and Epiphanius had a vision of the Mother of God: she entered through the church doors, escorted by St. John the Forerunner and St. John the Theologian and preceded by a host of angels. She stopped at the ambo (the great elevated pulpit in the center of the church) and knelt there in prayer, praying fervently and with tears. She then entered the altar and prayed again, and finally removed her veil and held it out over the faithful as she ascended from them. They concluded from this that her intercession would be a protection to the faithful in this, their hour of trial. And so it happened, as the feared military menace was averted.

The feast today reminds us of the maternal and invincible protection of the prayers of the Most Holy Mother of God and how she always prays fervently to her Divine Son for those who honor her as Theotokos.

St. Romanos the Melodist

Romanos was born of Jewish origin in Emesa, Syria, in the fifth century and served as a deacon in Beirut. He did not have the good voice usually needed by deacons for singing their part of the liturgy and was looked down on by many of them on account of this. He did possess, however, a great spiritual gift for writing hymns. In 468 he moved to Constantinople and served the church there. It is said his prayers for a more melodious voice were answered by the Mother of God. He would pray weeping to her for a better voice with which to glorify God. In a dream one night, she appeared to him, blessed him, and gave him a scroll with glorious hymns written on it. In his dream, he ascended the ambo in church and sang beautifully and with joy. When he awoke, the dream was fulfilled—he was able to sing beautifully and without his former inferior monotone. Romanos, "the melodious one," wrote a thousand hymns, including the kontakion for Christmas, "Today the Virgin gives birth to the Unapproachable One." Romanos died in peace in 530.

~: OCTOBER 2 :~

St. Andrew, Fool-for-Christ

Andrew was born a Scythian and brought to Constantinople as a slave in his childhood. He lived a holy life as a fool-for-Christ. His master, not understanding him and his vocation, thought him mad and released him from his service. Andrew wandered the streets of Constantinople, enduring hardship and insults and praying for all the world. Through his prayers he was given the gift of prophetic insight and received divine visions—including finally a vision of the Most Holy Theotokos's protection when at church at an all-night vigil (see October 1). He lived in holy deprivation for sixty-six years, dying in peace in 911.

Ss. Cyprian and Justina

In the mid-third century, a beautiful young girl named Justina lived in Antioch. Though a pagan and the daughter of a pagan priest, she was converted to the Christian Faith through the teaching of a certain Praulius, who served as a deacon of the church there. After being baptized by the bishop, Optatus, she decided to devote the rest of her life to holy chastity, prayer, and asceticism as a deaconess.

A young man named Aglaidas, a pagan, had fallen in love with her and was greatly distressed at her decision. He resorted for help to a certain man named Cyprian, who made his living in the occult sciences as a magician and seller of spells. Aglaidas hoped that, through his spells, Cyprian could influence the young Justina to fall in love with him. Though Cyprian tried all he could to use his arts to this end, nothing availed, for Justina was protected by the power of Christ. At length, Cyprian acknowledged the superiority of the Christian God and sought to learn more about this religion. Eventually he too was converted. He publicly burnt his magic books and received baptism. When the persecution fell upon the Church, Cyprian and Justina also were arrested, tortured, taken to Nicomedia, and finally beheaded.

OCTOBER 3

Hieromartyr Dionysius the Areopagite

When St. Paul came to preach in Athens, he was brought to the Areopagus, the local civic council, to explain his new teaching, and there he preached the gospel. Some sneered at his teaching, but some joined him and believed, including Dionysius (Acts 17:19–34). Dionysius was one of the council (an "Areopagite") and therefore an older man of distinction, learning, and power. He later became bishop of the Christian church in Athens. Such was his learning and wisdom that later writings (written about 500), which expressed the gospel in terms of Neoplatonic learning, were ascribed to him. (These works, which later included the influential and brilliant books *On the Celestial Hierarchies* and *On the Divine Names*, were sent to the church in Gaul, and their author was further confused with another Dionysius, a martyr of Paris who died about 286.)

OCTOBER 4

St. Hierotheus, Bishop of Athens

Hierotheus, like Dionysius (feast day October 3), was also one of the local civic council of Athens, the Areopagus (i.e., Hill of Ares, or Mars). He too was converted by St. Paul's preaching. He became the leader of the small Christian community in Athens, being succeeded by Dionysius, his colleague. He lived in holiness, teaching his flock as a true pastor. He died in the first century.

Our Holy Father Paul the Simple

Paul was a disciple of St. Anthony the Great. He may have been somewhat mentally handicapped but had great spiritual power. He worked as a simple and ignorant farm laborer for sixty years. Then, finding his wife was unfaithful to him, he fled to the then-famous Anthony to become a monk.

At first Anthony would not receive him as a monk, because he feared one of Paul's age would not be able to stand the rigors of the desert. But Paul was determined and stayed three days and nights outside Anthony's cell. Anthony then decided to test him. He told Paul to pray and not stop until he was told. Paul obeyed and prayed all day and night, not moving from his place, enduring the blazing heat of noon and the cold of the night. Anthony brought supper for the then-famished Paul and said, "First let us chant psalms and pray," which they did. Then he said, "Well, we've looked at the food, and that's enough for our supper. Now let us retire to bed." Paul obeyed without a murmur. When Anthony saw such obedience, he accepted him as a monk.

One day, Anthony and some monks were discussing Christ and how He fulfilled the words of the prophets, and Paul asked in simplicity, "Were the prophets before Jesus Christ or Jesus Christ before the prophets?"

Anthony was embarrassed at such stupidity from his attendant, reddened, and told him to go away and be quiet. Paul quietly received the quick and careless utterance as if it were a spiritual directive. He went to his cell and maintained silence. Anthony saw him there and asked, "Why are you here, silent in your cell?"

Paul replied, "Father, you told me yourself to go away and be quiet."

Anthony told his visitors, "Paul condemns us all—learn from this man what obedience to God ought to be. If I say anything, he does it instantly and cheerfully. Do we behave like this to our God?"

Paul received the prophetic gift of insight and could see men's hearts. Also, when Anthony could not exorcise a demon from a man, he sent him to Paul, and Paul drove out the demon instantly. Paul died in peace at a great age in the fourth century.

⁓ OCTOBER 5 ⁓

Holy Martyr Charitina

Charitina was a servant of a man named Claudius in Pontus. Though not yet baptized, she believed in Christ and loved Him. When she was denounced as a Christian, Claudius was reluctant to hand her over for trial, for he was truly fond of her and lamented her certain death. But she bade him to cheer up, saying she would pray for him. When Claudius surrendered her to the arresting soldiers, he asked her, "Remember me before the heavenly King."

Brought to trial, Charitina confessed herself a Christian. Her hair was cut off, and burning coals were poured over her head. She was then thrown into the water to drown, but she clambered out. She said, "This is my baptism!" The governor then had her teeth knocked out and her hands and feet cut off. She suffered for Christ as one of His faithful and inherited the crown in about 304.

⁓ OCTOBER 6 ⁓

Holy Apostle Thomas

Thomas was also called the Twin. He was a sensitive, impulsive man who felt deeply and spoke quickly. When he thought his Master planned to go to Judea to die, Thomas instantly said to the other apostles, "Let us also go, that we may die with Him" (John 11:16). During the Last Supper, when the Lord said they would know the way He was to go, he spoke out, "Lord, we do not know where You are going; how can we know the way?" (John 14:5, RSV). After the Resurrection, Thomas was not with the others when Christ appeared to them and, being emotionally wrung out from the strain of the last days, he was too numb to accept the apostles' testimony to Christ's

Resurrection. He said he would not believe it unless he could see His wounds for himself on His risen Body. Christ came to the apostles and offered to show Thomas His wounds. Thomas fell down in joy, crying out, "My Lord and my God!" (John 20:24–29). He ended his life as a martyr for his Lord.

~: **OCTOBER 7** :~

Holy Martyrs Sergius and Bacchus
These were two friends who were also army officers and Christians. They served in the household of the Emperor Maximian. The emperor one day entered the temple of Jupiter to offer sacrifice and noticed that the two officers remained outside. Suspecting them of being Christians, he ordered them to join him in sacrificing to the god. When they refused, he had their military insignia plucked off (meaning they were dishonorably discharged) and further humiliated them by having them dressed in women's clothes and paraded through the city. Still they remained firm. They were then sent to the city of Resapha. Bacchus was scourged until he died. Sergius was made to walk in boots with nails in them to tear his feet. He was then killed with the sword. They suffered for their Lord, brothers in the Spirit and in the martyr's crown, in about 301.

~: **OCTOBER 8** :~

Our Holy Mother Pelagia the Penitent
Pelagia was a famous actress and dancer in Antioch. She was very beautiful, dressed and conducted herself with great luxury and style, and was a popular sensation. She was also a prostitute and very wealthy. The people of Antioch nicknamed her Margaret (or "pearl"), since she wore such adornment. A group of bishops was meeting in Antioch one day, and Bishop Nonnus saw her. He looked long at her as she rode past, and then said to the other assembled bishops, "Wasn't she beautiful?"—and he began to weep. He explained to them, "She was a delight to see. It seems to me God placed her here

to judge us—for she spends so much time and effort to be physically beautiful, and we don't spend such time and effort to become spiritually beautiful."

The next time Nonnus spoke in church, Pelagia was there (for the first time), listening to his sermon. She was cut to the heart by his words and saw her life in all its ugliness and shame. She began to cry and later sent word to Bishop Nonnus, "To the holy disciple of Christ—a sinner and disciple of the devil sends greeting." She asked in her letter to be received into the Church. Nonnus rejoiced and appointed a deaconess, Romana, to be her sponsor. Pelagia was baptized and soon after gave all her wealth to the Church to give to the poor. The eighth day after her baptism, she laid aside her white baptismal robe and left Antioch—not to return to sin but to live in asceticism in Jerusalem. She lived in solitude as a hermit, pretending to be a man, Pelagius, so that she might remain safe. She was discovered to be a woman after her death. She died in peace in about 460.

OCTOBER 9

Holy Apostle James, Son of Alphaeus

James was the son of Alphaeus and one of the Twelve. (He is called James the Less or the Little to distinguish him from James the son of Zebedee, as he was the shorter of the two). He preached the gospel in foreign lands. Some say he died a martyr in Egypt in the town of Ostracina.

OCTOBER 10

Holy Martyrs Eulampius and Eulampia

When persecution against the Christians broke out, Eulampius, a young boy, along with others fled Nicomedia and hid in some caves. When food ran out, Eulampius was sent back to buy some more food. It was hoped that he would escape detection because of his young age. While there, he stood still to read an edict, just posted, which ordered all to sacrifice to the gods. When soldiers spoke to him, he panicked and ran away. They caught him and arrested him as a Christian. He refused to sacrifice to the gods and insulted the gods in his young boy's zeal. He was hung up, and a girl broke through the crowd, crying and throwing her arms around his neck. It was his sister, Eulampia. She was immediately arrested with him, and the next day the two were executed with the sword. They died for the truth in the early fourth century.

OCTOBER 11

Holy Apostle Philip

Philip was one of the seven men ordained as deacons by the apostles (Acts 6). He was a man of vision and a Hellenistic Jew. After the stoning of Stephen, Philip fled Jerusalem and went about preaching the gospel even to the Samaritans and baptizing them, driving out demons and healing the sick and the paralyzed. Even Simon the Sorcerer, a local cult figure, was baptized and attached himself to Philip, amazed at his miracles. Philip, led by the Spirit, went to Gaza, preached the gospel to an Ethiopian eunuch, and baptized him. Afterwards the Spirit caught him up, like the prophets of old, and took him to the next town of Azotus. He later settled in Caesarea and had four daughters who prophesied. He was a true evangelist, preaching the gospel everywhere. He later served as Bishop of Tralles. Philip died in peace at a great age.

OCTOBER 12

Holy Martyrs Probus, Tarachus, and Andronicus

These three martyrs were arrested at Pompeiopolis in Cilicia. Probus was from the town of Side in Pamphylia; Tarachus was a Roman citizen and retired soldier from Claudiopolis in Isauria; Andronicus came from a noble family of Ephesus. All were convicted of being Christians and refused to renounce their Faith.

Probus stood firm and told his interrogators not to waste their time trying to make him renounce Christ, but to torture and kill him immediately. He was flogged until his blood ran, and when urged to save himself only said, "This bloodshed is oil and perfume for me to anoint myself with joy for further contests." Tarachus, despite his old age, suffered by having his jaw broken by stones. Andronicus, the youngest, was hung on a gallows and had his limbs cut with thin blades, his sides burnt, and salt thrown into his wounds.

During a second interrogation, Tarachus was hung upside down above a brazier while a corrosive mixture was poured into his nostrils. Probus was burnt by red-hot irons, scalped, and had his tongue cut out. The three were then reserved for the gladiatorial shows, to be thrown to the beasts. Because of their wounds, they had to be carried into the arena. When the animals refused to hurt them, the governor ordered the gladiators to cut them to pieces. Thus did these three heroes for Christ inherit the incorruptible crown of glory in God's Kingdom. This happened in 304. They continue to shine in Christ's Church as a beacon of courage.

St. Martin of Tours

Martin was born at Sabaria in Pannonia in about 315. He was the son of a soldier and joined the army himself at age fifteen. Martin's parents were pagans, but he felt an attraction to the Christian Faith and enrolled in the Church as a catechumen. Martin was a boy of determined and extreme enthusiasm who did whatever he did with all his heart. When his corps was at Ambianum in Gaul in the dead of winter, he met a poor beggar who was freezing; his clothes were mere rags. Though his fellow soldiers jeered, Martin impulsively took his sword and cut his own cloak in two in order to have at least something to give the beggar.

That night in a dream he saw Christ seated on His throne and wearing the half-cloak Martin had given the beggar. He said to His heavenly court, "Martin is only a catechumen, and see—he clothes Me with his garment!" Martin finished his catechumenate and was baptized two years later, when he was eighteen. He remained in the army until he was twenty, his conscience driving him toward asceticism. He said, "I am Christ's soldier; I am not allowed to fight." He left the service just before a battle, and his fellows said he was leaving out of cowardice. He indignantly denied this was the reason and offered to prove it by standing, unarmed, between the two opposing armies.

Martin was discharged and went to Poitiers under St. Hilary. Hilary made him an exorcist—a minor order—as Martin in humility refused the greater order of the diaconate. He went to Pannonia to visit his parents and succeeded in converting his mother to Christ (though his father continued a pagan). Martin returned to Poitiers and to his mentor Hilary, and Hilary settled him in a monastery called Liguge. In 371, the see of Tours became vacant and, much against his will, Martin was elected its bishop. He remained a monk even after this, living in a cell near his church (though he later moved to a more secluded spot at Marmoutier, where he lived with eighty disciples). Through his influence, many other monasteries were founded as well.

As missionary bishop, Martin went everywhere, preaching to the pagans and opposing Arianism. He traveled to remote areas to preach the gospel to all and performed miracles through his prayers. He also was unusual for his enthusiastic acts of mercy. One day he heard that a number of men were to be tortured and executed for some crime the next day. He went to Tours to plead for the condemned and found the ruler responsible for them asleep in bed.

Martin threw himself on the ruler's doorstep, hands raised in supplication, and cried aloud for the men until the magistrate awoke. There he saw the aged bishop prostrate on his doorstep, hands raised in supplication. Moved to pity, he pardoned the condemned men. At other times, Martin also refused to support the persecution of Priscillian heretics by the state, saying that excommunication by the Church was enough. Martin died in peace in 397 after a long life of hard labor for his Lord. He was a true evangelizer and a man of God.

OCTOBER 13

Holy Martyrs Carpus and Papylus

Carpus was the son of pagan parents. He converted and eventually became the Bishop of Pergamum. Papylus came from neighboring

Thyatira. He was converted by Carpus, instructed by him, and eventually served as his deacon. They were both arrested during the persecution of Decius by order of the governor. After fearlessly confessing Christ, bishop and deacon were punished by being harnessed behind horses and forced to run forty miles to Sardis. There were tied up and flayed. When asked by their tormentors how they still endured with serenity, Carpus replied, "I have seen the glory of the Lord." The two suffered martyrdom for their Lord in about 250 and so entered the Kingdom.

⁓ OCTOBER 14 ⁓

The Holy Martyrs Nazarius, Gervase, Protasius, and Celsus

Nazarius was baptized in Rome in the late first century. When he was twenty years old, he left Rome, and for ten years he went through the cities of Italy, preaching the gospel. While in Milan, he visited two confessors who were imprisoned there, Gervase and Protasius, and he encouraged them to remain steadfast in the Faith.

When persecution caused Nazarius to flee from the city, he went to the city of Cimiez. He came to be entrusted with a young child by one of the local dignitaries there. He named the young boy Celsus and raised him as a Christian. Persecution befell them there too, and they fled to Trier, then found their way back to Milan, where they met Nazarius's old friends Gervase and Protasius. All four were arrested and beheaded. Their holy relics were eventually discovered by St. Ambrose, Bishop of Milan, in the late fourth century, and they became a source of healing for all those trusting in the power of Christ.

Our Holy Mother Petka

Petka was born in Serbia of wealthy and pious Christian parents. She left home and traveled to Constantinople and thence to Palestine, where she lived to old age in ascetic holiness. In her old age she returned to her native village of Epibata and died two years later, full of years and sanctity. She lived in the eleventh century.

~ OCTOBER 15 ~

Holy Martyr Lucian of Antioch

Lucian was born at Samosata in Syria of Christian parents, though orphaned at the age of twelve. As an adult he was ordained priest in Antioch and worked hard as a scholar, studying Hebrew and preparing accurate translations of the Holy Scriptures. When Maximian raged against the Church, Lucian was arrested (being betrayed to the authorities by a heretical fellow priest) and was taken to Nicomedia. There he was tortured grievously in the stocks so that his legs were dislocated and his back lacerated and pierced. He died on the floor of his cell, unable to use his legs.

On the day before he died, when the Feast of Theophany had come, Lucian's friends wanted to receive Holy Communion with him one last time but feared to bring a table into the cell to use as an altar. They did not know how they could conceal such an illegal celebration of the Eucharist beneath the very eyes of the guards. Finally Lucian said, "This breast of mine shall be the Table, and I think it will not be less esteemed by God than one of inanimate material, and you shall be the church over it, standing around me." Thus they crowded around their priest, their bodies shutting out from view of the guards the liturgy which the priest celebrated one last time using his own body as the altar. All received Holy Communion and sent some to the absent Christians also, as was customary. Lucian died the next day, suffering for God in about the year 312. His body was thrown into the sea, but the Church recovered the holy relics fifteen days later.

~ OCTOBER 16 ~

Holy Longinus the Centurion

The centurion who stood by our Savior's Cross and confessed Him to be the righteous Son of God (as He claimed) is called in the apocryphal Gospel of Nicodemus by the name Longinus—probably

Latinized from the Greek word *longche* ("spear")—since soldiers carried a spear with them. The centurion came from Cappadocia before serving the Emperor Tiberius in his army. It is said that he died a martyr. The confession of faith the centurion uttered as he stood by the Cross was a pledge that many others of the Gentiles—including those in the Roman armed forces—would acknowledge Christ crucified and offer their lives to Him.

⁓ OCTOBER 17 ⁓

Holy Prophet Hosea

Hosea was a prophet in the northern kingdom under King Jereboam (782 BC onwards). He preached against the evils of the kingdom's idolatry and heartless injustice to the poor. When opposition increased against him, he fled from the king to the southern kingdom of Judah in the reign of Uzziah and his successors (777 BC onwards).

Hosea's personal life held much tragedy, which God used to teach him in his prophetic ministry. He was told to marry a prostitute, Gomer, and have children of harlotry by her to enact the living lesson that Israel was a harlot and unfaithful to her divine husband, Yahweh, by worshipping other gods. Hosea named one of his children Jezreel, to show that God would punish Israel for the unjust slaughter that took place at the field of Jezreel. He named two other children Lo-ruhamah ("not pitied") and Lo-ammi ("not My people") to show that God would not pity His people and that He would disown them and let them be judged by foreign destroyers.

Gomer fled from Hosea and returned to her life of sin. Hosea later found her for sale at the slave market, and he was commanded by God to buy her back in order to show how God forgives His people and buys them back after a time of judgment. Hosea was a prophet of God's love, and he shows us that God loves us passionately as a Bridegroom loves his Bride, granting us His eternal forgiveness.

OCTOBER 18

Holy Apostle and Evangelist Luke

Luke was a Gentile born in Antioch of Syria. He became a physician and early joined the Christian movement, traveling as a companion to St. Paul on parts of his missionary journeys and staying with him in Rome during his first imprisonment. Luke was with Paul also at the end during his second imprisonment. He got to know the Lord's family and the people of the gospel narratives intimately through his research, so that he produced a two-volume history of the Lord and His Church—the Gospel of Luke and the Acts of the Apostles.

Luke painted some portraits of our Lord's Mother, becoming the father of iconography and an image for the apostolic origins of the art. After the death of his companion St. Paul, he continued to travel much in his preaching of the gospel. He ended his earthly course as a martyr. His relics were translated to Constantinople in 357. He was a man of compassion, and his gospel portrait of his Lord stresses especially his Master's concern for the poor and helpless.

OCTOBER 19

Holy Prophet Joel

Joel may have lived in the postexilic period of Israel's history and was probably a resident of Jerusalem. Israel was then threatened with complete destruction by an imminent plague of locusts, and Joel announced the judgment as the Day of the Lord, calling on the people to sanctify a fast and repent if they would be saved. He prophesied also of their subsequent restoration—of the days of the Messiah, when God would bless them by pouring out His Spirit upon all people, even the humblest of servants (Joel 2). This prophecy was fulfilled when Christ poured out the Spirit on the Day of Pentecost. St. Peter refers to this prophecy in his first sermon (Acts 2).

~: OCTOBER 20 :~

The Holy Great Martyr Artemius

Artemius was a Christian, born of a noble family, and was appointed military commander over Alexandria by Emperor Constantine the Great. Constantine's successor, Julian, attempted to restore the old pagan ways and began to persecute the Church. When Emperor Julian was in Antioch, preparing for his war on the Persians, he ordered two Christian priests of Antioch to be beaten. Artemius, as a military commander, had arrived in Antioch to help with the military effort, and he was offended at the beating given to the Christian clergy. He therefore rebuked his emperor for this, denouncing the pagan gods as lifeless idols.

Julian was furious at this rebuke from one of his officials. He had Artemius's badges of office torn off and Artemius arrested. Artemius was beaten and thrown into prison. At length, Julian had him brought forth and promised him restoration to his office and other honors if only he would renounce his faith and join the emperor in his restoration of paganism. Artemius was adamant. Julian therefore had him imprisoned with further tortures, as red-hot skewers were run through his body. When Artemius refused to disown Christ, he was finally taken out and executed by beheading. The great martyr and soldier for Christ suffered for his Lord in the fourth century.

~: OCTOBER 21 :~

Our Holy Father Hilarion the Great

Hilarion was born of pagan parents in the village of Tabatha south of Gaza in Palestine. Sent to Alexandria for an education, he was there converted to Christ. When he heard of the fame of St. Anthony in the desert of Egypt, he visited him and became his disciple, wanting to imitate him. Then, when he was a boy of fifteen, his parents died. He gave away the wealth they left him and entered the desert of Maiuma near Gaza.

Hilarion was of delicate health, and his friends feared for his health and safety in the dangers of the desert, but he persevered in his life as an ascetic hermit. Eventually, from about 329, others gathered around him in their own cells. Hilarion lived in a small hut, cut his hair only once a year (at Pascha), and wore his clothes until they were in rags. He knew the Scriptures by heart, living in holy solitude until he was sixty-three. Many came to visit him and seek his prayers for healing miracles, including some bishops and clergy. In about 360, in quest of solitude, Hilarion traveled to Egypt, Sicily, Dalamatia, and Cyprus. He died in peace in Cyprus at the age of eighty. As a successor to St. Anthony, he was a father of monks in Palestine even as Anthony was in Egypt. His relics were taken to Maiuma, where he was buried. He entered the Kingdom in about 372.

~: OCTOBER 22 :~

St. Abercius, Equal-to-the-Apostles

Abercius was Bishop of Hieropolis in Phrygia in the second century. The church of Hieropolis was very small amid a great many pagans. Through Abercius's steadfastness in preaching and his wonderworking prayers, many in the town came to the Faith. He died in peace at a great age in his see of Hieropolis.

Abercius must have been a tremendous preacher of poetic power. An inscription claiming to be his contains the words, "I am a disciple of the pure Shepherd who pastures His flocks on hills and dales, and who has great all-seeing eyes. He it is who taught me the faithful Scriptures of life. Faith was everywhere my guide. Everywhere Faith served me a fish of great size, from a most pure water-spring, that was caught by a pure Virgin. Faith ever gives her friends to eat of it, and has an exquisite wine that she gives with bread."

OCTOBER 23

Holy Apostle James, Brother of God

James was "the Lord's Brother"—that is, his kinsman, being (possibly) the son of St. Joseph's brother. Though originally not believing in Christ (John 7:5), he came soon to believe in Him, and Christ appeared to him after His Resurrection (1 Cor. 15:7). James was the first Bishop of Jerusalem and as such presided over the Apostolic Council of Jerusalem, which met to decide whether uncircumcised Gentiles might be admitted to the Church (Acts 15). He wrote one of the first New Testament epistles to the then-Jewish Church scattered abroad.

James was an ascetic pastor whose holiness was recognized even by the unbelieving Jews of Jerusalem, among whom he was known as James the Righteous. This no doubt inflamed his enemies all the more. One Passover he was asked to address the assembled crowd and speak about his kinsman Jesus who had been crucified, to clarify and dissuade Jews from the Christian Faith. James replied, "Why do you ask about Jesus the Son of Man? He sits in heaven at the right hand of the Majesty on high and will come again in the clouds of heaven." His foes, enraged at this, threw him down from the high place of the temple on which he stood. He was not killed outright by the fall, but struggled to his knees and prayed for them. One of them took a launderer's club and beat his brains out with it. Thus the brother of the Lord died a martyr for his Lord in about 62 at the age of sixty-nine. He was buried on Mount Olivet.

OCTOBER 24

Holy Martyr Arethas

Arethas's name in his own tongue was Abdallah-Ibn-Althamir. An old man distinguished for his Christian piety, he was the governor of the town of Negran in Omir in southern Arabia. In the political upheaval of those times, the town was besieged by an unbelieving king, Dzu Nowass (Latin *Dunaan*), who was urged to the persecution by Jewish advisors. When the town resisted the siege, the king resorted to treachery and promised that the town would be spared if they surrendered and paid an annual tribute. The town believed him and surrendered. It was destroyed even so, the property pillaged, and its Christian people slain—as many as 4,200 men, women, and children. Arethas, their governor, was beheaded with them. They suffered, confessing Christ their God in 523.

~: OCTOBER 25 :~

Holy Martyrs Marcian and Martyrius

In the fourth century, when the Arian controversy raged, Emperor Constantius became an Arian. Marcian and Martyrius were of noble birth and were appointed secretaries to the Patriarch of Constantinople. Marcian was a reader and Martyrius a subdeacon at the cathedral, and they opposed Arianism vehemently and defiantly. When their foes could not win them over to Arianism, the two were condemned and beheaded, suffering for the Lord in 355. When the peace of the Church was restored and Orthodoxy triumphant, St. John Chrysostom built a church over their tomb.

~: OCTOBER 26 :~

Holy Great Martyr Demetrius

Demetrius was a Christian born of wealthy parents in Thessalonica. During the persecution of the Church, he was arrested and taken to be imprisoned. Emperor Maximian was going to Thessalonica that day and ordered the Christian detained until he could be investigated and tried.

Maximian then went to the arena for the games to watch his favorite gladiator, the champion Lyaeus. The emperor offered a reward to any man who could defeat his favorite champion. An unknown young man named Nestor, having asked Demetrius's blessing, jumped into the midst and accepted the offer. The emperor, knowing the gladiator Lyaeus to be much his superior, tried to dissuade the young man, but he insisted on fighting him. Much to everyone's shock, Nestor killed the huge Lyaeus with one blow.

Furious at so losing his favorite champion, Maximian rose up in a huff and stormed out without giving Nestor the promised reward. When his officers met him and asked him what was to be done with the Christian Demetrius awaiting him, he angrily replied, "Run him through with your spears!" Thus Demetrius perished without trial, a martyr for the Lord. This happened in about 306. His relics were treasured in Thessalonica and a church built in honor of him by Leontius, Christian prefect of Illyria, after the peace of the Church.

~: OCTOBER 27 :~

Holy Martyr Nestor, Companion of St. Demetrius

When St. Demetrius (feast day October 26) suffered for his Lord, Nestor suffered at the same time. For the Emperor Maximian was at the gladiatorial games in Thessalonica, delighting in his favorite gladiator, Lyaeus. During this time, he had Demetrius, a notable and wealthy Christian, imprisoned nearby, awaiting trial.

Nestor had visited Demetrius in prison and was full of zeal for him and the cause of Christ. When at the games the emperor offered a great reward to anyone who could defeat his champion, Lyaeus, Nestor jumped up, offering to take him on. Entering the arena, Nestor cried, "God of Demetrius, help me!" When the great Lyaeus lunged at him, Nestor stepped nimbly aside and stabbed him in the heart, killing him with a single blow.

The emperor was furious at this and left in a huff, without giving Nestor the promised reward. Rather, hearing that Nestor had identified himself with Demetrius and his Christian God, he had him arrested and beheaded outside the city. Nestor and Demetrius suffered for the Lord and inherited their incorruptible and eternal reward.

❦ OCTOBER 28 ❧

Holy Martyrs Terence and Neonilla

Terence and his wife, Neonilla, lived with their seven children as believers in Christ. The persecution broke out upon the Church in pagan times, and they too were arrested and brought before the governor. When they refused to renounce Christ, they were tortured, and vinegar and salt were rubbed into their wounds. In the midst of their tortures, they kept on encouraging one another to hold fast to Christ. They were finally beheaded and entered the heavenly courts in triumph.

Holy Martyr Paraskeva

Paraskeva was born in Iconium of wealthy and pious parents. After their death, she gave away much wealth to the poor. When Diocletian persecuted the Church, Paraskeva also was arrested. When asked her name, she only replied, "I am a Christian." She was rebuked for not answering the question and replied, "This is my name in eternal life. Do you want my name in this transitory life?" For her defiant confession of the Faith, she was flogged, imprisoned, and tortured terribly. She was finally beheaded and went to eternal life in about 304.

❦ OCTOBER 29 ❧

Our Holy Father Abraham the Recluse

Abraham was the son of wealthy parents in Mesopotamia, near Edessa. He was married to a beautiful young girl and began a life of wealth and influence. But his heart desired only the holiness of solitude, and so a week after his marriage, he secretly fled to the desert. His parents and wife were in shock and searched for him everywhere. At last, after seventeen days, they found him and urged him to return to his former life, but to no avail. He remained in the solitude of a hermit. When his parents died, leaving him their wealth, he had his friends use it to help the poor.

The local Bishop of Edessa wanted to use the holy man to help evangelize a nearby pagan village. So he ordained Abraham priest and sent him there. He preached to the people, but they would not hearken or convert. At last he destroyed their idol, and they formed a mob and beat him until he could not move. He continued to preach and urge them to the truth, and at last they relented and became Christians.

Abraham stayed another year there, strengthening them in the Faith, before returning to his cell after a four-year absence. He also raised his niece, an orphan named Mary, and led her in the ascetic way. She fell away, however, and turned to a life of prostitution in Assos. Learning of this, Abraham disguised himself and went to reclaim her for God. She lived with him in repentance and prayer. He died ten years later at the age of seventy. Mary lived on for five years after her uncle's death and also died, inheriting with him the crown of life. This happened in about the fourth century.

OCTOBER 30

Hieromartyr Zenobius

Zenobius was born of wealthy Christian parents in Aegae in Cilicia and became Bishop of Aegae. He distributed much wealth to the poor and served as a pastor of healing to his flock. During the persecution he was arrested and given a choice. The judge said, "I offer you the two, life and death: life if you sacrifice to the gods, death if you do not."

Zenobius replied, "Life without Christ is not life but death, and death for Christ is not death but life." He was tortured for this faith, his sister Zenobia also suffering with him. They were finally both beheaded for their Lord in about 285.

OCTOBER 31

Priest-Martyr John Kochurov

John Kochurov was born on July 13, 1871, in the village of Bigildino-Surka of the district of Danky in the Ryazan region of Russia, the son of a priest, Alexander. Even at theological school John stood out from others as an example of piety and righteousness. His pastoral heart burned with missionary zeal, and so after graduating in 1895 and being ordained, he was sent to serve in the American diocese.

Fr. John arrived in America with his wife to begin missionary work. He served in a parish in Chicago that consisted of Russians, Galicians, Hungarians, Arabs, and Bulgarians. Eventually he built a church temple with funds gathered in Russia and served as true shepherd of his flock.

In response to the desire of his ailing father-in-law in Russia (who served as a priest in the St. Petersburg diocese and wanted John as his successor in his parish), Fr. John returned to his native Russia in 1907. He served in Neva, teaching in the church schools, and then as a pastor in Tsarskoye Selo, a parish of the imperial court. But shortly after his assignment there, the Communist Revolution broke out, and the chaos spread to affect John's life also. In the vortex of violence that spread throughout the land, Fr. John was arrested and shot by the Bolsheviks on October 31, 1917, a martyr for Christ and His Church during terrible times.

Holy Martyr Epimachus

Epimachus lived as an ascetic in the deserts of Egypt. In zeal for the Faith, he left the desert, entered the city of Alexandria, and overturned the altar of idols. He was arrested and languished a long time in prison, suffering horribly from scourging. He was finally beheaded and inherited eternal joy in 250. To his last breath, he continued to mock the idols and confess his Lord.

NOVEMBER 1

Holy Unmercenaries Cosmas and Damian

These were two brothers who came from the region of Ephesus. Their father was born a pagan, but he later converted to the Christian Faith. His early death left the two boys in the sole care of their mother, who had been a pious Christian since her childhood. As youths they devoted themselves to the study of medicine, and as Christian physicians, they prayed with their patients and healed them in the name of Jesus. They did not insist on payment but would tend the sick for the love of Christ, sometimes even refusing payment when offered. They were wonderworkers, God using their ministrations to work miracles of healing. They died leaving an example to all of the selfless service of love. With other holy healing physicians (such as St. Panteleimon), they are invoked by the Church today, that through them Christ may continue to heal His people.

NOVEMBER 2

Holy Martyr Akyndinus and Companions

Akyndinus and Anempodistus were court officials who served under the Persian King Sapor in the fourth century. They were Persian Christians and suffered in the persecution when the king raged against the Christians in his kingdom. The bold servants of Christ confessed their Lord faithfully, even though cruelly tortured (one account says they were laid on beds of red-hot iron). Others suffered in that persecution along with them, including a soldier named Aphthonius and a government official named Elpidephorus. They all suffered with honor and were executed in about 355.

NOVEMBER 3

Hieromartyr Akepsimas, Bishop of Naeson

In the fourth century, King Sapor of Persia raged against the Church, killing the Christians—as many as sixteen thousand. One of the bishops taken was the eighty-year-old Akepsimas, who suffered along with several of his clergy, such as his priest Joseph (aged seventy) and his deacon Aithalas (aged sixty). When Bishop Akepsimas was arrested, he was asked by one of his household what he wanted done with his property and house, for they knew he would be killed. He replied, "It's no longer my house; I'm going to a better house and will not return." Akepsimas languished in prison before finally being beheaded. He suffered with his fellow clergy in 350.

NOVEMBER 4

Our Holy Father Joannicius the Great

Joannicius was born of poor parents in Marykata, a village in Bithynia, in 765. He worked in youth as a pigherd. He later became a soldier and led a dissolute life. He repented and, though still in the army, began to lead a life of repentance, fasting, and asceticism, sleeping on the bare earth. After a campaign against the Bulgarians in which he distinguished himself for bravery, Joannicius renounced the world, left the army, and entered a series of monasteries. He learned to read and live as a monk. He then returned to Mount Olympus, living outdoors, exposed to the elements.

After twelve years he entered a monastery again in Eristae and was formally tonsured a monk. God gave him the gift of prophetic insight and miracles, and many came to visit him. After the iconoclasts were defeated in the Church, Joannicius urged that they be dealt with mercifully and with clemency, as erring brethren and not as enemies, because he once had iconoclast tendencies himself before he was enlightened as to the proper use of icons. He died in peace at the age of eighty-one in 846.

NOVEMBER 5

Holy Martyrs Galaction and Episteme

Galaction lived in Emesa in the mid-third century. Though he was a Christian, when he was twenty years old, he found himself, through his father, betrothed to a pagan girl named Episteme. Though he married her in obedience to his father, he refused to live with her as husband with wife because she was a pagan. Eventually he managed to convert her to his faith in Christ. In response to a vision, Episteme decided they were called to continue to live as brother and sister, and she in turn convinced Galaction of this. Accordingly, they sold their goods and went off to seek lives of holiness in a desert monastic community.

During the persecution that fell upon the Church in that time, the couple also were arrested. When they refused to renounce their faith, they were horribly tortured: Episteme was publicly stripped and had reeds driven under her nails, and both had their hands and feet cut off. They were finally beheaded and together won the crown of glory from their heavenly Bridegroom. Galaction was thirty years old when this happened, and Episteme was sixteen.

Holy Apostles Patrobus, Hermes, Linus, Gaius, and Philologus

Patrobus was Bishop possibly of Puteoli.

Hermes is thought to have served in Philpopolis.

Linus was Bishop of Rome (mentioned by St. Paul in 2 Tim. 4:21).

Gaius used his home to host all Christians passing through his city (see Rom. 16:23). He served, it is said, at Ephesus.

Philologus is said to have been Bishop of Sinope. All served the same Lord in their various callings and labors and inherited the same Kingdom.

NOVEMBER 6

St. Paul the Confessor, Patriarch of Constantinople

Paul was a young secretary to the Bishop of Byzantium in the days before that city was elevated to be the capital city of Constantinople in Constantine's empire. Paul was elected Patriarch of Constantinople in 336, but later the Arians persuaded Constantine to banish him to Pontus. When Constantine died in 338, he returned to his see. An Arian council condemned Paul, and he was banished again to Treves. He worked in the West, supporting the cause of St. Athanasius and Nicene Orthodoxy. In 342 he was again restored to his see.

The Arian Emperor attempted to expel him again, and the general sent to carry out this order was slain in a tumult of the people. Paul was condemned for this and sent in chains to prison. He was restored again at the insistence of Constans, the emperor of the West. When Constans died, Paul was again taken away to die in exile in Armenia. He was strangled there with his own episcopal pallium (or stole), dying a martyr for Nicene Orthodoxy in 351. In 381 his holy relics were translated to the capital.

NOVEMBER 7

The Holy Thirty-Three Martyrs of Melitene

Hieron was born in Tyana in Cappadocia. He was seized, brought before the governor of Melitene, and imprisoned along with thirty-three other Christians. All except one—Hieron's kinsman Victor—held fast and confessed the Faith and received the crown of martyrdom. As they were led away to execution, they all sang Psalm 119 together, "Blessed are the undefiled in the way, who walk in the Law of the Lord." As undefiled martyrs, they inherited the crown of life, suffering for their Lord in 298.

NOVEMBER 8

Holy Archangel Michael and All the Bodiless Powers

Archangel Michael is considered to be the leader of all the angelic hosts. This day commemorates all the angels. The angels are assigned by God to oversee and guide all the powers and energies of the created world. In addition, each nation has its angelic protector (Michael is warrior protector of the people of God), and each individual Christian has a guardian angel assigned to guard, guide, and pray for him. Angels are arranged in ranks as a heavenly army—with such ranks as seraphim, cherubim, thrones, dominions, virtues, powers, principalities, archangels, and simple angels. Monday of each week is devoted liturgically to commemorating the angels as the unseen protectors of our lives in Christ.

Matushka Olga of Alaska

Olga was born in 1916, a Yupik of Alaska. When her husband, the village postmaster, was ordained priest, Olga found herself mother not only to her own children (she would bear thirteen children, of whom eight survived), but also spiritual mother and matushka to those in her parish village. Olga served quietly, working as midwife in her village and constantly caring for the needy. Though her own family was poor, she often gave away her children's clothes to those who were poorer.

Matushka had a special gift in working with those who suffered abuse, especially sexual abuse. In her quiet ministry as midwife to the village, she was known for her ability to discern when a woman was pregnant, even before the woman knew herself. After her repose on November 8, 1979, many people experienced her coming to them in dreams, bringing her healing gifts. Matushka Olga's sanctity reveals the possibilities for genuine theosis and holiness, even for those living in the world.

NOVEMBER 9

Holy Martyrs Onesiphorus and Porphyrius

In the early third century, these two confessors were arrested during the persecution under Diocletian and Maximian. When they refused to renounce their Faith, they were stretched upon a gridiron and tortured with fire. They were then tied by their feet to horses and dragged over rough and thorny terrain. They died under their tortures and surrendered their souls to God, suffering with honor in about 308. Their bodies were recovered by local Christians and buried in the village of Panceanon.

St. Nectarius, Metropolitan of Pentapolis

The future saint of Pentapolis was born Anastasius Kephalas in Thrace in 1846. He was very poor, so he went to work for a tobacco merchant in Constantinople when he was fourteen years old. In 1875, he was tonsured a monk at the Nea Moni Monastery on Chios, with the name Lazarus, and later ordained a deacon, with the name Nectarius. After ordination to the priesthood, Fr. Nectarius left Chios and went to Egypt, where he was elected Metropolitan of Pentapolis. Some of his colleagues became jealous of him and accused him before the patriarch of plotting to become patriarch himself. For this he was suspended, though the order said only that he had been suspended "for reasons known to the patriarchate."

Nectarius bore all this with supreme patience. Seeing that it was creating a scandal in the Egyptian Patriarchate of Alexandria, he moved to Greece, only to find that the false rumors had preceded him. He was therefore only able to secure a living as a preacher in the humble diocese of Vitineia and Euboea, though he did eventually succeed in being appointed director of the Rizarios Seminary in Athens. The noise of the big city oppressed his spirit, and he yearned for monastic solitude. He therefore found an abandoned and tumbledown monastery on the island of Aegina, which he repaired with his own hands, eventually founding a community of nuns there.

Nectarius's health began to fail, and in 1920 he was admitted to a state hospital for the poor in Athens. The admitting intern would hardly believe that the old man in black robes was a bishop. He was heard muttering, "For the first time in my life I see a bishop without a panagia or cross, and more significantly, without money."

St. Nectarius died in holy apostolic poverty and simplicity in 1920 at the age of seventy-four. His relics were found for a long while to remain incorrupt. He was a true wonderworker, both before and after his death. His intercession is especially sought after by those suffering from cancer.

St. John the Dwarf

John was born of poor parents in Tese in about 339. He was very short (hence his name) and came to the desert monastery of Scetis with his brother Daniel when he was about eighteen years of age. He had quite a temper and struggled with anger. Whenever he felt anger with a brother, he would run away until he had cooled down. When he was a young monk, he wanted to go to the desert and live in great zeal, saying, "I long to be an angel! I will go and lead the angelic life in the desert!"

In a few days, though, he tired of it and returned to his brother Daniel at the monastery. He knocked at the door of Daniel's cell, but his brother did not answer.

"Who is it?" asked Daniel.

"It's me, John!" he said.

Daniel replied, "That can't be—John isn't a man anymore, he has become an angel!" John understood the lesson and learned humility.

One time he was rebuked by an irritable brother who said, "A little pitcher full of spite—that's what you are!"

John replied gently, "Ah friend! There are worse things in this pitcher than spite if you could peep inside." He attracted great attention and fame for his holiness. After 407 he moved to Suez and the mountain of St. Anthony. He died in peace in the fifth century.

✧ NOVEMBER 10 ✧

Holy Apostles Olympas, Erastus, Quartus, Herodion, Sosipator, and Tertius

Olympas was a Christian of Rome (see Rom. 16:15) and suffered in the same persecution as Peter and Paul. Erastus was a companion of St. Paul and later, it is said, served in Paneas in Palestine.

Quartus was a Christian of Corinth and may have served in Beirut.

Herodion was a Jew, a "kinsman" of St. Paul. He served, it is said, as Bishop of Thessaly, and was martyred by having his face crushed with stones and being run through with a sword. Sosipator served in Iconium after Tertius. Like, Herodion, he was a Jew.

Tertius was the secretary for St. Paul as he dictated his Epistle to the Romans (Rom. 16:22). He later served in Iconium.

✧ NOVEMBER 11 ✧

Holy Great Martyr Menas

Menas was an Egyptian and served in the Roman Army. When persecution began against army officers, he left the army and retired to a place of refuge with other Christians. When the persecution broke out against the general Christian populace in 303, he emerged from his solitary refuge and returned to the city of Cotyaeus. When martyrs were suffering in the arena, he shouted as loud as he could, "I was found by those who sought me not" (see Is. 65:1), and on examination confessed himself a Christian like the others. He was imprisoned and scourged the next day. He was torn with iron hooks and finally burned alive. He suffered with honor, a true soldier of Christ, in about 304.

✧ NOVEMBER 12 ✧

St. John the Merciful, Archbishop of Alexandria

John was born of wealthy parents in Cyprus. After his wife and all his children died, he used his wealth to help the poor. He was elected

Patriarch of Alexandria and immediately asked to see a list of his masters. When asked, "What masters?" he said that he meant the poor who needed his help. He built hospitals and visited the sick himself. He was a man of peace and humility.

One day John had to excommunicate two clergy who had a fistfight with each other. One bore it humbly, but the other resented John. Next Sunday, as the patriarch was serving liturgy, the deacon began the offertory prayer for the Gifts, and John remembered the Lord's words, "If you bring your gift to the altar, and there remember that your brother has something against you, leave your gift there before the altar, and go your way. First be reconciled to your brother, and then come and offer your gift" (Matt. 5:23–24).

John told his deacon to keep on saying the offertory prayer until he returned, and then he left the altar. He sent to have the resentful cleric brought to meet him in the vestry. There, in full vestments, the aged patriarch fell on his knees before the cleric, bowed down, and said, "Forgive me, my brother!" The man, ashamed of himself, flung himself at his patriarch's feet and, weeping, asked his pardon. They embraced in peace, and the patriarch returned to the altar to continue with the liturgy.

When the Persians invaded Egypt, John fled home to his native Cyprus. He fell ill on the way and died in his native town in 620 at the age of sixty-four. He ruled his patriarchal see for ten years.

ᛝ NOVEMBER 13 ᛝ

Our Father among the Saints, John Chrysostom, Archbishop of Constantinople

John was born in 347 in Antioch. He was raised a Christian and baptized at the age of eighteen by Meletius, Patriarch of Antioch. John wanted to live as a hermit, but Patriarch Meletius refused to give his blessing for this, so he served as an acolyte and then as a reader.

After three years of John's urging, Meletius finally relented and allowed him to go and live as a hermit. He went to a cave, denied himself proper sleep, read the Scriptures constantly, and spent two years without lying down. His austerities ruined his health, and his kidneys were damaged by the cold. Sick, he returned to Antioch, and Meletius sent him to a doctor.

John served as deacon for six years and in 386 was ordained priest by Flavian, Meletius's successor. He preached in the common language of the street, and his sermons touched everyone who heard them. His sermons began to draw crowds. God gave him a spiritual gift to touch people's hearts, and he was so eloquent that he would gain the name *Chrysostom*, that is, "golden mouth."

In 387 the people of Antioch held a tax revolt, during which they destroyed the imperial statues. This was a capital offense. Over a period of days the imperial soldiers executed many citizens. Bishop Flavian went to Constantinople to plead for mercy, and John preached a sermon series, "On the Statues," calling people to repentance and hope in God's eternal Kingdom. They city listened to him with renewed attention.

In 397 John was transferred to Constantinople to be the new patriarch. The previous patriarch had been easygoing and lax, but John was not. He insisted on holiness from his clergy. He did not give or attend lavish parties. He sold some of the new furniture in the patriarchal residence to build a hospital. He preached against luxury and greed. Many opposed him, including the empress.

The Archbishop of Alexandria, Theophilus, also resented John and conspired to ruin him. Appearing in Constantinople, he convoked a synod and had John banished on false charges. John refused to defend himself but committed his cause to God. He went into exile. But on the next day there was an earthquake, and he was restored. John did not change; still he preached against sin and vanity.

When the empress erected a statue of herself opposite the church, John denounced the vanity and said, "Again Herodias dances, again she rages, again she demands the head of John!" The empress was furious and again banished John. As he left, he begged his clergy to obey his successor for the sake of peace: "As you bowed your heads to John, so bow to him." He was old and in ill health, and they banished him to the Caucasus in Armenia.

John kept in touch with and was supported by the wealthy deaconess Olympias. His fame and influence grew with his exile. His enemies, wishing to harass him to death, made him move further out in the dead of winter. The strain was too much, and he died on the way. His final words were "Glory to God for all things!" The liturgy ascribed to him is testimony to the debt the Church owes to the patriarch whose grace, shining forth from his lips, has enlightened the whole world. He died in 407. His relics were returned with honor to his cathedral in Constantinople in 438.

~: NOVEMBER 14 :~

Holy Apostle Philip

Philip was a native of Bethsaida in Galilee. He was a friend of Andrew and joined him immediately as a follower of Jesus, persuading his friend Nathanael to join them also (John 1:43–51). He was chosen to be one of the Twelve. He had some Greek in his background, and when Greeks wanted to see Jesus, they went first to Philip (John 12:21–22). After the Resurrection, he went and preached in Phrygia, especially in Hieropolis, where he was martyred.

St. Gregory Palamas, Archbishop of Thessalonica

Gregory was born in Constantinople in 1292 of noble and wealthy parents. His mother died when he was young, and he became a ward of the emperor. As such he had before him a brilliant career at the imperial court. When he was about twenty, he left all the intrigue of life in the capital to enter the monastic life on Mount Athos. There he lived in peace and learned the ways of stillness and of hesychasm, celebrating the transfiguration of human nature through prayer.

The hesychast monks were attacked in 1333 by a Greek theologian of southern Italy named Barlaam, who thought their doctrine and claim that man could see the uncreated light was ridiculous. Barlaam felt their teaching denied the transcendence and unity of God. Gregory supported the monks and wrote his *Triads* in their defense. Barlaam was very powerful and influential, and Gregory was condemned and excommunicated. As he would not be silent about his teaching, he was also imprisoned.

Later, when a new emperor assumed the throne, Gregory was restored and appointed Archbishop of Thessalonica. Councils were held at Constantinople to examine the hesychast doctrines, and Gregory and his teaching were vindicated in 1351. It was proclaimed that God is one—His inner essence is transcendent, but His energies can be known, experienced, and seen as uncreated light. Thus, man can genuinely experience the transfiguring power of God. Gregory returned to his see in Thessalonica in 1356. Worn out by all his sufferings, he died in 1359. He was glorified as a saint nine years later.

NOVEMBER 15

Holy Martyrs Gurias, Samonas, and Abibus

In the persecution of the Church by Emperor Diocletian, Gurias and Samonas, two Christians of Edessa, were arrested. The prefect came, and the two confessors were brought before him and ordered to sacrifice to the gods. When they refused they were hung up with stone weights attached to their feet. They remained thus suspended without crying out for several hours until they fainted and were thrown into a dungeon, without light or sufficient food, for three days.

Upon being brought before the judge again, Samonas was so firm in his refusal that the judge lost his temper and ordered him again suspended in such a way that his hip would be strained and dislocated. Gurias, a man of more delicate constitution, had almost died from his previous suffering and so was spared this. They were then both executed by beheading in 299. Later, a deacon of the same church named Abibus gave himself up to the authorities and confessed himself a Christian. He was condemned and burnt alive. His half-burned relics were buried with those of Gurias and Samonas. They all suffered with honor for their Lord.

NOVEMBER 16

Holy Apostle and Evangelist Matthew

Matthew, also known as Levi, was a tax-collector. When our Lord called him, Matthew gave Him a feast to which he invited other notorious tax-collectors and impious friends. He left his old ways to become one of the Twelve. Clement of Alexandria said that Matthew embraced an ascetic way, never eating meat but only vegetarian fare. He remained in Palestine for fifteen years after the Resurrection and wrote down the teaching of Jesus for his fellow Jews in Aramaic, which was later translated into Greek. The gospel ascribed to him was written by him or by a teacher in his community.

Matthew seems to have gone as far as Ethiopia (or, some say, to the area around the Caspian Sea). Some say he was martyred there. His gospel is the most Jewish of all the gospels and testifies to Jesus being the fulfillment of Jewish messianic hopes.

NOVEMBER 17

St. Gregory of Neo-Caesarea, the Wonderworker

Gregory was born with the name Theodore, of pagan parents in Pontus. They moved to Caesarea, being attracted there by the fame of Origen. The family learned the Christian Faith from Origen, studying under him for five years. Gregory left Caesarea for his native Pontus and was ordained Bishop of Neocaesarea. He was of great personality and piety and received the grace to work miracles by his prayers. When the persecution under Decius broke out against the Church, he hid himself until it had passed. He encouraged his flock to keep the martyrs' festivals. In 253, a plague hit Asia Minor, and Gregory tirelessly ministered to the sick and dying of his see, which selfless charity converted many pagans to the Church. By the time of his death, there were only seventeen pagans left in his town—which was just the number of Christians that had been in his flock when he began his episcopate there. He died in peace in 270.

NOVEMBER 18

Holy Martyr Plato

Plato was born in Ancyra in Galatia. His brother Antiochus also suffered as a martyr. When Plato was brought before the governor Agrippinus on charges of being a Christian, he zealously confessed the Faith. He was beaten by twelve soldiers and tortured terribly, being laid on red-hot iron plates and having his sides burned until his skin blistered and bled. Every time he was offered release if he would deny his faith, he replied, "Christ is my life, and to die for Him is my gain." He languished in prison for eight days until he was finally beheaded. He suffered with honor in about the third century.

NOVEMBER 19

Holy Prophet Obadiah

Obadiah was a contemporary of Elijah the prophet. He lived in the ninth century BC, during the reign of King Ahab. He served in the court of the king but was a secret worshipper of Yahweh. When the royal persecution of Yahwism under Ahab began, Obadiah took one hundred of His prophets, hid them in a cave, and fed them until the crisis had passed. He was charged by his king to feed and save the livestock during the drought Elijah had called on the land as a judgment for their sin. Obadiah served Yahweh faithfully and died in peace.

New Martyr Daniel of Moscow

Fr. Daniel Sysoyev, born in 1974, was rector of St. Thomas Church in southern Moscow. His heart burned with zeal to bring all men to Christ, so that he worked tirelessly among the Muslims, neopagans, and Protestants of Russia to bring them all to Holy Orthodoxy. Such was his zeal that he founded a school for street preachers in Moscow. He was especially well known for his work among the Muslims, having baptized more than eighty of them, and engaging in public debate with one who converted to Islam. Though breaking the boundaries established by the politically correct in Russia, Fr. Daniel felt that the love of Christ constrained him to bring the gospel to all. Although he received many death-threats from Muslims, he always said the word of Christ was more important to him.

On the day of his death, Fr. Daniel was in his church at 10:40 PM. A masked Muslim fanatic rushed into the church, demanding to see him. When he came forward, the gunman shot him four times. He died on November 19, 2009, at the age of thirty-four, leaving a wife and three children. Patriarch Kyrill praised him as a confessor of the Faith and a martyr for preaching the gospel.

~: NOVEMBER 20 :~

Our Holy Father Gregory of Decapolis

Gregory was born in Isaurian Decapolis of pious parents. Though his parents wanted him to marry and begin a life of wealth and ease, he had a heart for monasticism. He renounced the world and went to live in the desert, where he became a monk. He lived in various places, such as Rome and the monastery of Mount Olympus, and was a friend of Joseph the Hymnographer (feast day April 4), who accompanied him to Constantinople. After a long and ascetic life of healing prayer, he died in peace. Gregory lived in the ninth century.

~: NOVEMBER 21 :~

The Entrance into the Temple of the Most Holy Theotokos

This feast commemorates the holiness and the spiritual preparation of the child Mary to be the Theotokos. According to the poetic account in the Protoevangelium of James, Mary was taken as a child of three to live in the temple, led there by a procession of maidens bearing torches. She entered the Holy of Holies and was fed by an angel. The Church tells us by this that Mary was not a random choice, but was chosen and prepared for her work from an early age—even as was her kinsman, John the Baptizer. Her entry into the Holy of Holies poetically tells us that she is the true Holy of Holies, the true temple in which Christ God was to dwell.

NOVEMBER 22

Holy Apostle Philemon, Ss. Apphia, Archippus, and Onesimus

Philemon was a wealthy householder in Colosse in the first century. He lived with his wife, Apphia, and his son, Archippus. Philemon was a bishop of the local church, one who opened his home to meetings of the church. His son, Archippus, served as his deacon. One day Philemon's slave Onesimus ran away and took refuge in Rome. There he was converted to the Christian Faith by St. Paul, who sent him back to Philemon, Apphia, and Archippus, and their church, to find reconciliation and peace. (The New Testament Epistle to Philemon preserves Paul's work on the slave's behalf.) It is said that Philemon and his family died as martyrs. Today's feast testifies to the gospel's power to reconcile and transform families so that they become vehicles for the glory of Christ.

St. Cecilia

Cecilia was a wealthy lady in Rome and founded a church in the Trastevere quarter of the city. In the third century, she was, it seems, taken in a persecution of the Church and martyred along with others, Valerian, Tibertius, and Maximus. In the early ninth century her relics were translated to the church of her name that she founded.

NOVEMBER 23

St. Amphilochius, Bishop of Iconium

In 374, much to his father's disappointment and annoyance, Amphilochius allowed himself to be ordained Bishop of Iconium. He strove against the Arians and urged St. Basil to write his book *On the Holy Spirit*. He urged the emperor to resist Arianism and persuaded him to do so in the following way.

When Amphilochius was visiting the emperor and his six-year-old son, he greeted the emperor but ignored his son, who was seated next to him. When the emperor chided him for this, he did not honor the boy as royalty but merely stroked his cheek with his finger and said, "Good day, my child." The emperor was incensed and ordered Amphilochius thrown out for his impertinence.

As he left, he stopped by the door and said, "You, your majesty, cannot endure that your son should not receive the honor due him; how then can God the Father endure that His Son should be dishonored by the Arians?" The emperor was moved by Amphilochius's words and agreed with him that he would resist the Arians. Amphilochius died in peace in 395 and entered the courts of heaven.

NOVEMBER 24

Holy Great Martyr Katherine

Katherine was born of wealthy parents in Alexandria. The tyrant Emperor Maximin was seducing great numbers of women in Alexandria, and he desired to seduce Katherine also. She, as a Christian, refused his advances, despite all his urgings and threats on her life. She was prepared to suffer martyrdom and death rather than give in to him, and so he confiscated all her wealth. She was then finally beheaded, though some say she was sent into exile. It is said they tried to kill her by having her tortured on a wheel but that God saved her. Her relics were later taken to Mount Sinai's Monastery of the Transfiguration, which was renamed St. Katherine's in her honor. Katherine endured her suffering in about 307.

NOVEMBER 25

St. Clement, Bishop of Rome

Clement was a disciple of St. Peter and worked with St. Paul—he is perhaps the Clement mentioned in Paul's Epistle to the Philippians as his "fellow worker" (Phil. 4:3). As head of the Roman church, he wrote a letter to his sister church in Corinth, rebuking them for a schism, exhorting them to have humility, and recalling them to unity among themselves. He suffered for the Faith, dying, it is said, under the Emperor Trajan.

St. Clement, Bishop of Ochrid and Enlightener of Bulgaria

Clement was disciple and successor to the work of Cyril and Methodius. After Methodius's death, facing hostility from the German bishops, he left Moravia with four companions and went south across the Danube to stay in the region of Ochrid. He was sheltered there by King Boris Michael. Clement established his see in a monastic center in Belica and then moved to Ochrid. From there he began his apostolic labors, working to enlighten the people of Bulgaria, teaching them to worship God in their own vernacular language. He was assisted by many, especially his companion Nahum, who labored on the southern shore of Lake Ochrid, translating the Scriptures for the missionary enterprise. Clement died in peace in 916, and his relics lay in the church of the Mother of God—later renamed St. Clement after this holy apostolic man.

~: NOVEMBER 26 :~

St. Alypius the Stylite

Alypius was born in Adrianople in the early seventh century. His father died when Alypius was only three, and his mother placed him in the care of the local bishop, Theodore. At length he was ordained deacon. He served well in the Church but longed for the solitude of the desert. Alypius left the city to pursue the ascetic life in the Palestinian desert. He had not received his bishop's blessing for this, however, and Bishop Theodore pursued his deacon, caught up with him at Euchaita, and forced him to return home.

At length, when he was thirty years old, Alypius built a chapel and made a cell for himself nearby. He remained there for two years, praying, fasting, and waging spiritual battle with the demons. His fame spread, and many came to visit him and seek his counsel. To preserve his seclusion, he built a pillar, with a wooden hut on top of it, and made this his dwelling. He remained there for fifty-three years, his mother living at the foot of the pillar and his bishop dwelling in the city. A community grew up around the saint.

Once, when a poor man came to him, he took off his own tunic and threw it down for him, remaining himself atop his pillar, shivering in the cold. (His plight became known, and someone came to his assistance.) Alypius's health gave out under his austerities: paralysis seized half his body, and he was troubled by ulcers. He nonetheless remained steadfast, dwelling atop his pillar for another fourteen years. He died at the age of ninety-nine.

St. Innocent of Irkutsk

Innocent was born in about 1680 as John Kulchitsky in Volhynia in Russia. A pious boy, he went to school in Kiev, graduating from the theological academy in 1696. He entered the Kiev Caves monastery and was tonsured a monk, taking the name Innocent. He taught in school as pro-rector of the academy until 1719.

After this, he was chosen to lead the mission to eastern Siberia and China, replacing an archimandrite who had died. He was ordained bishop and began his journey to China. He went to Selenginsk, a city on the Chinese border, and waited there for permission from the Chinese to enter. The Chinese, influenced by Jesuit missionaries in China, refused to grant him permission to enter China, and so he remained in Siberia for three years. While he waited, he lived simply, fishing and trying to support himself and his small group of fellow monastic missionaries. At length, in 1727, the Holy Synod of Bishops reassigned him as Bishop of Irkutsk—telling him, in effect, to stay where he was and try to minister pastorally to those around him.

Thus Innocent continued his work among the local Buryats around Lake Baikal. He preached to these pagan people, learning their Mongol language and trying to lead them to Christ. He also worked with the people of Irkutsk, striving to teach them sobriety and non-violence and loving them with the love of Christ. The clergy, he said, should be "a light in darkness, the salt of the earth, trumpets that destroy the walls of the city of sin." The people of Irkutsk did not appreciate their new bishop and would not support him at first, forcing him to live in the Ascension monastery across the Angara River. Still he strove patiently to teach and guide them. He tried to teach his clergy also, laboring hard as the harsh weather affected his aging health.

In 1731 Innocent became ill and died in peace, after only four years in Irkutsk. He never complained or asked to be transferred but persevered at the work the Providence of God gave him to do.

❧ NOVEMBER 27 ☙

Holy Great Martyr James the Persian

James was born of noble rank in Elapa, a royal city in Persia. The local Bishop Abdias unwisely burned down a pagan temple, which prompted a persecution of the church there. James, not wanting to die, apostatized from the Faith. His wife and mother were much grieved and avoided him after that. They wrote him a letter urging him to repent. James was greatly affected by this and indeed repented of his apostasy. His renewed Christian dedication was made known to the king. James was sent for and this time confessed himself a Christian.

He was so steadfast at his interrogation that the king was furious and sentenced him to be hung up and his limbs cut off, joint by joint. As each joint was severed, James praised God as if for a great victory. Finally, all his limbs were cut off and his thighs were torn from his hips. He lay weltering in his blood, a bare trunk, having lost half his body, still muttering prayers to God. At last he was beheaded and entered whole and joyfully into the Kingdom, inheriting the crown in 421.

❧ NOVEMBER 28 ☙

Our Holy Father New Martyr Stephen

Stephen was born in Constantinople in 714 of wealthy parents. He was brought up by monks and was himself tonsured at the age of sixteen. Such was his piety that he became abbot at the age of thirty, but he left after twelve years to live in hermetic solitude. Stephen became very famous for his holiness, and when the iconoclasts condemned the icons, they sought his agreement with their position. He refused and so brought their persecution upon him. Stephen was arrested and assaulted. When he remained steadfast in his refusal to condemn the holy icons, he was banished to the island of Proconnesus.

Stephen's miracles and fame grew from his island exile, so that two years later he was ordered to a prison in Constantinople. There the emperor met him and asked him if men really did insult Christ Himself simply by trampling on His picture. Stephen took a piece of money and asked what punishment he would get if he were to trample the emperor's image on the coin. Would that not be to insult the emperor? "Is it," he asked, "so great a crime to outrage the representation of an earthly king and none to destroy the image of the King of heaven?" He was scourged and beaten and left half dead on the prison floor. Then he was dragged roughly through the streets, his brains were dashed out by a club, and his holy body was torn to pieces by the mob. He suffered with honor and inherited the crown in 767 at the age of fifty-three.

~: NOVEMBER 29 :~

Holy Martyr Paramon and Companions
In Bithynia, the governor had seized a number of Christians, and as they refused to sacrifice to the gods, he had them sentenced to death. Paramon came upon them as they were being led away to their suffering and denounced the governor for this slaughter of the innocent, saying, "How terrible to slaughter so many men as if they were just animals!" For this he also was seized and arrested along with them. The soldiers present mistreated him, sticking him with their spears and cutting out his tongue. At length he was martyred along with the others. They all suffered for Christ in about 250.

~: NOVEMBER 30 :~

Holy Apostle Andrew the First-Called
A native of Bethsaida, Andrew was the brother of Simon Peter and a fisherman with him on the sea of Galilee. He was a disciple of St. John the Baptizer (John 1:36–40) and through John's witness of Jesus, became Jesus' first follower, believing Him to be the Messiah. When Christ called him and Peter from their lives as fishermen to

be His disciples, they immediately left all and followed Him (Matt. 4:18–20).

Andrew was one of the Twelve and seems to have had a special knack for engaging individuals and introducing them to Christ. Thus he brought his brother Simon to Christ (John 1:41), introduced a little lad with five loaves and two fishes to Christ (John 6:8–9), and even, with Philip, introduced some Greeks to Him (John 12:20–22). In his later apostolic travels, he went as far as Scythia near the Black Sea (and is therefore hailed by Russians as their national patron). He established a church in Byzantium on his return. He then went to preach in Greece.

Andrew was finally martyred by being tied to an X-shaped cross, lingering for some time and preaching to all who saw him. This martyrdom took place probably in Patras in Achaia. His relics were at length translated to Constantinople. Some relics were taken by St. Regulus to Scotland in about the fourth century so that Scotland looks to Andrew as their patron as well.

~ DECEMBER 1 ~

Holy Prophet Nahum
Nahum was from the town of Elkosh and lived in the seventh century BC. The northern kingdom of Israel had fallen to the seemingly invincible Assyrians (with their capital at Nineveh), and Nahum prophesied to assure the people of Yahweh's sovereignty. He saw in the Spirit that the proud Assyrian capital would fall by the hand of God and that the evil empire would not last. He prophesied in about 650 BC. Nineveh fell in 612 BC.

~ DECEMBER 2 ~

Holy Prophet Habakkuk
Habakkuk means "embrace." He was a prophet in Judah and was probably a Levite connected with the temple (as he writes an ode and musical directions for the temple in the third chapter of his book). Habakkuk prophesied at the peak of Babylon's power and in a time of great injustice and wickedness in Judah. He proclaimed that God avenges evil—both the evil of Judah and that of Babylon. He saw a vision of God's glory, which became his song (recorded in the third chapter). He prophesied in about 600 BC.

~ DECEMBER 3 ~

Holy Prophet Zephaniah
Zephaniah lived in Jerusalem during the reign of righteous King Josiah of Judah in the seventh century BC. He prophesied to further Josiah's reforms and pure devotion to Yahweh. He wrote that God

would judge the people's sin and that He would also restore them—at which time the daughter of Zion would sing aloud and exult and rejoice, and God would dwell in her midst (Zeph. 3:14–15). This prophecy of salvation was fulfilled in the Incarnation of Christ through His Mother. Zephaniah prophesied in about 620 BC.

~: DECEMBER 4 :~

St. John of Damascus

John was born at Damascus in about 675, the son of an important Christian official at the court of the Muslim caliph Abdul-Malek. He was educated by a Christian monk, Cosmas, who had been taken prisoner and whom his father ransomed and made John's tutor. John also had the name Mansur ("victorious") among the Muslims. He became a monk and a priest at the monastery of St. Sava in Palestine.

John also labored, though reluctantly, at the caliph's court in place of his father in Damascus. When the iconoclast controversy broke out, his position there protected him from persecution, and he was able with impunity to write three treatises in defense of the holy icons. He lived the remainder of his life at the monastery of St. Sava, and he wrote there *The Fount of Knowledge*, the third part of which is his *Exposition of the Orthodox Faith*, which was greatly influential in the Church. As a mystic lover of God, John also wrote three canons—for Pascha, Ascension, and Thomas Sunday—as well as the office for the departure of the soul at death. He compiled the Octoechos, the Hermologion, and the Menologion. He died in about 750.

Holy Great Martyr Barbara and her Companion Julianna

Barbara remains in the Church as an image of virginity and steadfastness of faith even unto death. Some say Barbara lived and suffered in Heliopolis, others say in Nicomedia, others in Rome, and some in Tuscany. It is said that her pagan father, Dioscuros, turned her over to the authorities, resulting in her martyrdom, and that a young woman named Julianna, impressed with Barbara's steadfastness under torture, also confessed herself a Christian and was martyred along with her. Whatever the particulars of her historicity, Barbara abides as an inspiration to heroic faithfulness for all Christians.

The Glorification of Priest-Martyr Alexander Hotovitzky

Alexander Hotovitzky was born on February 11, 1872, in the city of Kremenetz, into the pious family of Archpriest Alexander. He was educated at the Volhynia Seminary and the St. Petersburg Theological Academy, graduating in 1895. After ordination, Alexander was sent to the American diocese, serving in St. Nicholas Church in New York City. He was known as an especially brilliant preacher and had great missionary success among the Uniates, even though he suffered physical violence from his adversaries.

After eighteen years of fruitful service in America, Alexander returned to his Russian homeland, serving in what is now Helsinki, Finland, before being transferred to Moscow. When the tumult of the communist revolution convulsed the land, Fr. Alexander was arrested a number of times. In 1922, he was one of those tried and condemned for "counterrevolutionary practices." He was imprisoned for a time and later suffered exile. He was arrested again in 1937, and oral reports say that he died a martyr. The place of his burial is unknown.

Alexander strove mightily for his Lord as a loving pastor. Those who knew him said that it seemed as if his glance penetrated a person's heart and embraced it with affectionate love.

~ DECEMBER 5 ~

Our Holy Father Sabbas the Sanctified

Sabbas was born of wealthy parents in Cappadocia in 437. His father was an army officer, and Sabbas was left in the care of his family. Dissension in the family prompted him to flee when nine years old to a monastery near his home at the foot of Mount Argaeus. He stayed there until he was eighteen and then moved to live a life of asceticism in the Palestinian desert. He attached himself to an old fellow Cappadocian by the name of Elpidius who lived there as a monk.

DECEMBER

Sabbas's piety was so great and his age so young that he was moved to the cenobitic monastery of St. Euthymius under the care of Theoctistus. He took care of the monastery's donkeys until he was thirty years old. Then, in 469, he was allowed to move to a hermitage nearby, where he spent the next five years. He lived there in solitude, returning to the monastery only on weekends for church services and to gather new palm branches for his weekday labors of handicraft by which he supported himself. He also was allowed to accompany the great founder of the monastery, St. Euthymius, when he went out to spend Great Lent in the desert.

After Euthymius died in 473, Sabbas withdrew further to the Dead Sea area. There in 478, inspired by a vision from God, he established a hermitage for himself in the Cedron gorge and spent five years in solitude and prayer. After much spiritual preparation, he decided to form his own monastic community, allowing other hermits to join him, and soon seventy monks clustered around him. He used a large double cave (built, it seemed, by God Himself). For his growing community, which soon numbered 150, the local patriarch blessed his efforts and allowed the cave to be used as a church, ordaining Sabbas as priest to serve it. There were Egyptians and Armenians in his community, and Sabbas encouraged them to celebrate their offices and liturgies in their own vernacular languages.

As his fame grew, the patriarch gave Sabbas leadership over all the hermits of Palestine, even as he gave his neighbor and friend Theodosius leadership over all the cenobitic communal monasteries in Palestine. During the Monophysite controversy, Sabbas (with Theodosius) supported their patriarch in upholding the Fourth Ecumenical Council of Chalcedon in 451. He was also sent by him to Constantinople on church missions and to obtain funds for the churches from the emperor. Sabbas died in peace, a true father to Palestinian monasticism, in 532 at the age of ninety-four.

~: DECEMBER 6 :~

St. Nicholas, Wonderworker and Archbishop of Myra in Lycia

Nicholas was born at the turn of the fourth century in Asia Minor, possibly in the town of Patara in Lycia. Some say that his uncle was bishop of this city and that he served for a while as a monk in a monastery there. It is likely that he suffered during the persecution of the Church prior to the peace of Constantine.

Nicholas was elected Bishop of Myra and served there as a faithful pastor. He may have attended the First Ecumenical Council of Nicaea in 325. Certainly he vigorously opposed Arianism—so much so that he is said to have punched Arius at the Nicene council! As Bishop of Myra, a busy seaport town, he was busy in charitable work. The story is told of how he anonymously gave three bags of gold to a needy family with three daughters who otherwise would have had to send the girls out to earn a dishonorable living on the streets. Nicholas was a kindly and compassionate pastor to his flock and a model for hierarchs—so much so that, in the weekly calendar where each day is given a special liturgical theme, he shares every Thursday with the apostles. He died in peace in the fourth century, one of the most beloved of the Church's saints.

~: DECEMBER 7 :~

St. Ambrose, Bishop of Mediolanum (Milan)

Ambrose was born the son of a prefect in Gaul in about 340 and was raised in a powerful, ambitious, and influential family. As such, he was appointed governor of the province of Liguria when he was twenty-nine. As governor he ruled from Milan, and he ruled with wisdom, discretion, and fairness.

When the Bishop of Milan died, there was great confusion and striving for the office. As secular governor, Ambrose attended the election gathering and spoke calming words to the assembly. Then

DECEMBER

a child cried out, "Ambrose—bishop!" The cry was instantly taken up by the crowd, who wanted such a wise and fair governor as their church leader. Though yet only a catechumen, Ambrose reluctantly allowed himself to be elected. He was baptized and ordained bishop in 374. He was thirty-four years old.

One of his first acts as bishop was to request from St. Basil the relics of St. Dionysius. Western society in his day was falling to pieces, and the Church was locked in a struggle with the Arians. Ambrose set an example of holiness, fasting frequently and living simply. When he had to feed the poor as bishop, he sold the treasured church plate to raise the money. When this act was criticized as sacrilege, he simply said, "Which is more valuable—church vessels or living souls?" He strove against the Arians and suffered from their harassment.

Ambrose had always been close to his brother and sister, and when his brother died, he was overcome with grief. "What can I do now?" he exclaimed. "What is there worth living for?" He was depressed and comforted himself with thoughts of the future resurrection. He continued to be a good pastor to his flock. One of his most famous pastoral acts was the conversion and baptism of the then-young Augustine and his son.

Ambrose could also be stubborn and unyielding before secular powers. When Emperor Theodosius had a crowd of Thessalonian rioters massacred in 390, Ambrose excommunicated him and called him to repent of murder. Theodosius appeared at church, and Ambrose would not admit him. "How can you uplift a prayer with hands which still drip with blood? I say, repent!" Theodosius repented and did public penance, prostrating himself in church and weeping.

Ambrose continued to serve as a pastor to his flock. He introduced his congregation to antiphonal singing (which had been popular before in the East). He taught catechumens and wrote sermons for their instruction. The hymn Te Deum is ascribed to him. He discovered the bodies of the martyrs Protasius and Gervasius, long since buried.

When Ambrose fell ill with his final illness, he said, "I am not afraid to die, for we have a good Lord." He said that he saw the Lord coming to his bedside. He lay with his arms outstretched in the form of a cross and died whispering prayers, on Paschal eve in 397. He was fifty-eight and had governed Milan as bishop for over twenty-three years.

❧ DECEMBER 8 ☙

Our Holy Father Patapius
Patapius was born to pious parents in Thebes in Egypt. He early renounced the world and left for the solitude of the Egyptian desert. From there he moved to Constantinople, where he built a hermitage hut near the Blachernae church. His life of solitude and holiness led to his increasing fame, and soon many came to seek his counsel and healing prayers. He died in peace in the seventh century. His body was buried in the nearby monastery of the Egyptians. The presence of an Egyptian desert-dweller in the imperial city of Constantinople witnesses to the grace of Christ, whose light can shine through His saints wherever they are.

❧ DECEMBER 9 ☙

The Conception of the Most Holy Theotokos
This day commemorates the conception of Mary in the womb of her mother, Anna. Anna was barren and was enabled to conceive after she and her husband, Joachim, fervently asked God for a child. The feast (falling about nine months before the feast of Mary's Nativity on September 8) shows how Mary was chosen by God from the womb (like St. John the Baptizer) to be the Holy Mother of God and was prepared for this work by the Holy Spirit.

❧ DECEMBER 10 ☙

Holy Martyrs Menas, Hermogenes, and Eugraphus
In the days of the pagan Emperor Maximian, Menas was one of his counselors. When an uproar erupted in the city of Alexandria, Menas was sent to calm the turmoil and bring peace. Menas was an Athenian whose cultured education well suited him to this task. Though

outwardly pagan, Menas inwardly was drawn to Christ. Menas established peace in Alexandria, and also while there declared himself a Christian and used his position to bring the gospel message to many.

Alarmed, the emperor sent Hermogenes, his prefect, to arrest Menas and subject him to the usual tortures. Hermogenes obeyed. He entered Alexandria, arrested Menas, and subjected him to cruel interrogation, tearing off the soles of his feet, gouging out his eyes, and tearing out his tongue. Hermogenes, however, was not a cruel man, and these enormities affected him greatly. Impressed by the constancy of Menas and his radiant joy despite his torture, Hermogenes also converted to Christ.

The emperor was even more alarmed at this and hastened to Alexandria. Hermogenes was taken into custody and himself tortured. His arms and legs were cut off and his body pierced with spears. In the midst of these events, Menas's secretary, Eugraphus, also confessed himself a Christian like his suffering master. In exasperation, the emperor had him run through with a sword on the spot, while he had Menas and Hermogenes finally executed. All three martyrs suffered for Christ in the early fourth century.

Our Holy Mother Angelina

Angelina was the daughter of a prince of Albania and was married to Stephen, king of Serbia. She accompanied her husband in a life of trial, adventure, and hardship in Serbia, Albania, and Italy. When he died, she embraced monasticism and served in works of charity and the building of churches. She was popularly called Mother Angelina by her people, who loved her greatly. She died in the beginning of the sixteenth century.

DECEMBER 11

Our Holy Father Daniel the Stylite

Daniel was born at Maroutha in Syria in 409 and was raised by his pious parents to seek monastic holiness. When he was twelve he left home and entered a monastery not far away. He lived there until he was somewhat older and was finally tonsured as a monk with his parents attending the service. He visited the then-famous St. Simeon the Stylite and was enthralled by him. He ascended the pillar to speak to the great man and to get his blessing.

After the abbot of his monastery died, Daniel was elected abbot in his place, but he refused the honor and left to live elsewhere. He came finally to Constantinople in 452. He lived for nine years in the ruins of an old heathen temple nearby, attracting fame for his holiness and his healing prayers. He then had a pillar built for him and ascended it in imitation of his hero, Simeon the Stylite, who had died somewhat earlier.

Daniel was given the robe of the blessed Simeon and continued as his successor. The Patriarch Gennadius visited him and ordained him priest. Daniel celebrated the Eucharist from atop his pillar. Several houses were built nearby, and from these developed cells for his followers; later a monastery was built. Many great people came to visit the hermit and to seek his counsel. Daniel preached and spoke to all who came to him, speaking simply of the love of God, love for one another, and care for the poor. He only came down once in his thirty-three years on the pillar, to rebuke Emperor Basiliscus for the heresy of not supporting the Fourth Ecumenical Council of Chalcedon.

When he died, he left a letter for all. It said, "My children and brothers—I love you too much to leave you orphans. I leave the care of you to our heavenly Father. Embrace humility, keep the fasts, love poverty, and above all cherish love, which is the first and greatest commandment. Avoid the tares of heresy, separate not yourselves from the Church, our mother. If you do all these, you will be perfect." He died in peace at the age of eighty in 489.

~: DECEMBER 12 :~

St. Spiridon, Bishop of Tremithus

Spiridon was born in about 348 in Cyprus. He was a shepherd and was uneducated and unsophisticated. He had a wife and family. When he was chosen Bishop of Tremithus for his great piety, he continued to make his living as a shepherd. One day, it is said, a robber came to steal a sheep from his fold. Spiridon found him there, as it were, in the act. "So that you won't have had trouble for nothing," he said, "take a ram and go. But I wish you had asked first."

He was a simple man, but wise. A famous preacher of Cyprus was preaching and, in quoting the gospels, substituted the more luxurious word *couch* for the original more homely word used, *bed*.

"What!" Spiridon said in response, "Are you better than the Lord, who used the word *bed*, that you are ashamed to use His words?"

Another time a traveler came to him, much worn by his journey. Spiridon had no food to set before him except some salted pork. It was Great Lent, and the traveler did not want to break the fast. Spiridon replied, "You have good reason to eat. As St. Paul says, 'To the pure, all things are pure'"—and he began himself to eat the pork.

Spiridon traveled to the First Ecumenical Council in Nicaea in 325. He had no educated philosophical subtlety, but he had the shrewdness of spiritual wisdom. When two others were arguing philosophically, he interrupted and silenced them by saying, "Christ and His apostles left us not a system of logic, but a naked truth to be guarded by faith and good works." After the council he returned to his native Cyprus, where he died in peace in about 348. His relics were afterwards translated to Constantinople.

⁓ DECEMBER 13 ⁓

Our Holy Father St. Herman of Alaska
Herman was born in a merchant-class family in Serpukhov near Moscow in about 1758. He early entered a monastery and was tonsured a monk with the name Herman. In 1779 he moved to the famous Valaam monastery in Russian Finland. In 1793, Metropolitan Gabriel of Novgorod asked his abbot Nazarius to choose some monks for a mission team that was leaving to evangelize the natives of Russian Alaska. Herman was chosen to be one of the team from Valaam. The missionary monks journeyed for a year crossing Russia and landed on Kodiak Island in 1794. In their mission work,

Herman was chosen to run the school the monks set up to care for Native children.

The mission was dependent upon the local governor, Baranov, a man with no desire to have monks living with him and his rough, adventurous fur-traders. They were always at odds, as the monks supported the Native Aleuts and tried to save them from being exploited. The mission was underfunded and so did not have the success envisioned. Herman with the others continued, preaching the gospel and caring for those entrusted to him. The conflict with Baranov's men led him to move to Spruce Island sometime between 1808 and 1818 and to make it his "New Valaam." There he lived in ascetic solitude, praying, conversing with angels, teaching, and caring for his orphans and Natives.

They loved him and referred to him as their *apa* (or "grandpa"). Herman labored in ascetic holiness—he wore sixteen-pound chains, slept on a board, and wore the same patched cassock the year round. He was gifted with prophetic insight. Once, when a flood threatened the island, he took his icon of the Theotokos, placed it on the beach, and prayed. He told the people not to fear—the water would not rise past the icon. And it did not.

Herman was a great talker and often conversed with visiting Russians to bring them to fervent faith in Christ. One day he sat surrounded by naval officers and asked them what each wanted most. Some wanted wealth, some a beautiful wife, some other things. He said, "Isn't this what you all want—what you think best? And what could be better than Christ our God? Shouldn't we love God and want Him more than all?"

They all agreed. "How can we not love God?" they said.

Herman replied, "And I, poor sinner, have been trying more than forty years to love Him, and I cannot say I love Him properly."

The crew admitted they did not love Him as He deserved.

"Then," said Herman, "from this day, from this hour, from this moment, let us love God above all and do His will!"

Herman lived in holiness until 1837, when he died in peace. He was glorified in 1970, a wonderworker before death and after, a true light and North Star guiding the Orthodox in the new land he made his home.

~: DECEMBER 14 :~

Holy Martyrs Thyrsus, Leucius, and Callinicus
In the reign of Emperor Decius, Cumbricius, the governor of Bithynia, sought to enforce the decrees against the Christians. He arrested Leucius and Thyrsus among others in his journey through his jurisdiction. They were condemned and horribly tortured—Leucius was hung upside down, torn with iron hooks, and then beheaded. Thyrsus had his eyelids pierced and pulled out with rings and molten lead poured down his neck. A man named Callinicus witnessed the steadfastness of these martyrs and was himself converted. He also was arrested and executed with them. They all suffered with honor for Christ in about 250.

~: DECEMBER 15 :~

Hieromartyr Eleutherius
It is said Eleutherius knew and was influenced by Anacletus, Bishop of Rome. He was ordained to serve in Valona in Albania. When the persecution of Christians raged under Emperor Hadrian, he also was arrested and brought to Rome, where he suffered martyrdom after being tortured. He died for his Lord in about 120.

~: DECEMBER 16 :~

Holy Prophet Haggai
Haggai means "festal." He prophesied with Zechariah in the postexilic community around Jerusalem in 520 BC. The people had grown slack and cared for their own welfare and prosperity more than for God's house and honor. Haggai called them back to zeal in supporting the temple and promised God would be with them if they would honor Him. His prophecies were fulfilled finally in Christ, who made the

latter splendor to be greater than the former splendor (Hag. 2:9). His work prospered under the governor Zerubbabel. Haggai died in peace in the sixth century BC.

DECEMBER 17

Holy Prophet Daniel and the Three Young Men

Daniel was probably of noble descent and as a youth was taken in exile to Babylon, along with his three companions, in about 605 BC. The young men refused to compromise the Law's demands but with God's help kept themselves pure from ritual defilement by unclean food. For his zeal, God gave Daniel wisdom to interpret dreams. In the royal service of Nebuchadnezzar, he was able to interpret the king's dreams and so win royal favor and advancement. Daniel received angelic visitations and revelations of the future trials and restoration of Israel, predicting especially the persecution of Antiochus Epiphanes in the second century BC.

Colleagues who were jealous of his wisdom persecuted Daniel and got him thrown into a lions' den to be executed, but God closed the lions' mouths and preserved him unharmed. His friends, Ananias, Azarias, and Misael, also suffered persecution when they would not bow down to a royal image during a national religious festival. For this they were thrown alive into a fiery furnace, but God miraculously preserved them unharmed. Daniel survived all the trials of public office and died in peace, a true seer and man of wisdom. His visions show Christ and His Kingdom—especially his vision of Christ coming on the clouds as the Son of Man (Dan. 7).

DECEMBER 18

Holy Martyr Sebastian

Sebastian was born at Narbonne in Gaul but brought up in Milan, Italy. He served in the Roman army as head of the First Cohort. Certain Christian prisoners, Marcus and Marcellianus, were held in custody and were beginning to waver in their faith. Sebastian encouraged them to be steadfast and in so doing identified himself as a Christian. He too was arrested and condemned. He was shot with many arrows and died a martyr for his Lord, suffering in Rome in 303.

❈ DECEMBER 19 ❈

Holy Martyr Boniface

Boniface is said to have lived in Rome as a pagan servant to a dissolute woman named Aglais, with whom he had unlawful relations. He was sent by his mistress on an errand to Asia Minor and, while there, was converted to the Christian Faith by the constancy and witness of the martyrs. He repented of his former life and confessed himself a Christian, for which he was arrested and martyred. His body was returned to Aglais, and she too was sobered and embraced the Faith. Boniface suffered for Christ in about 290.

❈ DECEMBER 20 ❈

St. Ignatius the God-Bearer, Archbishop of Antioch

Ignatius was a convert of St. John the Theologian and succeeded Evodius as Bishop of Antioch in about 70. He was a prophet and had the nickname Theophorus (or "God-Bearer").

Ignatius established the custom of antiphonal singing by the church congregation, inspired by a vision he had of the worship of heaven. He was a passionate Christian, serving his flock with zeal and fervor. He was arrested under Trajan and boldly confessed himself a follower of Christ God. "Do you mean the one who was crucified?" asked Trajan derisively.

Ignatius replied, "I mean the One who by His death crucified sin and enabled those who bear Him in their hearts to trample on all the malice of demons!" For his confession of faith he was condemned to be thrown to the beasts and killed in the Roman arena. On hearing the sentence, he gave thanks to God and with joy put on his chains. He was taken with great roughness to Rome, passing through the cities of Asia Minor. To each of these he wrote letters, appealing to them to obey their bishop, to avoid heresy, and to live in peace and love. He also greeted Polycarp, Bishop of Smyrna, and they had time to talk of their days together with St. John the Theologian and of the love of God.

To the church of Rome for which he was bound, he wrote asking them not to try to interfere and prevent his martyrdom. "Of my own free will I die for God—unless you hinder me. I exhort you, don't be unseasonably kind to me. Let me be given to the wild beasts, for through them I can attain to God. I am God's wheat and am ground by the teeth of wild beasts that I may be found to be the pure Bread of Christ. Now I am beginning to be a disciple. Come fire and cross and grappling with wild beasts, wrenching of bones, hacking of limbs, crushing of my whole body; come cruel tortures of the devil to assail me! Only let me attain to Jesus Christ!"

Ignatius arrived in Rome and was presented to the prefect. His guards rushed him to the arena. Two lions were let loose, and they instantly devoured him. His bones were taken by the Church back to Antioch as a precious treasure. Thus did the God-Bearer attain to Christ and to eternal joy. He suffered in 107.

↶ DECEMBER 21 ↷

Holy Martyr Juliana

Though born to pagan parents of good standing, Juliana became a Christian. She exasperated her parents even more when she refused to marry a government official as arranged because he was not a Christian. Her father beat her severely, but she became ever more rebellious against his will. Finally he denounced her to the state, thinking that the terror of being threatened with torture in court would make her forget her Christian Faith and agree to marry as he had arranged. Juliana did not quail in court as he thought but rather boldly confessed Christ. For this she was beaten, tortured, and finally beheaded. She suffered for her Lord in about 309.

❦ DECEMBER 22 ❧

Holy Great Martyr Anastasia

Anastasia was a Christian girl, raised by a pagan father and a Christian mother. When she was young, she was married against her will to a pagan man, Publius, who, besides being pagan, was base and detestable. After marriage, she avoided his bed, claiming that she was sick. At night, she disguised herself as a poor working woman and went out into the city with a servant girl to visit the Christian confessors in the prisons. When at length her husband discovered that, far from being sick, she was going out on such an errand, he was furious and locked her up in his house.

Her husband, meanwhile, went off overseas. While he was on his way to Persia, his boat was shipwrecked, and he perished. Thus, after three months of forcible confinement at home, Anastasia was free to live as she pleased. She resumed her charitable work of visiting Christians in the prisons and of ministering to the martyrs there. She also traveled to Nicea in Bithynia and visited the Christian confessors imprisoned there. Eventually she too was arrested and executed. She suffered for her Master in about 304, joining the ranks of the martyrs she had ministered to for so long.

❦ DECEMBER 23 ❧

The Ten Holy Martyrs of Crete

In the mid-third century, a number of Christians in Crete were arrested for their faith: Theodulus, Saturninus, Europus, Galasius, Eunician (all from Gortyna, the main city of Crete), Zoticus from Knossos, Pompeius from the port of Leda, Agathopous from Panormus, Basilides from Khania, and Evaristus from Heraklion. Though from different places on the island, they were united in their fervent love for Christ. For thirty days they were taken around the pagan sanctuaries of the island and urged to sacrifice to the gods. When they continued to refuse, they were tortured and finally beheaded. Thus together they inherited the crown of glory as citizens of the heavenly Kingdom.

St. Nahum, Enlightener of the Bulgarians

Nahum was a disciple of Ss. Cyril and Methodius and a scholar of many languages. He traveled to Rome and then returned to Bulgaria. He worked with Clement and three other companions in Moravia until pressure from the Western bishops there drove them south to Bulgaria. He settled on the shores of Lake Ochrid with the help of Bulgarian ruler Boris Michael. He established a monastery on the lake's southern shore which became a spiritual center for the land. Nahum labored to translate the Scriptures into the vernacular Slavonic, working with Clement, Bishop of Ochrid. Nahum died in peace in the first part of the tenth century.

∻ DECEMBER 24 ∻

Our Holy Mother, the Martyr Eugenia

Eugenia was the daughter of an Egyptian government official and was born at Rome in the late second century. She fled from her family residence in Rome with her faithful servants, seeking freedom to follow an ascetic life. She cut her hair and joined a male monastic community, hiding the fact that she was a woman and going by the name Eugenius. At length, her secret discovered, she returned to Rome. When persecution broke out against the Church, Eugenia also was taken. She was martyred for her Lord and buried in the cemetery of Apronian on the Via Latina.

∻ DECEMBER 25 ∻

The Nativity of Our Lord, God, and Savior Jesus Christ

Bowing unknowingly before the sovereign purposes of God, Augustus Caesar decreed that all should be enrolled in a census, and thus all Israelites returned to their ancestral homes to be enrolled. Joseph, betrothed to the Virgin Mary, went to King David's hometown of Bethlehem because he was of the house of David. Mary went with him, and while there, she gave birth to her Divine Son.

The small town was crowded with people being enrolled for the census, and there was no room for them in the inn. They took refuge in a cave used for a stable, and it was there that Mary gave birth, wrapping the Child in the customary swaddling clothes and laying Him in a feeding trough. The angelic hosts rejoiced, proclaiming the news of the Messiah's birth to some shepherds who kept watch over their flock in the field that night. The angels announced God's glory in the heights and on earth, peace to men He had favored.

At the angels' word, the shepherds hurried to see the Child and to offer Him their gift of wonder. Later, magi (court astrologers and sages from the East) came to see the Child. They were made aware of His birth through researching the appearance of a new star in the heavens, and they came to Palestine to seek for Him. The court of Herod the king told them to look in Bethlehem for their universal messianic King, and so they also came to Christ and His Mother. Like the shepherds, they came to wonder—and to offer royal gifts of gold, incense, and myrrh. Thus all the world came to venerate the Christ Child—the humble shepherds of the earth and the wise and powerful of the nations.

☙ DECEMBER 26 ❧

Synaxis of the Theotokos

This day commemorates the role Mary played in our salvation in giving birth to Jesus our God. For the dispensation of our redemption could not have taken place without the faith and courage and labors of the Most Holy Mother of God. Thus all Christians are called upon today to give thanks to her for faithfully fulfilling her vocation. In accordance with her own word, we, with all generations, rise together and call her blessed (Luke 1:48)—ever blessed and most pure and the Mother of our God.

~: DECEMBER 27 :~

Holy Protomartyr Stephen the Archdeacon

Stephen was appointed by the apostles to be one of the seven deacons of the Jerusalem church. They were ordained as deacons to supervise the daily distribution of welfare to the widows cared for by the Church, and they were all Hellenistic Jews (as it was the Hellenistic Jewish widows who were being overlooked in the distribution).

Stephen argued and reasoned with his fellow Jews about Jesus being the fulfillment of Judaism with its Law and temple. In his diaconal ministry, he also prayed for the suffering and did great wonders and signs of healing. His popularity grew so much that he attracted persecution from the official Jewish Sanhedrin court. Stephen was arrested and brought before them on the charge of blaspheming against his ancestral religion.

At his trial he ably defended himself, showing that the Law and temple were never essential to God's people and were absent during much of their salvation history. He also rebuked the Jews for their hardness of heart, saying they now resisted God even as their forefathers had done. The council was furious at him. In his final hour, Stephen looked up and had a vision of Christ standing at the right hand of God. He cried out to them about what he saw of Jesus' glory as Messiah, and they madly rushed on him to stone him. As he was stoned by the mob, he cried out, "Lord Jesus, hold not this sin against them!" Stephen was the first to be martyred for the Lord and to inherit the crown.

~: DECEMBER 28 :~

The Holy Martyrs of Nicomedia

In the reign of Diocletian, a great number of Christians were assembled in church at the end of December to celebrate our Lord's glory. The pagans, raging against the Christians, closed the doors of the church, heaped firewood around it, and set it ablaze. The many martyrs inside perished, choosing to die inside rather than come out, surrender, and offer sacrifice to the gods. They perished in Nicomedia in about 303 and entered the Kingdom.

❦ DECEMBER 29 ❦

The Holy Innocent Children of Bethlehem

When the Magi from the East came to Herod wishing to venerate the newborn universal King, Herod sent them to search for the messianic King in Bethlehem, the town of David where the Messiah was prophesied to be born (Mic. 5). He asked them to bring word so that he might venerate Him also—though he planned instead to kill the Child as a rival to his own power.

The Magi were warned by God not to return to Herod, so they left the country after seeing Christ, without telling Herod where in Bethlehem the Child was. Herod, in a furious rage at having been so used, sent soldiers to kill all the young children of Bethlehem aged two years and younger, in order to be certain that he had killed the Christ Child also.

The small number of innocents killed in the little town of Bethlehem was nevertheless a crime of great proportion (hence the numbers poetically lamented: 14,000 in the Byzantine calendar; 64,000 in the Syrian calendar; 144,000 in the Middle Ages). This was not merely the slaughter of a few innocents but an eschatological outpouring of wrath predicted by the prophets, which would leave Rachel weeping for her children (Jer. 31:15).

❦ DECEMBER 30 ❦

Our Holy Mother Anysia

Anysia was a young girl of Thessalonica, born of noble parents. She was a Christian, and after her parents died, she gave away much of her wealth to live in holy asceticism and simplicity. She was very beautiful, and one day, while she was going out through the city gates, a pagan, taken with her beauty, lustfully accosted her and addressed her with lewd familiarity. Taken aback and afraid, she impulsively crossed herself and vigorously rejected his advances. When he asked her name, she would only say, "I am Christ's handmaiden and I'm going to church!" She pushed him away, trying to get away from him, and spat in his face.

Thereupon, seeing the one who rejected him was one of the hated Christians and furious at the rebuff, the man drew his sword and ran it into her side. She sank down and bled to death there on the spot. The Church treasured her holy memory of good deeds and righteousness. A generation or so later, a bishop of that city, Anysius, was so named after his see's illustrious martyr. Anysia died for Christ in about 300.

⁓ DECEMBER 31 ⁓

Our Holy Mother Melania the Roman

Melania was born in Rome in about 380 of a noble and wealthy Christian family. When she was fourteen, she married a young man named Pinianus (who was seventeen). She wanted to live with her husband in ascetic chastity as brother and sister. He resisted this idea until she was pregnant with their second child and in danger of death. Then he yielded and promised that if she survived they would live in chastity.

The child born died soon after (as had their first child). They then began to live as brother and sister in simplicity, giving away great sums to the poor, supporting monasteries, giving gifts to churches, and buying slaves their freedom. When the Visigoths invaded, the couple fled to their estates in North Africa, where they gave support to a monastery of eighty monks and one for one hundred nuns. They also visited St. Augustine of Hippo in his see. They lived in North Africa for seven years.

From there they went to Jerusalem and settled there. Melania visited the monks of Egypt and also St. Jerome while she lived in Palestine, adorning the church there with her presence and good deeds.

After her husband died in 435, she established a monastery for nuns and joined them in holy solitude and prayer. She also copied many books. She died in peace in 439 on the last day of the year.

Through the prayers of all Your saints, Lord Jesus Christ our God, have mercy on us and save us!

❦ READINGS FOR THE PASCHAL CYCLE ❧

PRE-LENTEN SUNDAYS

Zacchaeus Sunday
As we head towards the pre-Lenten Sundays of the Great Fast, the Church puts before us the story of Zacchaeus, from the Gospel of St. Luke, a story of desire, humility, and joy. Zacchaeus grew rich from tax-collecting—that is, from working for the hated occupying Romans and from gouging his people—and as such, he was a hated man. Yet within his heart lived a desire for something better, for a second chance.

So it was that when the famous rabbi from Galilee, Jesus the wonderworker, came to town amidst an immense throng, Zacchaeus had to see Him, even if it meant making himself look ridiculous by climbing a tree to see above the crowd. To his great surprise, Jesus stopped under the tree and looked up at him. And instead of rebuking him publicly for his notorious greed and dishonesty, He asked him for hospitality, saying He must stay at his place.

Zacchaeus was stunned—and jubilant. In the hastily arranged banquet for Him that followed, he dramatically stood up to announce to the Lord and his guests his new resolution: he would give away half his wealth to the poor and make good whatever he had defrauded, and then some. The Lord accepted his repentance, saying that today salvation had visited that house, for Zacchaeus, though hated as a sinner, was still a son of Abraham, and was called by God into the joy of His Kingdom.

Through his humility in sacrificing his dignity for a sight of Jesus, and through his decisive determination to change his life, the little

Zacchaeus found that repentance leads to joy. The Church puts that lesson before our eyes as we approach the Sundays of the Lenten Triodion.

Sunday of the Publican and the Pharisee

The period of the Lenten Triodion begins with this story from St. Luke's Gospel as the Church celebrates the first pre-Lenten Sunday. The Lord told this parable targeting those who trusted in themselves that they were righteous and looked down their noses at others.

It is the story of two men picked out from among the many who daily crowded the temple courts: one of them a Pharisee and one a hated publican, or tax-collector. All of our Lord's hearers knew (or thought they knew) which one God would favor and which one He would reject. The favored one was the religious one, the Pharisee, and he took his stand, giving thanks to God—for himself and how pious he was! His was not so much a prayer as a self-congratulation, as he exalted himself above those around him, disdaining them as so many extortioners, unjust, and adulterers. He especially rejoiced that he was not like that tax-collector he saw over there. Doubtless he went on for some time, but the Lord only follows his prayer for a sentence or two. (One imagines God lost interest in his prayer about the same time.)

That tax-collector whom the Pharisee especially despised offered quite a different prayer. In fact, it was not even a prayer: he could not even lift up eyes or hands to heaven (as everyone did while praying). All he could gasp out was the stifled and tearful cry, "God, be merciful to me, the sinful one!" It seems he was a very bad man.

Then came the surprise ending—it was this man, the sinful publican, who left the temple forgiven, and not the Pharisee. Because the publican humbled himself, God accepted him and lifted him up, and because the Pharisee exalted himself over others, God rejected him and brought him down. This is the lesson the Church offers her children as they begin their Lenten striving for righteousness: let us flee from the pride of the Pharisee and learn humility from the publican's tears.

Sunday of the Prodigal Son

Christ ate and feasted with tax-collectors and sinners, and this fact scandalized many. In response, He told stories of a man finding his lost sheep, a woman finding her lost coin—and a father finding his lost son. This final parable (all are found in St. Luke's Gospel) is particularly rich in detail, and it revolves ultimately around the conflict between the father's two sons. The Church focuses not on that conflict, nor on how the elder son should have rejoiced and feasted with his formerly lost brother, but on the love of the father.

The younger son was reckless and foolish. Leaving the love of the father's house, he wandered far from home and embraced a life of wantonness and sin. This choice led to its inevitable conclusion and left the boy desperate, destitute, and starving. To fend off starvation he was forced to take a job as a swineherd (the final indignity for a Jew), and even so he went to bed hungry each night. Then he came to his senses and decided to return home and humble himself before his father, not asking to be restored but simply asking for any job. With hunger burning in his stomach, he started the long way home.

While he was yet far off, the father spied him, for he was anxiously looking for any sign of his son's return. The father ran to him, threw his arms around him, and fell on his neck with joy. He did not even let him finish his rehearsed speech asking for a job, but insisted that the boy be restored, with festal robes, a ring, shoes, and a tremendous party, killing the calf that was fattening for just such an occasion. The boy, long feared dead, was alive and safe in the house of the father.

The Church offers us this story as we begin our Lenten repentance, for we also have scattered the riches the Father gave to us and need to return home to Him in repentance. The example of the prodigal son reveals what is awaiting us there: a loving embrace, restoration, and festal joy.

Sunday of the Last Judgment

This day is sometimes called Meatfare Sunday, since it is the last day meat is allowed before the great fast. The gospel for the day, from St. Matthew, focuses on the Last Judgment. In a parable, Christ tells of the day when He will return as King in glory to gather all the nations for judgment, dividing them into two groups, even as a shepherd would separate the sheep from the goats after they had intermingled. Both groups would be stunned by what they heard.

Those on the right hand of honor were commended for their deeds. They had fed Jesus when He was starving, given Him drink when He was dying of thirst. They came to see Him when He languished in prison and visited Him on His sickbed. They would have their just reward—the blessing of the Father as they inherited His Kingdom. But those rewarded spoke up in perplexity—when was Jesus ever starving? Or when did He languish in prison, or moan on a sickbed? Then came the stunning answer: each time they did these things to the poor, who were His humblest brothers, they did it to Him.

Those on the left hand had not heard this exchange, and the triumphant King turned on them in wrath. Let them get out of His face, fleeing like accursed men into hell, for when He was starving, they merely looked on; when He was languishing in prison, they didn't even visit Him, but let Him rot. These were as shocked as the first group and protested that they had done no such thing. The stunning answer came to them as well: each time they refused to help the poor, they affronted Jesus their King also.

The lesson for all is clear: eternal issues are involved in our earthly deeds. Let us walk in love and be abundant in almsgiving and good works, for by doing so we serve our King and save our souls.

Sunday of the Expulsion of Adam from Paradise

This last of the pre-Lenten Sundays is also called Cheesefare Sunday, since dairy is allowed on this final day before the fast. Often the Rite of Mutual Forgiveness is appended to the Sunday service, so that it is also called Forgiveness Sunday.

The gospel for the day is from Matthew's Sermon on the Mount, and it focuses on the right way to fast. We are to guard our hearts, so that our motivation for fasting is to please God, not to garner the applause of men. We must take all care not to flaunt our fasting before the eyes of the world—or the Church—as if their approval were paramount. For it is not. All that matters is that God sees our efforts and our hearts. We offer our appetites and efforts to Him to win His approval. Our abstinence from foods is the expression of our penitence; it is how we cry out to Him, "Have mercy on me, a transgressor, O merciful Lord!" It is God who will see our secret penitence and give us our reward.

~: SUNDAYS OF LENT :~

The First Sunday of Great Lent: Orthodoxy Sunday

This Sunday commemorates the restoration of the holy icons after the Church's long struggle with the iconoclasts, who banned and burned the icons, relentlessly persecuting those who made them and venerated them. The icons were restored on the first Sunday of Lent in 843, which ever after was dedicated to celebrating this restoration. (The readings for this Sunday, which focus on Christ as the fulfillment of the Law and the Prophets, have little to do with this theme, since the lectionary predates this restoration.)

This Sunday is called the Triumph of Orthodoxy because Orthodoxy centers on the Incarnation of the Divine Word, and it is this Incarnation which is proclaimed in the icons. With the Incarnation of God becoming Man in Jesus, the indescribable became capable of description, and the invisible God became visible, as He came to restore our fallen image by uniting it to His own divine beauty. Henceforth the Church would proclaim this saving Incarnation in both words and images.

The Second Sunday of Great Lent: St. Gregory Palamas, Archbishop of Thessalonica

St. Gregory's story can be found in the section for November 14.

Ever since the fourteenth century, this Sunday commemorates St. Gregory Palamas, archbishop of Thessalonica. St. Gregory was the great defender and theologian of hesychasm and of the uncreated light of Christ, and by commemorating St. Gregory a week after the Sunday of Orthodoxy, the Church enshrines his teaching and confirms it as a standard of Orthodoxy. The Lenten transfiguration we seek cannot be reached apart from godly and humble ascetical struggle.

The Third Sunday of Great Lent: Veneration of the Precious Cross

On this Sunday, midway through Great Lent, the Church brings out the precious Cross, lovingly adorned with flowers, to be offered to the faithful for veneration. As we endure the rigors of the fast, we are in need of renewed strength, of refreshment of spirit. The Cross gives us this strength, this refreshment, for it is through the Cross that joy has come into the world. Through the Cross we are granted victories over our spiritual adversaries. It is the glory of martyrs, the true adornment of holy monks, and the haven of salvation for the world. Through it, the sting of death and the victory of hell are vanquished, and we all enter again into Paradise.

The Fourth Sunday of Great Lent: Our Holy Father John of the Ladder ("Climacus")

St. John's story can be found in the section for March 30.

St. John was abbot of the Sinai monastery in the seventh century, and he wrote his *Ladder of Divine Ascent* for his monks. The volume became a classic whose value was recognized even by those struggling to serve Christ in the non-monastic world. The book was read by the monks of Sinai during the Lenten season, and this Sunday of Great Lent commemorates the writer with gratitude, thereby commending his work to the entire Orthodox world.

The Fifth Sunday of Great Lent: St. Mary of Egypt

St. Mary's story can be found in the section for April 1.

St. Mary of Egypt's story is recounted as the Great Fast draws to its conclusion. Her story inspires the faithful to repent of their sins, learning what a great reward awaits even the worst sinners as long as they come to God in repentance. Her transformation reveals that no one is beyond hope, and that Christ wills to save and heal all.

☙ PALM SUNDAY WEEKEND ☙

Lazarus Saturday: St. Lazarus the Resurrected

Lazarus was a close friend of Jesus, and he lived in Bethany with his sisters, Mary and Martha. When he grew sick, word was sent to Jesus to leave the safety of Galilee and come south to Judea to heal His friend. When Christ received word of this sickness, He said, "This sickness is not unto death, but for the glory of God," and He remained two days longer in the place where He was. Then He decided to make the two-day trip south to visit Lazarus, much to His disciples' alarm; they feared for His life if He should venture into Judea again. Christ was adamant, and, reluctantly, His disciples went with Him.

When Christ returned to Lazarus's home, His friend had been dead and buried for four days. Christ remained outside the town and sent word to Mary and Martha that He had returned. The sisters each went to see Him, grieving that He had not returned in time to save their brother from death. Christ assured them that if they would believe in Him, they would see the glory of God, as Lazarus would rise again.

Coming to Lazarus's tomb, Jesus wept, not only over Lazarus, but over the desolation and death that held the entire human race captive. Praying aloud so that all present would know that He worked His miracles by the power of God, Christ stood before Lazarus's grave and cried aloud, "Lazarus, come forth!" Lazarus sprang back to life, healed and fresh, and stumbled forth from the tomb, still bound hand and foot with the grave wrappings. Jesus commanded that the people unbind him and set him free.

Many believed in Jesus because of this, with the result that Jesus' enemies plotted to kill Lazarus too. Lazarus lived for years after this, dying, it is said, in Kition in Cyprus. It is possible that he moved to Cyprus to escape local persecution. His relics were later returned to Constantinople by the Emperor Leo the Wise (d. 912). Lazarus is honored on this Sunday as a foretaste of the Resurrection.

PASCHAL CYCLE

Palm Sunday

When it was apparent that Lazarus was sick unto death, the Lord Jesus discerned that this mortal sickness, occurring so close to the Passover, was to serve the glory of God. He realized that it was the Father's will that He raise Lazarus from the dead as an astounding testimony to His power and as a way of calling the attention of Jerusalem to His messianic authority.

Thus, after the raising of Lazarus, all Jerusalem was stirred and overwhelmed with the report of Jesus' miracle, and when He rode into Jerusalem six days before His Passion, the entire city was jubilant at the thought that their Messiah was coming to them, bringing the Kingdom of God. Our Lord entered the Holy City in humility, riding a donkey, not a warhorse, in fulfillment of the prophecy of Zechariah. He thus proclaimed that His Kingdom was not a military one but a spiritual one, and that He had come not to destroy Israel's national enemies but death itself, the enemy of all mankind.

Even the children rejoiced in Jesus' messianic Kingdom, shouting, "Hosanna to the Son of David!" as all the people threw their garments into the road and cut palm branches to strew His path with honor as He entered the Holy City. Thus the ancient prophecies were fulfilled as the Messiah entered Jerusalem in humility and in triumph, bringing the eternal Kingdom of God.

~: PASCHA THROUGH PENTECOST :~

The Great and Holy Pascha

It is on this day—the chosen and holy day, first of Sabbaths, queen and lady of days—that the Church blesses Christ forevermore. It is on this day that we shout with joy, exulting and commemorating the Resurrection of Christ with midnight vigil and exultant song. Pascha is the center and heart of Orthodoxy, the radiant fount from which all life proceeds.

Candlelit procession around the church culminates with the long-awaited cry, "Christ is risen from the dead, trampling down death by death, and upon those in the tombs bestowing life!" This cry ends our fasting, consoles our hearts, and dries all tears. With this cry the Church begins its liturgical and spiritual feast of faith, receiving the riches of God's lovingkindness and celebrating the universal Kingdom He has revealed. Christ is risen: life now reigns, and not one dead remains in the grave.

The Sunday after Pascha: Holy Apostle Thomas

Thomas's full story can be found in the section for October 6.

After the Resurrection, Thomas was not with the others when Christ appeared to them and, being emotionally wrung out from the strain of the last days, he was too numb to accept the apostles' testimony to Christ's Resurrection. He said he would not believe it unless he could see His wounds for himself on His risen Body. Christ came to the apostles and offered to show Thomas His wounds. Thomas fell down in joy, crying out, "My Lord and my God!" (John 20:24–29). Thus his hesitancy to believe confirmed the truth of the Resurrection for future generations.

The Third Sunday of Pascha: St. Joseph of Arimathea and the Myrrh-Bearing Women

St. Joseph of Arimathea was a disciple of Jesus and a member of the Sanhedrin, the council that ruled Jerusalem and Jewish affairs. He kept his loyalty to Jesus secret in the early days, since such loyalty was fiercely persecuted in Judea. After Christ's death, Joseph gathered up his courage and went to Pilate to ask for the body of Jesus to give it honorable burial. This was a courageous act, sure to invite persecution from his fellow Jews. Joseph nonetheless carried out the burial, wrapping Christ's body in a clean linen shroud and placing it in his own new tomb, which he had hewn out of the rock in a garden near Golgotha.

Mary Magdalene and Mary the mother of James and Joseph, with other women, saw where Jesus was buried, and they determined to anoint His body as a final act of love and devotion. They had some spices prepared but needed to buy more. Since the weekly Sabbath began immediately after Jesus' burial, they rested on the Sabbath, and

PASCHAL CYCLE

after the Sabbath, bought more spices. Early on Sunday, the first day of the week, they met at the tomb, determined somehow to have the stone guarding the door of the tomb moved.

When they arrived, they saw that the stone had already been moved and that the body of Jesus was not there. They saw a vision of angels in white who told them that Christ was not there but had risen. The angels told the women to tell this news to the apostles, assuring them that all should meet the risen Christ in Galilee. The women fled awestruck from the tomb. They told the disciples of their vision, though the apostles did not believe their word alone. The myrrh-bearing women remain in the Church as images of faithful love and courage, enlightened and rewarded by the joy of the Resurrection.

The Fourth Sunday of Pascha: The Paralytic

The story of the healing of the paralytic is one of the series of stories in John's Gospel that center on water. Pascha is the baptismal festival par excellence, and the Paschal season thus features these baptismal gospel stories.

In this story, a man long languishing in lameness waited by the pool of water near the Sheep Gate in Jerusalem, beneath five porticoes, for it was thought that when an angel stirred the water, the first one into the pool would find healing from any affliction. His attention was all on that pool, so that when Jesus found him and asked him if he really wanted to be healed, all he could think to ask was that He might help him into the pool the next time the angel stirred the waters.

In John's Gospel, the water here is an image of the Law (given by angels, having five books to parallel the five porticoes). The man is an image of the Jews, depending on the Law for their salvation. Christ redirects the man's attention to Himself and His word. He tells the man he doesn't need the pool anymore. Let him arise, take up his pallet, and walk home. And the man does—showing that healing and salvation come only from Christ. We also, whose souls are paralyzed by sins and thoughtless acts, can find the same salvation. We also can sing to Him, "Glory to Your majesty, O bountiful Christ!"

The Fifth Sunday of Pascha: St. Photini, the Samaritan Woman

Photini (or "enlightened") is the name given to the Samaritan woman whom Christ met at the well. She had a colorful history: she had had five husbands, and at the time she met Christ was living with another man who was not her husband. She was something of an outcast, which is probably why she had come to draw water at the sixth hour, the hottest time of the day. The other village women would have come at a cooler and earlier hour, and at noon she could be assured of being left alone.

As she was drawing water from the well, Christ asked her for a drink. Startled that a Jewish man was asking to drink from her water pot (for Jews had no such dealings with Samaritans, much less with Samaritan women), she began to speak with Him. Christ brought her to faith, speaking with divine prophetic knowledge of her past and of the things of God. She ran in haste to tell the others in her village of this man, who claimed to be the Messiah. Christ stayed with the villagers two days, convincing them that He was indeed the Messiah all were expecting.

Photini was evidently a woman of determination and spirit. It is said that she converted her four sisters and two sons to Christ and died a martyr. Her example reveals that we also, through baptism and faith, can find the spring of water welling up to eternal life. We also can drink abundantly of the water of wisdom and be ever glorified.

The Sixth Sunday of Pascha: The Blind Man

In the story of the healing of the blind man in John's Gospel, we see most clearly the salvation Christ offers all through baptism and faith. This man was born blind, with shriveled eyes and with no hope. Christ, who made Adam from the earth, again took earth, added spittle to make clay, and smeared it on the man's eyes, telling him to go and wash it off in the pool of the Siloam (Siloam means "sent," since the water was sent to that place through an aqueduct). He washed, and light flooded in through his eyes, ending his long darkness and giving him a new life. He came back to Christ seeing, confessing Him to be the messianic Son of Man, and worshipping Him.

The blind man thus becomes an image of every disciple, for all men are blind from birth in their spiritual eyes and need to call out to Christ in repentance. This call is answered in baptism: we also wash in the baptismal pool of Jesus, the One sent by the Father to be the Savior of the world. We also come back seeing and worshiping Him, confessing Him to be the Christ, the Light of the world.

The Ascension of our Lord and Savior Jesus Christ

For forty days after our Lord's Resurrection He presented Himself to His disciples alive, eating and drinking with them and speaking of the Kingdom of God. When the time came for His final departure from them into heaven, He led them out of Jerusalem as far as Bethany. As He lifted up His hands for a last blessing, He was carried up into heaven, having promised that the disciples would receive the Holy Spirit if they stayed in Jerusalem.

In His Ascension, Christ carried our human nature into heaven, thus completing our redemption. Though ascended in glory and sitting at the right hand of the Father, Christ still remains with us who love Him, crying within our hearts, "I am with you, and no one will be against you!" Our reception of the Holy Spirit He pours out into our hearts from His heavenly throne assures us that He is truly the Son of God, the Redeemer of the world.

The Seventh Sunday of Pascha: The Fathers of the First Ecumenical Council

When the heretical teaching of Arius spread like poison through the Church in the early fourth century, Emperor Constantine, who greatly valued the peace and unity of the Church, wanted to take action and help the Church resolve this conflict. He therefore summoned the Church to meet as a council (the classic way of resolving church disputes), and a council eventually met in Nicea in 325. Bishops came from throughout the empire.

It soon became apparent that the teaching of Arius was unacceptable, for Arius taught that Christ was not divine in any real sense, whereas the Church had always worshipped Christ as divine. But how to exclude Arius and his teaching? For he and his supporters (the Arians, as they were soon called) were adept at finding loopholes in any Orthodox formula that had been used.

At length the council Fathers, led by such lights as the young deacon Athanasius of Alexandria, drafted a creedal statement even the Arians could not wriggle out of. It proclaimed Christ as "light from light, true God from true God, begotten, not made, of one essence [Gr. *homoousios*] with the Father," saying that all things were made through Christ. This statement became the core of the Nicene Creed, which (along with later additions from a council that met at Constantinople in 381) abides forever as our Symbol of Faith. The 318 Fathers of the First Ecumenical Council are honored in the Church as the great standard-bearers of God's eternal truth.

Pentecost: The Descent of the Holy Spirit

Fifty days after Passover, on the Feast of Weeks (or Pentecost), Christ's disciples were waiting in Jerusalem for the coming of the Holy Spirit, the promised Comforter. The ascended and glorified Christ fulfilled His promise, pouring out the Holy Spirit upon His disciples with the roar of a mighty rushing wind and tongues of fire, enabling them to declare the mighty acts of God in foreign languages.

Filled with power to witness to Christ, the disciples eventually took the Good News of His Kingdom to every land. Though they were humble and rustic fishermen, God by His Spirit made them most wise, drawing the whole world into His saving net. Through them, all the divided nations are called to unity in Christ so that they may find salvation and glorify with one voice the All-Holy Spirit.

Glory to God for all things!

∾ ABOUT THE AUTHOR ∾

Archpriest Lawrence Farley is the pastor of St. Herman of Alaska Orthodox Church (OCA) in Langley, B.C., Canada. He received his B.A. from Trinity College, Toronto, and his M.Div. from Wycliffe College, Toronto. A former Anglican priest, he converted to Orthodoxy in 1985 and studied for two years at St. Tikhon's Orthodox Seminary in Pennsylvania. In addition to the Orthodox Bible Study Companion Series, he has also published *Let Us Attend*, *The Christian Old Testament*, *Following Egeria*, *The Empty Throne*, *One Flesh*, *Unquenchable Fire*, and *A Song in the Furnace*.

MORE BOOKS BY LAWRENCE R. FARLEY

from Ancient Faith Publishing

The Orthodox Bible Study Companion Series

The Gospel of Matthew: Torah for the Church

The Gospel of Mark: The Suffering Servant

The Gospel of Luke: Good News for the Poor

The Gospel of John: Beholding the Glory

The Acts of the Apostles: Spreading the Word

The Epistle to the Romans: A Gospel for All

First and Second Corinthians: Straight from the Heart

Words of Fire: The Early Epistles of St. Paul to the Thessalonians and the Galatians

The Prison Epistles: Philippians, Ephesians, Colossians, Philemon

Shepherding the Flock: The Pastoral Epistles of St. Paul the Apostle to Timothy and Titus

The Epistle to the Hebrews: High Priest in Heaven

Universal Truth: The Catholic Epistles of James, Peter, Jude, and John

The Apocalypse of St. John: A Revelation of Love and Power

Other Books

Let Us Attend: A Journey through the Orthodox Divine Liturgy

The Christian Old Testament: Looking at the Hebrew Scriptures through Christian Eyes

The Empty Throne: Reflections on the History and Future of the Orthodox Episcopacy

Following Egeria: A Visit to the Holy Land through Time and Space

One Flesh: Salvation through Marriage in the Orthodox Church

Unquenchable Fire: The Traditional Christian Teaching about Hell

A Song in the Furnace: The Message of the Book of Daniel

Ancient Faith Publishing hopes you have enjoyed and benefited from this book. The proceeds from the sales of our books only partially cover the costs of operating our nonprofit ministry—which includes both the work of **Ancient Faith Publishing** and the work of **Ancient Faith Radio**. Your financial support makes it possible to continue this ministry both in print and online. Donations are tax-deductible and can be made at **www.ancientfaith.com.**

To view our other publications,
please visit our website: **store.ancientfaith.com**

Bringing you Orthodox Christian music, readings,
prayers, teaching, and podcasts 24 hours a day since 2004 at
www.ancientfaith.com